GODDESS
❦ *Afoot!* ❦

MICHELLE SKYE

GODDESS
❧ Afoot! ❧

PRACTICING MAGIC WITH
CELTIC & NORSE GODDESSES

Llewellyn Publications
Woodbury, Minnesota

First Edition
First Printing, 2008

Book design by Donna Burch
Cover art © 2007 by Lin Wang
Cover design by Ellen Dahl
Interior Goddess illustrations © 2007 by Lin Wang
Illustrations on pages 7–8, 63, 86, 130, 209 and 263 © 2007 by Kerigwen
Llewellyn is a registered trademark of Llewellyn Worldwide, Ltd.

Library of Congress Cataloging-in-Publication Data for *Goddess Afoot! Practicing Magic with Celtic & Norse Goddesses* is on file at the Library of Congress.
ISBN: 978-0-7387-1331-1

Llewellyn Publications
A Division of Llewellyn Worldwide, Ltd.
2143 Wooddale Drive, Dept. 978-0-7387-1331-1
Woodbury, Minnesota 55125-2989, U.S.A.
www.llewellyn.com

Printed in the United States of America

OTHER WORKS BY MICHELLE SKYE

Llewellyn's Magical Almanac
(contributor, 2000, 2002, 2004, 2006)

Llewellyn's Herbal Almanac
(contributor, 2006, 2007)

Goddess Alive!
(Llewellyn Publications, 2007)

FORTHCOMING WORKS BY MICHELLE SKYE

Goddess Mantras
(Llewellyn Publications, 2009)

Goddess Magic
(Llewellyn Publications, 2009)

CONTENTS

ACKNOWLEDGMENTS

It takes the hard work of many people before a book is published and placed on bookshelves across the country. I first want to thank the editors and staff members at Llewellyn Publications for their compassion and attention to detail in the handling of "my baby." You make the editorial process easy and pain-free!

Many thanks to the people and organizations who work tirelessly to reclaim the myths of our ancient ancestors. They are (in no particular order): The Sisterhood of Avalon, The Troth, The Northvegr Foundation, The Camelot Project at the University of Rochester, the Internet Ancient Texts Archive (http://www.ancienttexts.org), The Internet Sacred Texts Archive (http://www.sacred-texts.com), the Corpus of Electronic Texts (CELT) and the Order of Bards, Ovates, and Druids. Without these people, *Goddess Afoot!* never would have left the stage of conception.

Lastly, I want to thank my family who gave me the space, courage, and inspiration to write. They truly are the backbone of this book! I love you guys!

WALKING
YOUR PATH

The Essence of Magic

What is magic? Is it pulling a rabbit out of a hat or causing the Empire State Building to disappear? Is it sending fluttery sparkles through the air or changing one's hair color from brown to red and back again? Is it shape-shifting into a wolf or altering someone else's shape—the proverbial frog into a prince? Magic is all of these things and none of them. It is the ultimate enigma.

Magic is the ability to manifest one's will in the world at large. This is easy to say but hard to do. How do you create your own reality with all of the possibilities and random chances that make up life, that compose our existence, our living amid billions of people and animals and plants? Perhaps the question should be: How do you not? In truth, we create our reality every day in thousands of small, subtle ways. We instinctively make miniscule choices without even thinking about them: Coffee or tea? Library or bookstore? Condominium or apartment? Boy or girl? These choices shape our lives, causing us to form our conscious reality with our unconscious desires. It is these unconscious desires that magic harnesses. Instead of keeping your wishes in the dark recesses of your mind, magic brings them into the sparkling brilliance of day and, rather like a magnifying glass in the sun, heats up those desires so that your focus on them is absolute. This focus or intent (in other words, your desire magnified) is then amplified with natural and mythic wonders and sent off into the universe to become your reality. Magic, in other words, is taking a completely normal, everyday activity and spiking it with power in order to give it kick.

PERSONAL RESPONSIBILITY

As magic is the realization of your will and your wishes, it is important to understand the implications of performing magic. Remember, everyone has the ability to cast magic spells, just as everyone has hidden dreams and desires. Your wishes are not necessarily the wishes of your best friend, or your neighbor, or your boss, or your teacher. These are individuals, separate from you and your conscious or unconscious desires. No matter how well-meaning you may be, it is generally not a good idea to perform unasked-for magic on another person. Their life lessons are their own. Who are you to decide that a relationship needs to be saved or that a job should be changed? How would you feel if someone made you their personal puppet on the stage of life? That's what magic does when performed on an unsuspecting bystander, it takes their power of choice away from them, relegating them to a supporting role in their own life story.

Are there exceptions to this precaution? Absolutely, but the repercussions must be considered, understood, and accepted before any magic can be performed. Consider this story, which occurred in my life when I was a new witch. I had two friends, one male and one female (we'll call them Jack and Jill for clarity), who became a couple. (*Sigh*, how lovely!) All was wonderful until Jack broke up with Jill. (Horrors!) Amid the tears and soggy handkerchiefs, Jill began to mention some of her past beaus and their… *unfortunate* accidents. One had been severely hurt in a mountain accident; another had lost all of his most prized possessions in a car fire. She told me that she used to lie in bed at night and think over and over and over, "I wish (*insert ex-boyfriend's name here*) would feel the pain that I am feeling right now." Jill was performing magic, even though she was not aware that's what it was called.

Naturally, I was a bit concerned by this darker side of Jill, but I worked on getting her simply to move past Jack's rejection. We never openly talked about magic, as I was very much "in the closet" as a Pagan. I was also not secure in my magical and spiritual knowledge. Weeks went by, and Jack mentioned to me that he had stumbled upon the opportunity of a lifetime. He was offered a position to live and sail on a replica of a historic two-masted sailing ship. Jack was ecstatic; his dreams were coming true! When Jill found out about Jack's new job (through mutual acquaintances), she began to talk a lot about hurricanes and storms at sea. Thinking back to Jill's other ex-boyfriends, I began to worry seriously about Jack's well-being. Could Jill destroy Jack's ship, possibly even killing him while at sea? She certainly believed she could, and belief in oneself is one of the cornerstones of magic. And, to be perfectly honest, after hearing the stories about her ex-boyfriends, I believed she could as well. I felt compelled to do something to combat Jill's negative, destructive spellwork. So I performed a magic spell without talking to Jack or Jill.

At the time, I believed I had no other options. I felt uncomfortable talking about witchcraft and magic with other people. Jack was oblivious to Jill's animosity and would have judged me insane had I expressed my fears. Jill was not responding to my rather thinly veiled suggestions to think positive thoughts and not dwell on the past. And I believe to this day that she had the power and the desire to seriously harm Jack. So I whipped up a spell to protect the ship from Jill's negative magic, creating a type of "astral shield." And the spell worked! The ship stayed completely protected. Jack was safe and secure … and on land. The funding for the ship's journey fell through, and the ship never left the dock. Jack was protected, but he had lost the chance to fulfill a lifelong dream.

Even now, years later, I cringe when I think about that foray into meddlesome magic. I feel badly that Jack was not able to achieve one of his dreams. (Although, who knows? Perhaps he has by now. One can always hope!) Yet what if I had ignored the situation? Would Jack be dead even now, having been swept overboard by a wave or crushed by a hurricane's pounding surf? I don't know. I do know that I interfered in his life path and changed its outcome. For good or ill … who can say? But the power of magic is strong, and when considering meddlesome magic, it is important to look at the options, accept the ramifications of any and all actions, and make a choice. You are taking someone else's life into your hands. You are affecting their wyrd, their fate. The power is yours, but so is the awesome responsibility. And never doubt that you will be called to task for it on the Other Side.

Any kind of magic, not just meddlesome magic, automatically comes with a responsibility clause attached. Every action, from brushing your teeth to paying a parking ticket, creates ripples in the pond of life. These everyday actions are tiny pebbles that, when thrown into the pond, make small, hardly noticeable ripples that will touch other people's ripples. When small, they affect only a limited number of people. For instance, if you decide not to brush your teeth on the weekend, probably only a handful of people will notice your stinky breath, due to the small size of your metaphorical stone. However, the pond's shoreline contains many sizes of rocks. There are tiny pebbles and palm-size skipping stones and heavy cobblestones and even boulders. Some of our actions affect lots and lots of people, meriting a bigger stone with bigger ripples. When we donate to the poor or spread malicious gossip, we drop in a skipping stone. If we pull a baby out of a burning house or kill someone with a semiautomatic weapon, down goes the heavy cobblestone. Sometimes the stone is so big and the ripples so strong that they splash to the side of the pond, and maybe even ricochet back to the center, to the root cause of the disturbance—to us. Thus, our original actions return to us, altering our physical, emotional, and spiritual lives. This concept is the basis for the magical Law of Return.

Figure 1: The ripple effect illustrates how the Law of Return works.

Like our everyday actions, our magical spells can affect others in large and small ways. However, since magic deals with the unseen threads of life that bind us all together, its repercussions are always greater and more far-flung than those of our small, everyday chores. Even the smallest spell creates strong ripples that will return back to us. Hence, the Law of Return: that which we send out into the universe comes back to us. Our positive and negative thoughts, emotions, and actions alter the world around us, especially when they are linked to the unconscious and the divine through magic. We reap many seen and unseen rewards and consequences that ripple far into our future and spread across many locations and lives. To perform magic lightly, without thought, is irresponsible and disrespectful to yourself and to other individuals around the world. Before casting any spell, you must prepare for the changes that will occur and you must freely accept them into your life. If there is any hesitation or question in your mind whether this is the correct course of action, stop and reevaluate your situation. You may be unwilling to accept the consequences, or you may not physically or mentally be ready for the spell. In either case, the magic will not work and you'll be wasting your time.

PREPARING TO WORK MAGIC

Performing magic takes research, courage, belief in oneself, and belief in the spell to be cast. If any of these are missing, the magic fizzles before it can soar to the universal consciousness of the Goddess. In order to perform magic, the magical practitioner must have an intimate knowledge and understanding of what is alternately known as the Witches' Pyramid, the Four Powers of the Sphinx, the Magician's Maxim, or the Rules of the Magus: the phrase "To Know, to Will, to Dare, and to Keep Silent."

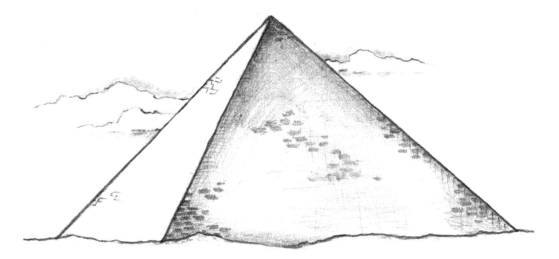

Figure 2: Crafted to be closer to the divine,
pyramids serve as perfect symbols to illustrate magical principles.

To Know: Knowledge Is Power

The first section of the maxim is the reason why many store-bought spell kits don't work very well. In order for magic to work, you have to be intimately connected to all its physical components. Magic often requires stuff. Candles, crystals, herbs, moonlight, midnight dark, chants, songs, glyphs, graphs, and secret names are elements of magic. If you don't know what they mean or what they stand for, your magic becomes meaningless. If you wish to attract love to your life with a talisman, you will need to research the correct herbs, oils, and stones to use. (These are often contained in "correspondence charts" in the back of books.) If you buy a love-attracting talisman, what does it mean to you? Exactly $12.95, plus tax.

The research time is a necessary part of magical practice. It gives you the space to see your situation from every possible angle and to notice if there are other avenues open to you that you have not yet pursued. Instead of crafting a love talisman, you may decide that you want to work on the mundane level first. Or, you may choose to focus all of your energy on attracting love, combining your mundane activities with your magical ones. Perhaps you will sign up for a speed-dating session or enroll in a gym. Rushing through the "to know" section of magical preparation is dangerous and ill-advised. And often, you will not achieve your desired end results.

To Will: Believe in Yourself

In my opinion, this is the hardest aspect of the Magician's Maxim to master and, incidentally, the most important of the four. New magic wielders fail in their early spells because of a tiny seed of self-doubt harbored deep in the subconscious. This seed, planted no doubt in their childhood, won't let them totally commit to the experience—to allow the forces of the universe to work through them, carrying them along on an eddying stream of power and strength. Thoughts detrimental to the spell flit through their minds. They can't believe that they can actually create their own destinies. And, even if they manage to quiet the questions, it is difficult to trust the experience. Perhaps, they think, *I'm making it all up in my mind.* And when the spells backfire or fizzle before fruition, the lessons learned only serve to confirm the original belief and self-doubt, stripping away even more confidence.

So how does one believe? Only through trust does belief flourish. Luckily, trust can be fostered with the help of magical objects and a spellwork routine. If you are finding it difficult to truly believe that you have the power to alter your reality, create a magical environment in which to perform your spells. Choose specific incense that you only use during spellwork. Smudge the room with sage in order to purify and bring you closer to the divine. Put on calming, meditative music and change into clothes that make you feel magical. All of these alterations in the outer world will help to change your mindset in the inner world. Over time, they will trigger a visceral reaction in your body as well as in your subconscious, letting you know that soon magic will be in the air. Your magic will begin to flow automatically as soon as the outside magical environment is created.

Before too long, your spells will manifest in the world around you and you will begin to truly trust your own power. At this point, you may find that you no longer have a need for the incense, sage, music, and special clothes. Your magic will be intrinsic to your personality and not dependent on magical tools or ritual environments. However, you may choose to continue using them anyway, as a way to remind yourself of the transformative journey you have undergone or as a link to all of the past magical success you have experienced. Whether you choose to continue with the creation of a magical environment or decide to simply perform your spells in the living room, you now have absolute belief in yourself and the power to manifest your dreams and create your own destiny.

To Dare: Accept Future Possibilities

Magic changes everything. As discussed earlier in this chapter, its repercussions can be felt by many individuals for a very long time and will eventually come back to you, for good or ill. Therefore, as a magical practitioner, you must be willing to accept any and all consequences of the magic you send out into the world. You must have the courage to live with the responsibility of your actions.

Consider this scenario: you are sitting home alone, watching the eleven o'clock news, when suddenly a scream pierces the night, followed by several expletives and a sob. What do you do?

A. Jump off the couch, throw on your fuzzy bunny slippers, and run outside to help the person in trouble, possibly picking up a baseball bat on your way out the door.

B. Jump off the couch, throw on your fuzzy bunny slippers, and reach for the telephone, dialing 9-1-1 as you open your front door and peer into the darkness.

C. Settle back onto the couch, kick off your fuzzy bunny slippers, and turn up the volume on the television.

Each of these answers indicates an acceptance of responsibility and a tolerance for magical backlash. If you chose letter C, you probably shouldn't be doing any magic at all, since you don't wish to upset your natural state of being. These people plan their lives down to the tiniest grain of rice and would be overwhelmed by the chaos that can sometimes result from a magical spell. Those who chose B are comfortable with life's changes, but only on their terms and in their comfortable environments. These people should be conscious of the Law of Return and should seriously consider every magical spell they perform. They should steer away from any controversial magic, which might tamper with the free will of another individual. If you chose A, any type of spell and any form of magic is open to you. These people have an understanding of consequences and accept the results of their rash actions. Despite this ability to live with the repercussions, letter A people should slow down when attempting a magical spell so that they can truly consider their actions. Magic should never be done thoughtlessly or heedlessly, as it will not only affect the magic wielder, but countless other people and experiences as well.[1]

To Keep Silent: Be Quiet

Simple: don't talk about your spell after you've cast it. Allow the magic to float up to the ethers and disappear until your desires are visible on the earth. But sometimes it's hard to keep quiet. We are proud of our spellwork and excited when it manifests in our lives. Yet we must understand that this is the ego talking and taking over our thought processes. Why is it important that others know how powerful we are? They can be equally as powerful, if only they choose to tap into their inner desires. If your only reason to talk about a spell is to gloat, don't do it. The universal consciousness may decide that you have plenty of everything and no longer need to create your inner desires in your life, and your magic will suffer. However, should you wish to discuss the details of your spell with other magic practitioners in order to receive their opinions and suggestions, go right ahead. It is only through this discussion that you will grow as a magician. You may also wish to share your spells with others who are having similar problems or issues. As long as you trust the individual, by all means, please share your spell. It is important to

---

1. I heard a variation of this magical-backlash test at a lecture by Silver Ravenwolf in western Massachusetts in 1995. From her lecture, and the subsequent discussion, I created the one viewed here.

know the individual because your energy is entwined with the creation of the spell, and you wouldn't want to be linked to just anybody.

Another reason to keep magic secret is doubt. Once you have cast the spell, it is sent up to the universe to gather the energy of the gods and goddesses. However, the spell is still linked to you. The spell contains your energy and thus is always connected to the energy housed within your body. Think of it as an invisible ribbon of light that unites you and the spell, serving as a homing beacon for the positive and negative repercussions of your magic. If you talk about your spellwork with a magical nonbeliever (and there are many in this world), the doubt seeded by that conversation travels up the invisible ribbon of light and invades your magic. This skepticism will infuse your magical spell and will slow down and possibly even destroy its manifestation in your life. You will have canceled out any belief in your own power by listening to the negative, detrimental words of another. So, in order to keep your magic pure and untainted by uncertainty, keep quiet!

TYPES OF MAGIC

Magic can take many forms and can be approached from many different directions. The end result, your subconscious desire, can be achieved through a multitude of actions. You have the choice to create any spell you wish. The options are limitless, which can be a bit daunting when first starting out. The following list is a compilation of the most common types of magic spells, each with a brief description. You will find that each of these types of spells (with the exception of sex magic, due to its controversial, adults-only nature) is represented in the following chapters, so you will have an opportunity to try them all firsthand. Most magic users gravitate toward one type of spell or another, due to personal preference and personality. As you read this list, make a note next to the magic types that most resonate with you right now. Then, as you progress through the chapters and perform the spells, see whether your interests stay the same or change. As your magic evolves, you will notice subtle changes in your spellwork; these changes reflect your growth. Magic helps us get to the heart of ourselves, find our hidden truth. It is important, then, to know where we began in order to see the growth of ourselves. The following types of magic are in alphabetical order and do not reflect the author's personal preferences. All magic works as long as you follow the Rules of the Magus; no one type of magic works better than any other type. They are all dependent on the desire, personality, and focus of the magician.

Candle Magic: Infusing a candle with your subconscious desires, so that when it burns your goals are manifested on earth.

Crystal Magic: Using the magical properties of crystals and gemstones to bring about a desired end result, either by inclusion in a talisman or in conjunction with other forms of magic.

Divination: Communing with the divine through a specific tool in order to access the future and effect change in your life. Types of divination include tarot reading, rune casting, ogham casting, palm reading, and scrying.

Elemental Magic: Accessing one of the four elements—earth, air, fire, or water—and harnessing its power to intensify and achieve your dreams.

Faery Magic: Calling on the denizens of faeryland and all of their characteristics and personal traits to aid you in manifesting your wishes on earth.

Herbal Magic: Using the magical properties of herbs to bring about a desired end result, either by burning through incense or in conjunction with other forms of magic.

Incantation Magic: Using the spoken word to focus your wishes and create them on earth. Can be performed as a song, poem, or short chant and is often repeated a specific number of times to correspond to the magical intent of the practitioner.

Incense Magic: Using the magical properties of scent to send your hopes and dreams on the smoke up to the universal consciousness.

Meditation/Creative Visualization Magic: Utilizing relaxation and breathing techniques to focus the mind on the desired goal by actually "seeing" the goal materialized.

Natural Magic: Using your natural surroundings and items found in nature to achieve your magical goal.

Physical Magic: Constructing a charm or talisman with the express purpose of manifesting your wishes and desires.

Rune Magic: Utilizing the divine power of the runes (a Norse divination system) to fulfill your wishes. Rune magic is best performed by a practitioner with knowledge of the runes.

Sex Magic: Accessing the energy that is built up during foreplay (known in Eastern circles as kundalini energy) to strengthen your magical intent.

Symbolic Magic: Using an item in the material realm to represent a person, place, object, or goal in your life. This type of magic is generally performed in conjunction with other forms of magic.

Sympathetic Magic: Altering your perception of a small object so that it becomes the larger person, place, goal, or object that you wish to magically affect. The best-known example of sympathetic magic is a voudou doll. However, changing bread and wine into the body and blood of Christ in a Catholic Communion ceremony is another example of sympathetic magic.

Tarot Magic: Accessing the archetypal knowledge and power of the tarot cards to manifest your desires. It is best to have a general understanding of tarot before performing this type of magic.

Written Word: Using the written word to manifest your desires on earth. This can be performed on paper, rocks, wood, people, or anything else that can hold the written word. If on paper, it is common to burn or bury the spell, in a time frame determined by the practitioner.

Not every magical practitioner would include divination in a list of types of magic. But I do. Magic helps us to crystallize our inner desires and manifest them in our lives. Divination focuses our whirling minds by giving us a firsthand, up-close-and-personal view of our lives from the divine perspective. Instead of being mired in the minutiae of everyday life, we are allowed a glimpse of the big picture. We briefly grasp what the God and Goddess have planned for us. This new knowledge gives us the opportunity to make changes in our lives in order to better fulfill our inner selves and realize our subconscious dreams and goals. Therefore, divination is magic, because it achieves the same goal of bringing forward our best selves in order to create our own reality. It is a powerful magical tool that can easily be used in conjunction with other types of magic.

HIGH MAGIC, LOW MAGIC, AND GODDESS MAGIC

There is a lot of debate in magical circles about the most important type of magic. In my opinion, the most important type of magic helps you manifest your dreams and become the person you were destined to be. We have only a short time in which to learn all of the lessons of our soul. Magic allows us to gain confidence and open ourselves to the myriad possibilities before us. It helps us to see that we are not locked into one life, one thought-form, one way of doing things. It gives us the power to create our ideal existence on the planet. And just as there are multiple types of magic, there are also multiple magical pathways we can take to achieve our goals.

High magic strives to create an ideal existence by working directly with the divine through a specific set of rules and correspondences. There is no guesswork or impromptu spell casting in high magic; everything is planned out weeks in advance. The high magician strives to create balance in the universe and order in life through accessing complex formulae, creating sigils, and calling on the power of the divine. High magic is very concerned with higher ideals, such as the shape of the soul or peace on earth or the protection of innocents. Magic is done in a ritualized setting, usually with specific incantations and invocations. The magical practitioner must prepare him or herself bodily and mentally for the magic to be cast by showering vigorously or fasting for an entire day. In high magic, all magic is done with the astrological, lunar, solar, and seasonal correspondences in mind. This means that magic is performed at all hours of the day and night, regardless of mundane responsibilities.

Low magic, on the other hand, is conducted to benefit the practitioner on the earthly plane. A spell is cast to benefit his or her life and make living enjoyable. The low magician tends to utilize common everyday items found around the house in performing a spell. There are no complex charts and graphs or incantations to be memorized, as instead there is a reliance on physical objects and the power that resides in them. This means that low magicians supplement their own inner power with the energy they find in the natural world, housed in ordinary objects and items. Many low magicians will cleanse themselves before performing magic, but strict adherence to this type of purification varies from magician to magician. Low magicians will pay attention to the moon phase and the seasonal shifts, but with less rigidity than in high magic. Instead of utilizing the energy residing in the cosmos and with the divine, low magic focuses on the energy found in the earth and in her objects. Thus, celestial information is not as vital as personal intuition and observation of the world around you.

Goddess magic combines high and low magic, striving to bring your true self out of your subconscious and into the sunlight of day in order to make everyday life more enjoyable. Mundane needs are addressed alongside esoteric concerns and desires. By attuning ourselves to a specific goddess whose realm of understanding overlaps our own, we are able to connect with the divine while keeping our feet firmly planted on the earth. Your energy and the energy of the goddess merge to create your dreams and desires right before your eyes.

Goddess magic begins with understanding the historic and mythological role of the specific goddess. Look with the same eyes and understand with the same knowledge as our ancestors as you read and research ancient stories of the goddess. Next, travel with her in meditation to her homeland, to an ancient hall or a chilly loch. And finally, invoke her presence through incantation and work magic in your life, your hands ever guided by hers. Using Goddess magic brings you closer to the divine female presence in the universe. It aligns your energy with hers, allowing her to teach you lessons and shower gifts upon you. It is a magic defined by love—love of self, love of others, and love of the divine. There is no room for fear, hate, jealousy, or anger in Goddess magic, as those will ultimately not bring you the joy of life that we all so desperately crave.

As Goddess magic is feminine-inspired, it pays close attention to lunar and earth energies. Therefore, the moon phase and the earth's seasonal cycle are of special importance. For each magic spell in this book, a suggested moon phase and season will be listed. These are guidelines only. Do not feel pressured to wait until the "right time" to cast a spell. If you have connected to a goddess and feel as though your goals need to manifest right now, disregard the moon phase and seasonal information and perform the Goddess magic. Your intuition is your best source of inner wisdom. Listen to it and allow the power of the goddess to aid you in the creation of your desired reality.

MEDITATION AS MAGIC

Guided meditation (also known as shamanic journeying) is one of the core components of Goddess magic, as it allows you direct access to the divine energy of a goddess. Reading and understanding a goddess's story help you connect with her on a mental level, while meditation aids you in connecting with her through your emotions and feelings. It is during the meditation that your energy mingles with the energy of the goddess, giving you deeper wisdom and insight. It is the combination of these two essences that will infuse your magic, giving it the power to manifest your ideal reality.

If you are new to guided meditation, the most important thing to remember is that you have the power to enter and exit a meditation at any time. So, if your journey into the Otherworld becomes too intense, emotionally painful, or difficult to follow, know that you can leave the meditation and return to it at a later time. No one is judging you. This is your experience, so do what feels right for you.

One of the best ways to remember your free will while performing a pathworking (or meditation) is to have a protective talisman. This is either a physical object or a thought-form that protects your spirit and body while you are journeying in the Otherworld. It could be a mantra or chant, a memory, or an ancestor, guardian angel, or spirit. You might find that your protective talisman is a stuffed animal; a picture of your daughter or son; a crystal, rock, or herb; or even a particular incense scent, like sage. Whatever form your talisman takes, it will remind you that should things become too uncomfortable in the Otherworld, you can leave and return to your own body at any time.

The following mini-meditation will help you find your protective talisman. As with all of the meditations in this book, I recommend recording the meditation onto a cassette tape or CD or having a friend or family member read it aloud, in order for you to truly experience the full power of the pathworking. Also, you might want to create a journal of some kind to record your experiences with each meditation. You can then look back on your notes and see if there are any connecting threads throughout the meditations or if they correspond to events that occurred in your everyday life.

Meditation to Find Your Protective Talisman

Take a deep breath, in through your nose, and out through your mouth. Take another deep breath, filling your stomach, your diaphragm, and finally your lungs. Hold this breath for five seconds... 1-2-3-4-5... and exhale, allowing the breath to exit your lungs first, then your diaphragm, and finally your stomach. Take one more deep breath, and as you breathe in, feel the energy and the wonder of the world around you in your fingers, your toes, your legs, and your shoulders, even the top of your head. Hold the breath for seven seconds... 1-2-3-4-5-6-7. As you exhale, feel all tension leave your fingers, your toes, your legs, and your shoulders, even the top of your head. Feel the ground under your body touching every nerve ending and muscle. The ground is warm and radiant. Continue breathing deeply, in through your nose and out through your mouth. Allow the earth to hold and support your body, cradling you in warmth and comfort. You have never felt so relaxed, so secure, so calm.

You are lying in a spring meadow. To your right is a forest. Birds play among the branches of the trees. You hear their sweet songs and see their intricate patterns against the sky. The sky is soft blue. Fluffy white clouds float above your head, cooling the rays of the bright, warm sun. You stretch and feel the heat suffusing every muscle in your body, making you more and more relaxed. A wooden staff of perfect height and weight rests next to you. It is made of oak and inscribed with symbols and glyphs of protection. (pause) You trace the carvings with your finger, and they glow with a golden gleam. You know that naught can harm you while the staff is nearby, guarding your resting form in a circle of light and security.

Inches from the staff, a bag rests next to you. Your fingers graze the soft material and pull the bag closer to you. Leaning up on one elbow, you look inside. What do you see there? A bouquet of wildflowers? A bird feather? A gleaming stone? Or something else, completely different? (pause) Whatever you see, take it out of the bag and lie down on your back. Rest the object on your chest, placing it over your heart. Feel the energy of your heart reaching out to this object, making it one with you and with the universe. (pause) This object protects you and is your gateway to the Otherworld. It allows you access to the houses of the gods, to the realms of angels, to the land of faery, and to the domain of our ancestors, where you can move and fly free. (pause) At the same time, this object connects you with your body here on the earth. If you should wish to return at any time, you need only touch the object and you will be once more in your body. (pause) The object sparkles brightly with the universal life force. It is warm and comforting in the palm of your hand. Squeeze the object lightly and place it in your pocket for safekeeping. Know that anytime you undertake a journey to the Otherworld, you need only reach your hand into your pocket and your protective talisman with be there.

Begin to focus once again on your breathing. Take deep breaths in and out, in and out. (pause) On the next deep breath in, feel the energy and the wonder of the world around you in your fingers, your toes, your legs, and your shoulders, even the top of your head. As you exhale, wiggle your fingers and your toes. Shake your legs and move your shoulders up and down. Take another deep breath and, as you exhale, move your head from side to side. Feel the ground under your body touching every nerve ending and muscle. Hear the rustlings of the people around you. Notice the movements outside. Continue breathing. Stretch your arms out above your head. You are returning to the present, to the here and now. Continue stretching. Continue breathing. When you are ready, open your eyes, blink and focus, and sit up.[2]

With your talisman in hand and your Witches' Pyramid intact, you are ready to embark on a life-altering journey into the realm of the Norse and Celtic goddesses! Each of the following twelve chapters focuses on a specific goddess and seeks to gift you with a deeper appreciation of self and a confidence that all is open to you in this world, if only you look within, unite with the divine, believe in yourself, and seize the opportunity. May the light of the Goddess shine down on you as you realize your full potential and create the life of your dreams!

---

2. The Meditation to Find Your Protective Talisman and the two paragraphs preceding it were taken from the author's book *Goddess Alive!,* 7–8.

LESSONS FROM THE WELSH

MEETING ARIANRHOD,
WELSH GODDESS OF THE STARS
Finding Your Magical Name

ARIANRHOD: GODDESS FOR THE MODERN WORLD

Out of all the goddesses in this book, Arianrhod (pronounced Ahr-ee-AHN-hrod) may be the most modern. She has setbacks and disappointments, such as brothers who undermine her self-esteem and children who, given up for adoption, unexpectedly arrive on her doorstep. She is embarrassed in public by family members who don't understand her true nature and her innate longing for something outside the roles of wife and mother. She takes her lovers as she wishes and rules her own kingdom. Her life is not perfect; it is messy and fraught with sadness and dejection. However, her power is undeniable. She works hard day after day to battle the constructs of society in order to come into her true self—in order to find her own definition of womanhood.

Arianrhod is a moon and star Goddess who also has close links to the earth and humanity. She suffers through the pain (and power) of birth on earth yet oversees the great Whirlpool of Creation in the sky. She lives both in Caer Sidi, a tower on a fortified island in the northern section of Britain, and in Caer Arianrhod, the star cluster known as the Corona Borealis. She is aloof and mighty as the keeper of the Wheel of Stars, a symbol of time, reincarnation, and karma. Yet as the Lady of the Silver Wheel (or full moon), she descends to the earth in her pale white chariot to watch over the tides of the seas and the ebbing and flowing of the tides of human fertility.[1] Both near and far, both of earth and of sky, Arianrhod teases us with a glimpse of her power and her beauty. Then, like the lovely coquette, she pulls away with a knowing smile, leaving us wishing for more.

An ancestral goddess of the ancient Celts, Arianrhod is the daughter of the mother goddess Don. Her father, like her consort, Nwyvre, is little discussed in relation to her mythos. Some sources list her father as Beli, the Celtic god of light and healing,[2] but she is always referred to as her mother's child, possibly harking back to a time of "mother-rule" in the distant past. Her brother is usually listed as Gwydion, a god of magic and trickery. However, Gwydion has two brothers, Amaethon, god of agriculture, and Govannon, god of smithcraft, who do not appear to be directly related to Arianrhod. This confusing family tree leads to the possibility that Don may have exercised her right to choose her lovers freely in a time when a queen chose and dismissed her consorts as she wished, without the constraint of marriage.

---

1. Ryewolf, "Arianrhod."
2. Jordan, *Encyclopedia of Gods*, 24.

If so, this "queen-right" explains the convoluted and conflicting passages relating to Arianrhod in the medieval Welsh book of mythology, *The Mabinogion*. Arianrhod appears to have followed her mother's example, as she lives by herself, without a husband, at Caer Sidi or Caer Arianrhod, with a court of women to attend to her needs. She takes her mates as she wishes and is even said to have slept with mermen on the beach near her castle.[3] However, when her brother Gwydion calls her to the court of their uncle, Math ap Mathonwy (Don's brother and a powerful magician), her brother claims that she is a virgin. When Math asks her if she is a maiden, Arianrhod replies, "I know not but that I am."[4] Math tests her virginity (and the truthfulness of her word) by asking Arianrhod to step over his bent magic wand. (The shape of the wand is important to note, because in the text, Math actually takes the time to bend his wand, perhaps giving it more potency or a more phallic shape.)

Without fear or hesitation, Arianrhod steps over the wand and promptly delivers one baby boy, Dylan Eil Ton, Sea Son of Wave,[5] who immediately crawls to the sea and is not heard of again until his uncle (half uncle?) Govannon kills him by accident. As Arianrhod heads to the door, another bundle of joy drops from her, unnoticed by everyone except Gwydion, who grabs the small child and wraps it in a silk sheet. The appearance of these two children seems to contradict Arianrhod's original claim that she is a virgin. In modern society, we, like Math, view virginity as a purely physical condition. However, if you accept the premise that a matriarchal culture existed at one time in the British Isles, then Arianrhod was not lying by calling herself a maiden. She saw virginity as a state of mind, rather than merely a lack of sexual contact. She believed herself to be a free woman, complete unto herself, without ties or obligations to any man. She was simply confusing (perhaps deliberately) her uncle's question and answering it on her own terms instead of his.

Years later, Gwydion arrives at Arianrhod's court with the boy he had wrapped in the silk sheet. She asks him who the child is, and he tells her, "This boy is a son of thine." Arianrhod replies, "Alas, man! What came over thee to put me to shame, and keep it as long as this?"[6] It seems startling that a mother would welcome her child in such a fashion, claiming that he "shamed" her and condemning Gwydion for taking care of him for so long.

---

3. Monaghan, *New Book of Goddesses and Heroines*.

4. Jones and Jones, *Mabinogion*, 54.

5. Ibid., 54.

6. Ibid., 55.

(She does not even treat her son as a person, but rather a thing, by calling him "it.") However, the answer to her puzzling behavior may stem from her immediate response to birthing her children at Math's court all those years before. If Arianrhod purposefully mistakes Math's question about her virginity, answering on her own terms of emotional and spiritual freedom rather than sexual purity, she chooses to hide her beliefs instead of stating them and confronting her uncle's culturally limited ideas. She outwardly conforms, concealing her true nature. The birth of her sons gives her the ideal opportunity to discuss her beliefs with her uncle, her brother, and all of the men of the court, yet she flees. Instead of gaining power from the birth of her sons and taking pride in her innate creative ability, she disavows them and runs away.

Arianrhod returns to her home, Caer Sidi, where her woman-centered, female-empowered ideas are understood and welcomed. Instead of reveling in her power as a woman at Math's court, she slinks away to a place where her beliefs are encouraged. She does not declare her right to have children with whom she wishes, and she does not proclaim her equality with the men of Math's court. Instead, she succumbs to their ideas about her and to the socially accepted views of womanhood. Arianrhod allows the men to alter her perceptions about herself. For a brief moment, she agrees with them about her "unnatural" sexual liberation, about her inability to rule a kingdom, and about her need to be protected by a male. It is this moment of weakness that shames Arianrhod. The boy is simply a reminder, and Gwydion, having suggested that Math send for Arianrhod all those years before, is the originator of the situation that caused her betrayal of herself. Gwydion's arrival at her court forces Arianrhod to recall her cowardly behavior; therefore, she lashes out at her son with a curse to never have a name unless she gives it to him.

The next day, Gwydion, in his trickster aspect, dupes Arianrhod into giving the young boy a name, Lleu Llaw Gyffes ("fair, deft hand"),[7] when he disguises the boy and himself as shoemakers crafting shoes made of gold. After Gwydion reveals their true shapes to Arianrhod, she announces that her brother may have won this round but that she will win the next. She exclaims, "I will swear on this boy a destiny that he shall never bear arms till I myself equip him therewith."[8] This curse seems less an angry statement

7. Ibid., 56.
8. Ibid.

against Lleu and more a proclamation against Gwydion. It is as if the two siblings are fighting over who is more powerful and the boy is merely a pawn in their game.

Years pass, and Lleu is trained in the martial skills of riding a horse and wielding a sword. When he is ready, Gwydion again disguises himself and the boy, this time as traveling bards, and they are welcomed into Caer Arianrhod to entertain the court. After singing songs and telling tales all evening long, Gwydion once again tricks his sister into breaking her own curse. The next morning, he creates the illusion of an invasion force surrounding Caer Arianrhod and convinces Arianrhod that every able-bodied man should be called to arms. She agrees and even straps the armor on her son, at the prompting of Gwydion. Once she has done this, her curse is broken and Gwydion makes the false fleet disappear. Astonished, Arianrhod admonishes her brother by stating that many of her men might have been harmed because of his deceit. He is unrepentant, and so, in a pique against her brother, Arianrhod lays the final curse on her son. She proclaims, "And I will swear a destiny on him, that he shall never have a wife of the race that is now on this earth."[9] This curse is foiled by Gwydion and Math. Working together, they create a wife for Lleu out of flowers, the goddess Blodeuwedd. (See the next chapter for more information on Blodeuwedd.)

Arianrhod's curses against her son never materialized for long, and perhaps she knew they wouldn't, since she is the goddess of reincarnation and fate. However, her struggle to have supreme control over her son and over herself shows her strength and her desire to be her own woman and be in control of her own destiny. Throughout time, women have struggled to find their own identity, separate from the roles of "wife" and "mother." Arianrhod calls us to remember that just because we, as women, have the ability to give birth, we are not defined by the act of creation. Arianrhod is a goddess who understands that other life goals and missions may take precedence over the ability to conceive and nurture a life within you. Just as Arianrhod made the decision to deny her son Lleu Llaw Gyffes, so we have the ability in our lives to decide our connection to mother-energy and our acceptance or denial of that energy. Women who struggle with the disappointment of infertility, the heartbreak of miscarriage, or the difficulty of abortion will find understanding and comfort in the arms of Arianrhod, the goddess who chose her own life separate from her son, her brother, and her uncle.

---

9. Ibid., 57.

Yet Arianrhod is no less a woman for her choices, no less warm, and no less caring. Finding peace within herself, she has the ability to give so much more to the world because she followed her own path. By staying true to herself, Arianrhod is able to be a better person, free of bitterness and disappointment, free of second-guessing and misunderstandings. In the end, when Lleu arrives at Caer Arianrhod at the end of his life, I envision Arianrhod welcoming him into her home, the waiting place of the spirits of the dead, with open arms and a knowing smile.

Round full-moon mother and strong independent woman, Arianrhod is all around us in the changing of the seasons and the turning Wheel of the Year. Harnessing the power of earth and sky, she brings them into herself to form the firmament of the universe, the shifting of time itself. She sees the past, the present, and the future equally, knowing they are all the same, save for the blink of an eye. She is a mother not defined by motherhood. She is a daughter and a sister not defined by patriarchal family obligations. She is Arianrhod, woman unto herself, goddess immortal!

A MAGICAL NAME

Names have always held magic. They define who we are, how we see ourselves, and how others see us. Names ground us in space and time to the present, to the here and now. When you say your name, you know who you are and accept all of your traits, both good and bad. You are yourself, whole and complete.

A magical name takes you outside of your everyday life and connects you to the sacred—the sacred inside yourself and the sacred of the divine. It represents the mystical part of your personality and amplifies it so that it shines through every part of your body. Your magical name connects you to the truly magical, spiritual being inside you. The name symbolizes all of the wishes, hopes, and idealized images that you ever had of yourself. You are the sorceress, the Merlin, the Lady of the Lake, the temple priest. Through your magical name, the power within yourself is brought to the surface, pushing aside all day-to-day worries and concerns. You find and access the sacred divine within yourself.

At the same time, your magical name allows you a deeper knowledge and understanding of the divine, in whatever form it takes. Gods, goddesses, nature, and the universal life force are suddenly on a first-name basis with you. With you! You can call on their energies to mesh with yours in any sort of mystical undertaking. Meditating, performing a magic spell or ritual, healing with energy or crystals, crafting a gift to the gods, and divining with tarot cards or runes will be times of open communication between yourself and the divine. By opening yourself to the divine and asking for their help and guidance, they will listen and respond. Suddenly, your magical name has opened up a whole new realm of possibility and achievement, linking you to the energy of the gods.

Since the magical name is such a strong conduit to the divine, many people choose to keep their name secret. They feel this keeps the channel to the deities open and uncluttered by other people's thoughts, feelings, and emotions. It also ensures that the magical name stays magical by using it only during sacred connection with the divine. Other people feel that all of life is magical and that utilizing a magical name in all aspects of life makes all of their actions divine and sacred. The choice is yours whether to keep your magical name a secret or not. However, should you choose to keep it a secret, know that you can always choose a "public" magical name for open circles, metaphysical classes, or tarot-card parties and keep a "secret" magical name for ritual, magic, and true union with the divine.

Also, don't limit yourself to one magical name. After some time with one name, you may feel it no longer resonates with you. Don't feel stuck with that magical name! You can add onto it or choose a totally different name. New experiences, new life passages, and new ideas can spark the need for an additional name, so allow your name to grow and change with you.

THE PATHWORKING

In this guided meditation, you will visit Caer Arianrhod, the stronghold of the Goddess Arianrhod. It is housed among the stars, at the Corona Borealis. This guided meditation will take you to the upper reaches of space and time. Traveling in space feels completely different from traveling along the earth plane, in the sky, or under the ground. There is a lightness of being and a lack of resistance that may feel uncomfortable and strange at first. Remember to hold on to your protective talisman, as it will remind you of the safety inherent in these meditations. Should you begin to feel dizzy, experience shortness of breath, or begin to hyperventilate, clasp your talisman and request to return to your body and the earth plane. You can always return to the meditation later, when you are feeling more secure in the experience.

This meditation gives you a few moments alone with the goddess Arianrhod in order to hear what magical name and magical tool or weapon she gives you. Try to listen closely to her words or to the images or feelings she is giving to you. If you don't understand the message, ask her to clarify. Arianrhod is a compassionate, caring goddess; you do not need to fear any repercussions or punishments. As a strong, independent goddess, she respects other strong and independent people. As long as you are respectful, your request is sure to be granted.

There is also a brief period here in which you will be allowed access to the Whirlpool of Creation, in order to look into the past, present, and future. You may find that confronting the Whirlpool is a challenging experience. Divining takes time and effort and it can be difficult to understand the images, thoughts, words, or feelings that are given to you. If you find it arduous to divine, try narrowing the topic of your divination before entering the meditation. Think about one aspect of your life or one question to which you would like an answer. When at the Whirlpool, accept whatever messages come forth. Don't try to analyze them while in the meditation. Pay attention to the images, sounds, or feelings, remembering as many as possible. You can explore their possible meanings once the meditation has ended and you are writing down your experiences in your journal. Also, do not be discouraged if the messages make no sense to you. They probably relate to your future, and thus you will understand their meanings later. Above all, get to know Arianrhod, stay alert, and enjoy the sensation of space travel. For most of us, it's the only way we'll ever get to experience it!

GUIDED MEDITATION: FINDING YOUR MAGICAL NAME

Take a deep breath, in through your nose and out through your mouth. Take another deep breath, filling your stomach, your diaphragm, and finally your lungs. Hold this breath for five seconds … 1-2-3-4-5 … and exhale, allowing the breath to exit your lungs first, then your diaphragm, and finally your stomach. Take one more deep breath and as you breathe in, feel the energy of the natural world around you in your fingers, your toes, your legs, and your shoulders, even the top of your head. Hold the breath for seven seconds … 1-2-3-4-5-6-7. As you exhale, feel all tension leave your fingers, your toes, your legs, and your shoulders, even the top of your head. Feel the ground under your body; sense the sky far above. The ground is soft and comforting, the sky spacious and inviting. Continue breathing deeply, in through your nose and out through your mouth.

Allow the earth to hold and support your body. Allow the sky to refresh your spirit with gentle winds and airy sighs. You have never felt so relaxed, so secure, so calm.

You are lying in a spring meadow amid soft grasses and fragrant flowers. A soft breeze blows about you, dancing with the flowers and playing among your hair. It feels like gentle fingertips tugging and massaging. Birds call to each other, their shrill voices echoing across the field. The sky is soft blue. Fluffy white clouds float above your head, cooling the rays of the bright, warm sun. You stretch and feel the heat suffusing every muscle in your body, making you more and more relaxed. You reach into your pocket and find your protective talisman. It might be the same talisman that you've always used, or it may look different from the last time you took it out and used its power to access the gateway of the gods and goddesses—no matter. Take the object and place it against your heart. Feel it warming in the palm of your hand. Feel its calming, protective energy. It is a part of you and will allow no problems to occur while you are visiting the castle and fortress of Arianrhod. Should you feel uncomfortable at any time while in the Otherworld, just touch your talisman and you will return to your own body immediately. (brief pause) Squeeze your object lightly and place it back in your pocket.

As you remove your hand from your pocket, you begin to feel light and free. It is as if tiny bubbles are growing under every part of your body, or perhaps the clouds are descending to the earth and billowing underneath you, or maybe downy-soft swan feathers are gathering beneath your resting body and buoying you upward. Whether bubbles, clouds, or feathers, you float upward softly, softly, safe and secure in a cocoon of warmth, along the breath of the Goddess. You are surrounded by the beautiful periwinkle blue of the sky. A stray cloud floats by, and you reach out a hand to touch its moist, silken texture. You sigh deeply, releasing any last bits of tension as you swing effortlessly in the hammock of the gods. You close your eyes and see the universe of the body behind your eyelids: Shooting stars of pink and yellow. Starbursts of purple and blue. Moonbeams of white and gray and silver. You open your eyes and see the same scene mirrored before you in the perfect beauty and wonder of the universe. You have never seen anything so wondrous, so beautiful.

To your left, a spiral configuration sparkles with pink, purple, and indigo light. It is made of the swirling stardust of the universe. This is the Corona Borealis, Caer Arianrhod, the magical land of the north, Caer Sidi, the seat of power for the Welsh goddess Arianrhod. You float closer.

She sits there, Arianrhod, the Lady of the Silver Wheel, of the turning of the year, of moon and stars, and of birth and death and reincarnation, beautiful and shining. She takes your breath away. Her throne is luminescent, silver in color, with flashes of purple and deep blue and green. The colors move along a pattern carved into the throne, weaving in and out of the armrests and feet and back of the high chair. Moons and stars peek out from the pattern, glimmering in the light. Arianrhod's hair flows down her back, resting upon a gown of white. Silvery green shapes weave themselves into the white material of her gown. Can you see their design? Are they Celtic knots or spirals? Pictish birds or dogs? Nature-based flowers or trees? Or something else, completely different? (pause) Pay attention to the design and remember it for later. It is the secret to Arianrhod's nature and the key to her home. (brief pause) The goddess smiles at you, her starlit eyes twinkling. You speak to her:

"Oh Arianrhod, keeper of the circling Silver Wheel of stars. All knowledge of past and future do you possess. Time has no meaning for you. The past, present, and future form one spiraling, circling web that cannot be separated. Forever joined, forever together. As the weaver, you control the interactions of our lives and the very act of creation. As the lover, you grant us the power to choose our fate and revel in its all-encompassing sensations. You are the goddess of fertility, the full moon, the stars, regeneration, and reincarnation. Your pathway is an eternal thread that has no beginning or end. I come to you with an open heart and an open mind, seeking the Whirlpool of Creation, that which grants prophecies and wisdom. Show me your love. Embrace me and grant me that which I seek. As you did name your son Lleu Llaw Gyffes, as you did arm him, give me my magical name, give me my magical tool."

The lady points to a swirling rainbow of stars at her feet. You float close to it and look within. (pause) Past ... present ... and future ... do you see. (long pause, three to five minutes) You feel the lady's arm surround you, resting on your waist. (pause) Her breath tickles your ear. (pause) She whispers to you, giving you your magical name, giving you your magical tool. (long pause, three minutes)

You turn your eyes away from the mesmerizing starlight swirls and look into the face of the goddess Arianrhod. With awe and wonder, you thank the goddess for her insight and wisdom. (pause) She nods her head. You begin to float away from the Corona Borealis, away from the magical land of Caer Arianrhod, away from Caer Sidi, the homestead of the beauteous goddess. You close your eyes on the shooting stars of pink and yellow, the starbursts of purple and blue, and the moonbeams of white and gray and silver. Behind your eyelids, the world of the body takes shape: rounded hills of green, soft clouds of white, the all-encompassing sky of heather blue. (pause) You hear the twitters of birds and smell the perfume of wildflowers, tended only by the graceful hand of Mother Nature. You gently land on the soft grass of the spring meadow, and as you do, the bubbles, clouds, or feathers disappear without a trace. You open your eyes. You are back in the meadow with your protective talisman in your pocket. You reach into your pocket and feel your talisman, which allows you access into and out of the astral realm of the gods and goddesses. It is whole and safe and warm. You squeeze it and let it rest in your pocket, where you know it will remain, ready to guide and protect you on your next visit to the deities.

Now take a deep breath, in through your nose and out through your mouth. Take another deep breath, filling your stomach, your diaphragm, and finally your lungs. Hold this breath for five seconds … 1-2-3-4-5 … and exhale, allowing the breath to exit your lungs first, then your diaphragm, and finally your stomach. Breathe deeply once more, and as you breathe in, feel the energy and the wonder of the world around you in your fingers, your toes, your legs, and your shoulders, even the top of your head. As you exhale, wiggle your fingers and toes. Shake your legs and move your shoulders up and down. Take another deep breath and, as you exhale, move your head from side to side. Feel the ground under your body touching every nerve ending and muscle. Hear the rustlings of the people around you. Notice the movements outside. Continue breathing. Stretch your arms out above your head. You are returning to the present, to the here and now. Continue stretching. Continue breathing. When you are ready, open your eyes, blink and focus, and sit up.

INVOCATION TO ARIANRHOD

Goddess Arianrhod,
Moon mother, Star Goddess,
Shining one, Divine!
You are known as:
Daughter of Don,
Mother of Dylan and Lleu Llaw Gyffes,
Sister of Gwydion,
Niece of Math ap Mathonwy,

Half-sister of Amaethon and Govannon,
Daughter of Beli,
Wife of Nwyvre
But you are so much more!

Ruler of Caer Sidi and Caer Arianrhod,
The portal to the Otherworld opens at your fingertips.
Custodian of the Whirlpool of Creation,
Fate encircles your head in a glistening crown.
Keeper of the Wheel of Stars,
Past, present, and future blend in the folds of your robe.
Lady of the Silver Wheel,
Love and creation live in the depths of your heart.

I honor you, Arianrhod,
Goddess Divine,
As the woman you are—
Independent, strong, caring, loving.
May I follow my own path,
As you followed yours.
May I accept my own power,
As you accepted yours.
May I choose my own life,
As you chose yours.
May my words and actions honor you
As I honor myself for the (wo)man I am.

Hail Arianrhod, Goddess immortal, Woman unto herself!
Hail (*your name here*), Spark of the Divine, (Wo)man unto (her/him)self!

MAGICAL ACTIVITIES

Physical Magic: Create a Crown of Stars

Items Needed: Star garland, scissors, curly ribbon, paper (optional), pen or pencil
(optional)

Moon Phase: Full
Seasonal Cycle: Any

To celebrate Arianrhod's association with the stars in the sky and to represent your own innate power (your inner royal queen or king), you can create a crown of stars to wear in ritual, while stargazing, or when attending Renaissance festivals or Sabbat celebrations. This spell is designed to boost your ego and connect you to the aspect of Arianrhod that rules a kingdom and chooses her own life path, regardless of societal pressures. You want the crown to symbolize your own right to rule your life, regardless of the ideas and expectations of others. It is a very simple craft but, when performed with intention, can profoundly affect your life and your self-worth. And, once you have the materials, you can complete it in less than a half-hour. Children also find this craft easy to make and, due to its hands-on nature, find the magical aspect accessible and easy to understand. This spell is especially potent when self-confidence becomes an issue, so don't be afraid to bust out the curly ribbon with your preteen or teenager.

Go to your local craft store and look for the decorative trim and garland section. If your store has a wide variety, then it will undoubtedly have many different designs and colors. You want garland that is made of thin foil-wrapped wire (about the width of florist wire) and has variously sized stars attached to it. My garland is made by Westrim Crafts, is nine feet long, and comes in over five different colors. Since green, white, and silver are the colors most associated with Arianrhod, I would look for those colors first. However, don't despair if your store only has gold and purple. Any color will work well for this craft. While at the craft store, if you don't have curly ribbon at home, look for some to complement the colors of your star garland.

After you have gathered all of the materials, take some time to explore your sense of self, your accomplishments, your positive characteristics, and your skills. You can do this in your head or on a piece of paper, whichever is easiest for you, but make sure you can remember them all. Whether in your mind or on a piece of paper, be aware that it is often very easy to focus on those things we want to improve in our lives but difficult to list those things we do well. Allow yourself some time to gather your thoughts and ideas. Remember that you bring beauty into the world just by being you. Whenever you start to question the positive traits you are listing, remind yourself of your importance to your family and friends. They love you. Now it is time to love yourself.

Once you've gathered your materials and listed at least twenty positive characteristics and accomplishments, take the star garland and unravel a section. Wrap it around your head, either at your forehead or a little above your forehead, measuring the circumference of your head. This will form the foundation of your star crown, so make sure that you don't make it too small or too big. Mark the place where it meets itself with your finger and bring the star garland, now in the shape of a circle, into your lap. Keep the circle shape intact by twisting the end of the garland around the place marked by your finger. You now have a circle the size of your head attached to a long string of star garland.

Loop the star garland around your circlet, creating a thicker circle of stars. As you do this, begin to focus on the wonderful characteristics and traits you bring into the world. You can say them out loud or think them to yourself. Focus on general ideas like your creativity, your sense of style, or your positive attitude. After two or three loops, cut the garland so that the end matches up to the place where you twisted the garland earlier. Give yourself a little extra wire so that you can twist all of the loops together. The twisted section will be the back of your crown, so don't worry if it's not particularly neat. If you want to use more than one color of star garland, limit the number of your loops to one or two per color. Any more than five loops of star garland will make your crown look bulky and awkward.

Hold the looped star garland in your hands and gaze at it for a moment. Really see the colors, the shapes, and the shiny foil. For each star on your crown, say or think one of your items on your list of positive attributes and deeds. Be sure to hold the star in your hand when you do this, since you are effectively "naming" it, attuning it to your own positive energy, past, present, and future.

After you have named each star, use the curly ribbon to decorate your star crown. Start in the back of your crown, knotting the ribbon securely in place. Weave the ribbon around all of the sections of star garland, bringing them loosely together. When you return to the back of the crown again, either knot the ribbon in place or continue to wrap around the crown. The curly ribbon seals the magic in place, attaching the naming to each star. As you wind the ribbon, creating your queen or king of myself crown, say or think the following:

My power stays, true and bright. I dismiss the dark of night. I strive to reach my truest height as I become the Queen/King of Might.

Once you have looped the curly ribbon to your satisfaction, leave a long tail or streamer at the back of your crown so that it will hang down your back and frolic joyfully in the breeze. You can make the streamers as curly or as straight as you like, depending on the amount of pressure you place against the curly ribbon. To make the ribbon curly, use the flat edge of your scissors or a ruler. Notice how the ribbon naturally wants to curl. Take your flat edge and run it along the length of the underside of the curl. This should cause the ribbon to curl even more. If the ribbon seems to straighten, don't panic! Simply take your flat edge and run it along the other side of the ribbon, and your ribbon should curl up nicely.

When you're done with the star garland and curly ribbon, you should have a beautiful, simple star crown that fits your head perfectly. These crowns are fragile and will not last for years, so enjoy your crown now! Utilize its power to remind you of your Goddess-given skills and talents. It will remind you of all you have accomplished and of all the positive energy you bring into the world. If you take care of your crown, it should last you several months. And remember, you can always make another.

Divination: The Power of Fate

Items Needed: Paper (at least three sheets) and a pen or pencil
Moon Phase: Dark or new
Seasonal Cycle: Autumn, especially the end of October and beginning of November

While many people receive their magical name during meditation or journeywork or in dreams, some may not be able to "hear" the will of the Goddess, the name she bestows. This is especially true if you typically experience meditations in a visual format (like a movie or a series of snapshots) as opposed to an audio or sensory format. If you performed the guided meditation and didn't receive your magical name, don't despair. You can access the knowledge of the Goddess by utilizing intuition and fate with the following activity.

Take a piece of paper and write down all of the things that first attracted you to Goddess spirituality. Write down colors, sensations, and emotions. Include random phrases that pop into your head, descriptions of scenes, and people and places that influenced you. Now add to your list all of the gods and goddesses, angels, faeries, and spirit guides (including animals) to which you feel drawn. Incorporate flowers, trees, and herbs that hold meaning for you, as well as any celestial bodies that attract you.

After you've covered the sheet of paper with as many words and phrases as you can, turn it away from you so that the blank side is face-up. Ground and center as you normally do, taking as much time as you need but making sure you relax for at least five minutes. When you feel calm and centered, flip the piece of paper over and allow your eyes to scan the words on the page. Don't read them; just have your eyes float over the page. Your eyes will naturally be attracted to certain words and will pause briefly at them. Write these words down on small scraps of paper. When you have between five and ten words, stop looking at your list and put it aside. Fold up the small pieces of paper. Now comes the fun part!

Draw a moon, a pentacle, or a Goddess symbol on a blank piece of paper and place it in front of you. Gather your small pieces of paper together and hold them in your hands. Take a deep breath and focus on your goal of finding your magical name. Blow your breath onto the pieces of paper, raise them above your head, and then let them fall in front of you. Some will fall on your sacred design; others will ricochet off the walls or the floor or your pet kitty or guinea pig. Open only the papers that fell on your design and write down the words that appear. Do this as many times as is necessary to achieve seven (or nine or thirteen) appearances of the same word. Ta-da! You have just found your magical name.

Incantation Magic: Claiming Your Magical Name

Items Needed: Two small bowls, salt, water (in a pitcher or cup), a red candle and holder, lavender stick incense and holder, eyeliner of any color, sparkles, a lighter or matches, a picture of the universe

Moon Phase: Waxing or full

Seasonal Cycle: Early spring

You have traveled to the Corona Borealis, visited with the goddess Arianrhod, and received your magical name. Now it is time to embrace that name and, in the presence of the elementals and the gods and goddesses, claim your new name. By claiming your magical name, you will introduce your energy to the universe, opening up profound portals and channels. Many people experience a stronger connection to the divine, more powerful spellwork and energy healing, and greater accuracy in divination after accepting and owning their magical name. Do not be surprised if you have vivid dreams or enhanced intuition. Pay attention to the messages sent by the universe and write them down in your journal or Book of Shadows.

Since this spell deals with profound, universal energies, I have included a circle casting and a calling of the quarters along with the actual spellwork. You can skip directly to the spellwork if you prefer. Since this spell is opening yourself up to the energy of the universe and inscribing your name into every fiber of your being, I prefer a more stylized and ritualized format. The choice is entirely up to you.

Begin by sitting or kneeling before your altar. Have all of the necessary items on the altar ahead of time. Ground and center yourself as you would before any meditation. Really feel your connection to the earth, rooting you in the present and in the here and now. Expand your heart chakra and your heart energy beyond your physical body to your astral body, your aura, and your chi, and feel it flow smoothly and effortlessly, soft and warm. Continue to push out your heart energy to the plants and animals around your home, to the tops of the trees, to the fluffy clouds in the sky. Make sure that your link to Mother Earth still remains strong, even though you have shifted your focus up to the realms of the sky gods. Once you feel as though your focus on the blue sky is clear, extend your heart chakra up to the twinkling, star-strewn universe. Honor the universe and ask that a portion of its energy return with you when you call back your heart chakra to the earth realm. Spend as much time in the universe as you would like, and when you are ready, bring your heart energy down from the stars, down from the fluffy clouds and the tops of the trees. Call your heart chakra back into yourself, inward and away from the animals and plants around your house, in through your chi, your aura, and your astral body, to rest once again in your physical self.

Open your eyes and focus on the picture of the universe on your altar. Feel its energy pulsing inside you and all around you. Feel it creating a sacred sphere around you and your space. It holds in the energy and separates you from the outside world. You truly sit between two worlds. Light the lavender incense and walk around your altar clockwise, holding the incense. When you return to your altar, place the incense in its holder and say:

O rushing winds and gentle breezes,
Ye sylphs and birds and faery folk,
I am called (your magical name).
I honor you and ask for your guidance and protection
In all my magical work.

Take a few moments to feel the cleansing beauty of the element of air before lighting the red candle. Hold the candle in both hands and walk clockwise around your altar. When you return to where you started, place the candle in its holder and say:

> *O dancing flame and burning torch,*
> *Ye salamanders and snakes and dragons,*
> *I am called* (your magical name).
> *I honor you and ask for your guidance and protection*
> *In all my magical work.*

Relax and feel the purifying heat of the element of fire. When you are finished with the visualization, pour the water into one of the bowls on the altar. Holding the bowl of water, walk around your altar in a clockwise direction. When you return to where you started, place the bowl on the altar and say:

> *O misty rain and living flood,*
> *Ye undines and fish and mermaids,*
> *I am called* (your magical name).
> *I honor you and ask for your guidance and protection*
> *In all my magical work.*

Breathe deeply and feel the soothing calm of the element of water. After a moment, place a handful of salt into the remaining bowl and, holding the bowl, walk around the altar clockwise. When you return to where you started, place the bowl on the altar and say:

> *O forests green and mountains dark,*
> *Ye gnomes and bears and white buffalo,*
> *I am called* (your magical name).
> *I honor you and ask for your guidance and protection*
> *In all my magical work.*

Ease any tension in your body and feel the stable security of the element of earth. Focusing on each of the elements and on the universe, state your intention to embrace and accept your magical name. Say:

> *The Star and Moon Goddess Arianrhod is the giver of names.*
> *She has given me my magical name and I honor it.*

May my name connect me to the elements of air, fire, water, and earth.
May my name link me to the energy of the universe and its boundless vision.
May the gods and goddesses know, protect, and guide me by this name.

Take your eyeliner and write your magical name on your skin. It can be on your arm, your leg, your hand, your foot, or anywhere else you feel is appropriate. While you are writing, focus all of your energy and will on your new name. Feel it sinking into your skin, seeping into your blood and bones. When you are done, dust your name with a light sprinkling of sparkles, signifying that it is now a part of the realm of the divine. Say your name three times out loud in a clear, proud voice.

Honor the elements by placing your hands over your heart and bowing slightly to each one. Thank them individually for attending your magic, and honor them by walking each element counterclockwise around your altar. You do not have to say or do anything fancy; simply give the elements the respect they deserve. After each element has been honored, visualize the universe that is all around you. Hold your arms out and, in a sweeping gesture, release the universe by guiding it upward through the atmosphere and into the immensity of space. Keep the elements and the picture of the universe on the altar until the incense and the candle burn out. If you need to leave the house or the room, please blow the candle out and relight it at a later time. Ideally, the candle should be burned all the way down right after the spell is performed. However, a candle should never be left alone in a room: you don't want to catch your house or apartment on fire.

Once the incense and candle have burned out naturally, take the candle stub, the incense ashes, the salt, and the water and bury them in a respectful manner. If you don't have any place to bury them, it is possible (but not ideal) to throw them in the trash. Should you dispose of your ritual elements in the trash, please honor the elementals with a fluorite stone left outdoors for the faeries. (And remember, every plant loves water, so you can definitely recycle that element.)

Your magical name is now a part of your body, your mind, and your spirit. It is the name by which the universe, the elementals, and the gods and goddesses know you. Rejoice! Your connection to Spirit grows stronger every day.

MEETING BLODEUWEDD, WELSH GODDESS OF SEDUCTION AND CHOICE

Accepting Your Shadow Self

BLODEUWEDD: CHANGING GODDESS

There is nothing more difficult to accept than change. Daily life assumes a relaxing, natural, rhythm and then *wham*! Something occurs to destroy your bubble of peace and security. We can thank Blodeuwedd (pronounced blow-DYE-weth) for that. Blodeuwedd is a goddess who welcomes change, alteration, transformation, and variation. Not content with a devoted husband, a beautiful castle home, and a secure life, Blodeuwedd chooses the excitement of true love over the sanctuary of marriage. She realizes that a refuge can just as easily become a prison.

In *The Mabinogion*, the Welsh medieval mythological epic, Blodeuwedd is created by Math ap Mathonwy for his nephew, Lleu Llaw Gyffes. Lleu has been cursed by his mother, Arianrhod, with never having a human wife. Greatly upset by this curse, as it would preclude him from ever being considered a "true man," Lleu and his foster father, Gwydion (Arianrhod's brother), ask Math for help. Math, a great magician, crafts a woman out of flowers. In *The Mabinogion*, Math creates her from three flowers, "the flowers of the oak, and the flowers of the broom, and the flowers of the meadowsweet."[1] Robert Graves, in his seminal work *The White Goddess*, states that nine flowers were used in the formation of Blodeuwedd: the sacred flowers of the oak, broom, meadowsweet, primrose, cockle, bean, nettle, chestnut, and hawthorn.[2]

After her birth, Blodeuwedd is immediately married to Lleu in the traditional way. In short, there is a feast and a consummation between man and wife. They settle into the castle of Tomen Y Mur, but before long, Lleu decides to visit his uncle Math, leaving Blodeuwedd by herself in her castle with her servants. Not long after Lleu leaves, a hunting horn sounds outside the castle walls. Undoubtedly bored, Blodeuwedd sends a messenger out to the hunting party to find out the name of the lord. The messenger returns with the name Gronw Bebyr, lord of Penllyn, who is busy hunting, slaying, and dressing a stag. Gronw works until dusk, and Blodeuwedd, seeing his hard work and understanding he is far from home, extends hospitality to him and his men, inviting them to stay in her home for the evening.

Over dinner, Blodeuwedd and Gronw exchange glances and, without warning, are immediately overwhelmed with love for each other. Their love is so sudden and so sharp that they sleep together that very night. For two days and nights, Blodeuwedd

---

1. Jones and Jones, *Mabinogion,* 58.
2. Graves, *White Goddess,* 41.

and Gronw live in an ecstasy of bittersweet love, constantly looking over their shoulders and hoping Lleu will not arrive home. It is at this time that Blodeuwedd begins to understand that she holds innate power within herself. Each day, Gronw suggests that he should leave. Blodeuwedd counters with the phrase "Thou wilt not go from me,"[3] and Gronw obeys. On the third day, Blodeuwedd gives her consent to Gronw's departure but agrees with his plan to find out how to kill her husband so that she may be free to marry her new lover.

The very day that Gronw departs, Lleu arrives home, blithely unaware of his wife's intentions. That evening, Blodeuwedd is unresponsive to Lleu's amorous gestures, and he questions her about her obvious distress. She sighs that she is worried about his possible death. Laughing, he explains to her that he can be killed by no mortal means. "One must needs be a year making the spear wherewith I should be smitten, without making anything of it save when folk were at mass on Sunday," Lleu explains.[4] He continues with the series of events that must take place in order for him to die. He must be neither on land nor in water, inside nor outside, on the earth nor in the air. "By making a bath for me on a river bank, and making a vaulted frame over the tub, and thatching it well and snugly beside the tub, and bringing a he-goat, and setting it beside the tub, and myself placing one foot on the back of the he-goat and the other on the edge of the tub. Whoever should smite me so, he would bring about my death."[5]

Blodeuwedd sends the instructions to Gronw and waits a year for the spear to be made. Once Gronw has finished fashioning the spear according to Lleu's instructions, Blodeuwedd again feigns anxiety over Lleu's possible death. To ease her fears that such an event is unlikely, he creates the scenario necessary for his death and actually stands with one foot on a he-goat and one foot on a tub. Naturally, Gronw is ready with his spear, and his aim is true. When Lleu is pierced by the poisoned spear, he shape-shifts into an eagle and flies away.

With Lleu gone, Blodeuwedd and Gronw are free to be lovers, and they move into Tomen Y Mur together. After a time, Gwydion and Math become concerned that they have not heard from Lleu. They fear evil tidings, yet with all their magic, they cannot discern the fate of their young relative. Gwydion stumbles across a sow that is apparently

---

3. Jones and Jones, *Mabinogion*, 59.

4. Ibid., 59–60.

5. Ibid., 60.

caught up in some magic. He follows her one morning to a tree that is surrounded by rotting flesh and maggots. In the limbs of the tree rests a shriveled, diseased eagle who is none other than Lleu Llaw Gyffes. Gwydion brings the eagle to Math, who with a touch of his wand transforms him back into a man. For several months, Lleu is nursed back to health.

Once Lleu is whole again, the three men descend upon Tomen Y Mur, but Blodeuwedd has already fled to a nearby mountain. However, she is no match for the two magicians and one warrior. They catch up to her, and Gwydion changes her into an owl, a bird that is feared by all other birds. Gronw escapes to his homeland of Penllyn and begs Lleu for peace. Lleu, however, will not be satisfied with anything other than the opportunity to kill Gronw in the same manner in which he was killed. And so Gronw is killed by a spear thrown by Lleu on the banks of the Cynfael River.

Many scholars, including Robert Graves in *The White Goddess*, have suggested that Blodeuwedd fulfills the function of the archetypal Earth Mother or May Queen in relation to her husband's role as sacrificial king. Lleu's bedding of Blodeuwedd to make them husband and wife would then be seen as a ritual in which he pledges his life to the Earth Mother in order to ensure her fruitfulness.[6] This is a common theme in legends from pre-Christian Europe and the pre-Islamic Middle East and may indicate a time when a king was indeed required to sacrifice his life for the good of his people and the good of his land. One need only think of the legend of King Arthur, a story that originated in *The Mabinogion*, to see strikingly familiar patterns.

However, while King Arthur dies and Guinevere and Lancelot live on, though as mere shadows of their former glorious selves, Lleu does not die. He is resurrected by his magical uncle Math ap Mathonwy, while Blodeuwedd's love, Gronw Bebyr, is killed. Therefore, Blodeuwedd's story does not fit perfectly within the structure of the true sacrificial king motif.

Another viewpoint on the myth of Blodeuwedd comes from the women's spirituality movement. Feminist historians and writers have connected Blodeuwedd's story with that of physically and mentally abused woman. They view Blodeuwedd as a victim who is forced to marry against her will. In response, she lashes out against her situation, fighting to free herself from her husband and choose her own life. The feminist perspective stays truer to the original story; however, there is no indication that Lleu

---

6. Graves, *White Goddess*, 41, 332, and 447–448.

abused Blodeuwedd or that Blodeuwedd was unhappy in her marriage. Thus, feminist historians attach a modern philosophical cause or issue to the story that is not indicated in the original text.

Blodeuwedd indeed chooses to reject her marriage for the excitement of true love, but not for the reasons the feminists claim. She does it because she realizes she can. Blodeuwedd loves Lleu, just as she loves herself and Gronw Bebyr. However, her love changes and mutates when confronted by the shifting energies of her lovers. She loves them both, just differently. Accepting that love can have many faces allows Blodeuwedd to understand the many faces of herself. Once Blodeuwedd mentally and emotionally grows as a woman, she can admit that she is not all flowers and springtime and happiness. She realizes that the owl lurks within as well, bringing with it midnight and death.

Through her relationship with Gronw, Blodeuwedd comprehends that there is more to her character than she originally presumed. She has power, but with that power comes awesome responsibility and a necessary acceptance of all sides of her complex personality. Without her dalliance with Gronw, Blodeuwedd would never have thought to cuckold her husband and plan his death, despite the fact that these actions were always within her nature to achieve. Reaching into the dark places of her true self, Blodeuwedd unlocks her inner needs and desires and seeks to manifest them in her life.

Blodeuwedd teaches us that balance and transformation are necessary aspects of life. She grants us permission to accept our darker halves, to realize that we have power beyond that which we can comprehend. Fanciful, sexual, and lively, Blodeuwedd encourages us to live life to the fullest and to acknowledge our faults along with our positive attributes. We are all made up of flowers and owls. If we only have the courage to unite our two halves, we will be amazed by our innate strength and power.

THE TRUE YOU: ACCEPTING YOURSELF

The world is made up of black and white, good and bad, night and day. Without one half of the pair, the other would appear meaningless and devoid of worth. How could we revel in the warmth of the sun without knowing the chilly dark of the night? How could we appreciate the tender glow of a shooting star without first experiencing the garish heat of the sun? We couldn't. We, as humans, are creatures of the natural world, and like day and night, we each have darkness and light within ourselves. To deny one of these aspects is to leach power from our inner selves.

Accepting the darkness within can be difficult. It is not easy to acknowledge a raging temper or an underhanded, sly demeanor. We set ourselves up as models of perfection, and climbing down from that lofty perch can be precarious and dangerous. There is always the possibility of succumbing to the darkness and drowning in the inky murk, without any hope for rescue or survival.

Recognizing your shadow side is not about giving yourself over to your least desirable qualities. Rather, it is a process of accepting your true nature and loving yourself despite (maybe even because of) your faults. Like Blodeuwedd, your darkness makes you a complete person—a person full of wonder and power and choices beyond belief. You have the ability to ascend higher than you have ever dreamed, but only if you have the courage to delve first into the slippery shades of your inner being.

THE PATHWORKING

Visiting Blodeuwedd is rather like eating as much candy as you want without realizing the dentist is waiting for you just around the corner. Tomen Y Mur is beautiful and lush, with riches beyond your imagination. However, Blodeuwedd is not a goddess content with your surface personality. She wants to know you—all of you. She wants to know the true you that you keep stashed in the recesses of your mind and soul and heart.

Near the end of your journey, Blodeuwedd will ask you to look deep into a goblet of wine and see your shadow self. Your shadow self may appear as a child, an old man, a tree stump, or even a monster. Do not be afraid. Remember, this dark aspect is you, and you can control it once you have accepted it wholly and unconditionally. Blodeuwedd will ask you not only to meet your dark half but also to "become whole." You can do this in any number of ways, and the meditation allows you to create your own journey. However, to "become whole," your shadow self should no longer exist separately from the rest of yourself.

It may take several meditations to truly recognize your connection to your other half. Don't worry if you are so surprised by the physical appearance of your dark half that you immediately come out of the meditation without working on acceptance. Shadow work takes time and cannot be rushed. Take as much time as you need, for Blodeuwedd is always there for you.

GUIDED MEDITATION: ACCEPTING YOUR SHADOW SELF

Take a deep breath, in through your nose and out through your mouth. Take another deep breath, filling your stomach, your diaphragm, and finally your lungs. Hold this breath for five seconds... 1-2-3-4-5... and exhale, allowing the breath to exit your lungs first, then your diaphragm, and finally your stomach. Take one more deep breath, and as you breathe in, feel calming earth energy enter you, supporting your fingers, your toes, your legs, and your shoulders, even the top of your head. Hold the breath for seven seconds... 1-2-3-4-5-6-7. As you exhale, feel all tension leave your fingers, your toes, your legs, and your shoulders, even the top of your head. Feel the fertile earth under your body, moist and green. The land supports you, giving you strength and guidance. Feel any stress and anger seep from your body into the welcoming, waiting ground, where it is converted into positive, healing energy. Continue breathing deeply, in through your nose and out through your mouth. Allow the earth to hold and support your body, removing any remaining fear and anxiety. You have never felt so relaxed, so secure, so calm.

You are standing at the foot of a large, earthen mound covered with soft green grass. At the top of the mound rests a stone fortress, well kept up, neat, and tidy. A heavy oaken door is closed against the wind that whips across this open, lonely country. The clouds scuttle overhead, streaks of gray cotton pulled taut by the fingers of a celestial weaver. The sun hides behind the light gray curtain of the sky, and all of the colors in this wild and desolate place are muted and damp.

You walk around the earthen mound, looking for a way to ascend to the relative comfort and safety of the stone fort. Then you notice a set of narrow stone stairs, partially obscured by the lush grass. The stairs wind around the hill, following its gentle rise and swell, until they reach the very top of the mound. You place your foot on the first stair just as a huge gust of wind rolls across the valley and over the mound. You are almost knocked backward off the stair, and you fight to hold your balance and stay upright. Your vision is obscured by the hood of your cloak, and you realize, rather suddenly, that you are wearing a warm, woolen cape. There is a pocket on the inside front flap, and you tentatively reach inside. Your hand closes around a familiar and welcoming shape—your protective totem for journeys into the Otherworld. You give your totem a tender squeeze and begin to quickly climb the stairs.

The stairs lead you to the front of the stone fortress. The oaken door looms before you. It is even larger than you thought. It looks to be newly made, although the hinges and door handles are old in design. They are black and made from heavy iron in a pattern that resembles medieval scrollwork. You half-expect a brown-robed cleric to open the door and ask your business. But one does not appear. In fact, no one appears. You knock at the door, but there is no answer. You crouch down, huddling to stay warm, and stare out at the vast expanse of nothingness that surrounds this green mound of earth.

You wait for what seems like forever. Your nose is raw from the unceasing wind, and your fingers are blue from the cold. You can no longer feel your toes, and your feet and legs are cramped from holding the same position. You realize that you must make a decision. You must leave this wind-tossed mound and search for a warm, smoky tavern, or you must enter the stone fortress. You scan the uninhabited countryside and know that there is only one choice open to you. You slowly unbend from your crouched position, shaking your arms and legs to return the flow of blood to them. Taking a deep breath, you stride over to the oaken door and push it open.

A flood of warmth rolls over you, and you are blinded by bright, dazzling white light. You struggle backward, throwing your arm over your eyes as a shield. You turn to find the stairs and leave this strange place, but a force tugs you toward the fortress. Against your will, you are softly pulled into the blinding light. The door slams behind you.

A voice speaks: "You almost fell off the edge." The voice is taut with worry and strain, yet you sense hints of softness hidden within. You open your eyes to see a dazzling display before you. A heavy mahogany table stretches the length of a giant hall. Chandeliers sparkle overhead, lit by the flickering flames of hundreds of candles. They cast rainbows all around the room. The walls are covered with rich tapestries woven in fantastical designs. Burgundy wine, forest green, sea blue, golden yellow—the colors swirl around and through each other. Take a moment to study the designs and colors. What do you see? These images are clues to the goddess Blodeuwedd's true nature and your own inner self. (pause)

Tearing your eyes away from the tapestries, you are confronted with an enormous feast laid out on the table. You wonder if it was there beforehand but shrug off any feeling of disquiet as your stomach rumbles noisily. Several turkeys, bowls of potatoes, quail, rabbit, mince pies, vegetable stews, and carrots in butter sauce cover the length of the table. The aroma is delectable, and your mouth begins to water. You step up to the table, ready to eat the item closest to you, when a thought makes you stop with your mouth wide open: is it polite to begin a feast without talking to the host first?

"Feel free to eat," the voice from before whispers into your ear, now sounding seductive and slightly amused. "This feast is for you." A large plate appears at your elbow. You pick it up and heap as much food as you would like onto it. At the far end of the table, away from the oaken door, an open doorway beckons you. Diffused candlelight softens the darkened recesses of the side room, and you can make out the outline of a plush sofa. Quietly, stealthily, you step inside.

Far to the back of the room, a fire blazes invitingly. Although you are no longer cold, the sofa looks warm and inviting, the perfect place to enjoy an afternoon feast. As you move toward the fireplace, thick fur rugs pad your feet, muting your footsteps. Large portraits of people long dead loom above you, their eyes fixed and staring. You see a heavy chest against one wall, intricately carved with knotwork and spirals. As you look, the patterns seem to shift, moving of their own accord. New designs, just as beautiful, emerge. You shiver despite the warmth of the fire.

You sit on the sofa and unhook your cape to get more comfortable. You eat, enjoying the taste and texture of every morsel of food. Carrots, turkey, stew! This is the best food you have ever eaten! (pause) You move your hand to wipe away some stray butter sauce that has dribbled down your chin, and a cloth napkin appears before your very eyes. You gasp, startled, and look away from the food. There, sitting next to you, handing you a napkin, is a tall, striking woman. She is dressed in white, and her light-brown hair waves down her back and around her shoulders. Her face has a strong bone structure that precludes the use of the word *beautiful* but lends her an earthy, capable air. Her mouth is wide, with full, expressive lips, and her light gray eyes are watchful, yet full of cheer. She shakes the napkin, a hint of a smile playing about the corners of her mouth. You take it from her.

"I am the goddess Blodeuwedd," she says, leaning back against the sofa and wrapping a paisley-print shawl around her shoulders. "Flower-face, Owl Queen. Welcome to my home, Tomen Y Mur." You stammer your thanks to her (pause) but she waves them off with a dismissive gesture. "My home is always open to those who seek with their true heart." She smiles wolfishly, and her hooded eyes darken. "Do you seek with your true heart?" You answer her as best you can. (pause)

Satisfied with your answer, Blodeuwedd thrusts a shimmering goblet into your hand. It is filled to the brim with deep red wine, the color of garnets and pomegranates and blood. You look into the goblet and feel lost. You feel as though your very essence could be sucked deep into the darkness of the wine. You glance over at Blodeuwedd. Her hands twirl in the air around her, forming ancient glyphs and shapes. They sparkle with golden faery lights before fizzling into darkness. She is looking at you, the golden lights reflected in her gray eyes.

"Stare into the goblet," Blodeuwedd instructs you, "for there you will know your other half. Light and dark. Good and bad. Earth and sky. Fire and water. Go and meet your shadow self and become whole."

You stare into the cup of wine. (pause) You see the flickering light and shadow from the fire. (pause) You see the bursting golden faery lights. (pause) You see your own eyes reflected back at you. (pause) And then the picture alters slightly and you see something completely different. (pause) Give in to this other image. Study it. Become it. And then allow yourself to be pulled into the world of the wine goblet. (long pause)

As you finish your work with your true self, you look up and see the faery lights of Blodeuwedd's patterns. You follow the glyphs with your eyes, (pause) and when you look away from them, you find you are once again on the wind-tossed summit of the hill of Tomen Y Mur. You look around you, wondering how you got there, and hear Blodeuwedd's throaty, full-bodied laughter on the wind.

"Life is a surprise," she chuckles. "Love it. Accept it. And live it!" Her voice flies away from you and you are alone once again in the gray light. You shrug the woolen cape farther up on your shoulders for warmth and, smiling, begin the circular descent back down the grassy mound.

Now take a deep breath, in through your nose and out through your mouth. Take another deep breath, filling your stomach, your diaphragm, and finally your lungs. Hold this breath for five seconds … 1-2-3-4-5 … and exhale, allowing the breath to exit your lungs first, then your diaphragm, and finally your stomach. Breathe deeply once more, and as you breathe in, feel the energy and the wonder of the world around you in your fingers, your toes, your legs, and your shoulders, even the top of your head. As you exhale, wiggle your fingers and toes. Shake your legs and move your shoulders up and down. Take another deep breath and, as you exhale, move your head from side to side. Feel the ground under your body touching every nerve ending and muscle. Hear the rustlings of the people around you. Notice the movements outside. Continue breathing.

Stretch your arms out above your head. You are returning to the present, to the here and now. Continue stretching. Continue breathing. When you are ready, open your eyes, blink and focus, and sit up.

INVOCATION TO BLODEUWEDD

Flower-face,
Owl woman,
Goddess of old,
Goddess renewed.
Reborn in a flurry of feathers,
In a flash of lightning,
I honor your darkness.
I honor your light.

I feel the prick of your dagger,
The blood surging full,
And the brightness of a spring day,
The flower wafting sweet.

Help me to open my eyes,
To see the truth of myself.
Help me to become complete.
Courage and honor,
Deception and death,
I accept them all
Into myself,
Into my blood, singing
Of another place
And another world
And another time.

I am Flower-face
Owl woman,
God/dess of old,

God/dess renewed.

I honor my darkness.

I honor my light.

MAGICAL ACTIVITIES

Symbolic Magic: Become One with Your Shadow Self

Items Needed: Thirteen chocolates, cookies, or cups of coffee or tea

Moon Phase: Waning or dark

Seasonal Cycle: Winter

Perhaps you listened to the meditation and had some difficulty in integrating your shadow self. Or, maybe you were able to connect with your darker half but still have lingering doubts about the meditation. If so, then this exercise is one more way to accept your true, complete personality.

Gather together thirteen small pieces of chocolate. If you are allergic to chocolate, you can use ginger or molasses cookies or even cups of hot black tea or coffee. (If you like alcohol, rum works well too.) I like the number thirteen because of its mystical, magical, often-misunderstood connotations. Like the owl, the number thirteen was considered sacred in the ancient past. There are thirteen moons in the year, and the Celts had a thirteenth month that occurred right around the time of Samhain or All Hallow's Eve. However, if you wish to choose a different number of chocolates, cookies, or cups of tea or coffee, feel free.

Take one of the chocolates, cookies, or cups of hot tea or coffee and name it as one of your less-than-desirable attributes. For instance, you might say, "This chocolate is my insecurity. It began when I lost GI Joe at the toy store and realized that life is unpredictable. I accept my insecurity, loving myself for all of my faults as well as my positive traits. Only through acceptance can my insecurity grow into strength and power." After you have named the chocolate, eat it. Take your time. Think about your insecurity. Relive that traumatic day in the toy store. Focus on your less-than-desirable quality and realize that it can be sweet as well as dark, like the chocolate melting in your mouth. Ask yourself and your higher power what can be done to turn this characteristic into a part of your inner power. Write down any images, words, or feelings that come to you.

Do this exercise for thirteen days in a row, choosing a different negative trait every day. If you can't think of thirteen traits, then repeat some of the attributes that you feel are especially difficult to accept. When you are done, gather together all of the suggestions on accessing your inner powerful self from the past thirteen days and choose to work on one. Set realistic goals, and don't get discouraged if you ignore them for a day or two. Remember, working with the shadow self is a lifelong process. Accept your shortcomings, love them, and live life completely!

Physical Magic: Create a Coin of Truth

Items Needed: A plain wooden coin and either magazines and decoupage glue or a wood-burning tool and shellac

Moon Phase: Full or new

Seasonal Cycle: A time of balance, the spring or autumn equinox

A coin of truth is a simple divination device as well as a tool for personal growth. You will need to purchase a small, unfinished wooden coin. Many unfinished-furniture stores and craft stores will carry them. If you can't find a wooden coin, purchase a wooden dowel that is at least two inches in diameter. Using a saw, you can cut off a section of the dowel so that it resembles a coin. If the prospect of using an electric or manual saw is overwhelming, use a quarter or half-dollar as a template and trace around the coin on a heavy paperstock. Then cut out the circle using scissors.

Whether you decide on a wooden or paper coin, it is now time to decorate. On one side of the coin, you should decoupage, paint, or wood-burn an image that makes you happy. This can be as simple as a sun or as complex as the last family gathering you attended. This is Blodeuwedd's flower side, and you can also feel free to decorate the coin in honor of Blodeuwedd by using the image of a flower. The other side of the coin should be an image that is darker in subject matter. It may be a representation of your shadow self, an owl for Blodeuwedd, or a skull and crossbones. Use your imagination. Once your images are finished, seal the coin with laminating paper (if a paper coin) or shellac (if a wooden coin). If using decoupage, the glue used to hold the images will also seal the design.

Your coin of truth can answer simple yes-or-no questions. While thinking of the question, flip the coin in the air using your thumb and catch it on the way down. Slap it onto the back of your nondominant hand. If the sun or flower is staring up at you, the answer is "Yes." If you see the darker image, the answer is "No." The coin of truth is especially reliable when trying to get to the bottom of a situation, understand the root of a problem, or ferret out hidden agendas or half-truths.

The coin of truth is also extremely helpful when coming to terms with your dark aspects. You can carry it with you, using it as a worry stone or talisman. Holding it or putting it on your third eye while meditating is very effective in activating all of your personality traits. It is even a good idea to place it on your altar to charge it with the energy of the divine. This will help you to remember that the Goddess created you exactly as you are and that you are sacred in her eyes. Your coin of truth is a reminder of your true self and the power that is innately yours.

Candle Magic: From Darkness Comes Light

> Items Needed: Thirteen white spell candles and candle holders; purification oil, sage oil, or sweetgrass oil; two white pillar candles and two black pillar candles and holders; several chocolate brownies; a cup of milk; a sweetgrass braid; a lighter; and a needle or sharp knife for inscribing the candles
> Moon Phase: Full
> Seasonal Cycle: Summer

Once you have identified and integrated the shadow side of your personality, it is important to understand its role in your life. The shadow lingers within as a reminder of who we are and what we have endured. It is a source of strength and power and is often left untapped due to fear or indecision. After all, what do you *do* with those parts of yourself? If you bury them deep in your psyche, they manifest throughout your life in strange and unexplained ways, so they cannot simply be ignored. If you embrace them, making them the prime focus of your life, you reject all that is bright in your life, choosing to live in a world of complaint and negativity. All you can do is accept the shadow, turning its energy from dark to light, using its power to better your life and create your goals and dreams.

The following spell works with the thirteen shadows that you identified and integrated into yourself in the Symbolic Magic spell above. It is imperative that you perform that spell first before crafting this spell. This spell is best performed during a full moon, when the monthly light is at its greatest, or at noon, when the daily light is brightest. Although it uses fairly simple magic, I have included a circle warding and quarter calls for you to perform before the actual spell. Since this spell involves working with the darker aspects of yourself, it is important to feel comfortable and confident in your sacred space. You don't want to be wasting energy on wondering whether negativity is seeping into your spellwork.

Begin by placing the pillar candles at the directions, alternating the colors: black-white-black-white. Place all of the other objects in the center of your ritual space. Take several deep, calming breaths and ground and center as you normally do. When you feel relaxed, take the plate of brownies and the cup of milk and place them some distance away from your ritual area. These are an offering to the darker energy of the world. Acknowledge that this energy exists and is necessary for balance in the world. Respectfully say, "I acknowledge your importance in the world of men and the world of spirits. I request that you accept my offering and do not interfere with the casting of my spell." Bow politely to the darkness of the Otherworld and return to the center of your sacred space.

Light the braid of sweetgrass and carry it clockwise around your circle, beginning in the east. You will probably want to carry your lighter with you and relight the braid at every direction, as sweetgrass burns quickly and dies out faster than sage. Walk to the east candle, light it, and say:

Power of the East, I ask that you
Clear my way as I turn darkness into light.

Feel the winds of change enter your soul, and when you are ready, walk to the south. Light the candle and say:

Power of the South, I ask that you
Illuminate my way as I turn darkness into light.

Feel the heat of transformation on your body. When you have basked in the flames long enough, walk to the west, light the candle, and say:

Power of the West, I ask that you
Smooth my way as I turn darkness into light.

Feel the rushing water of persistence in your heart. When it has softened your resistance, walk to the north and light the candle, saying:

Power of the North, I ask that you
Free my way as I turn darkness into light.

Feel the stable nature of the ground under your feet. When it has strengthened your resolve, return to the center of your sacred area. Twirl around three times in a clockwise direction with your arms extended, creating a protective ward around your sacred space.

Take your first white spell candle and carve one of your thirteen shadow aspects on one side of it. Turning the candle over, inscribe a way to transform that shadow into light, now that you have integrated and accepted it as a part of yourself. For instance, if insecurity is one of your shadow aspects, you might etch *knowledge* or *daring* as your transformative word. (*Knowledge* would indicate that knowledge is power, while *daring* would show that you will take more risks despite your immediate misgivings.) Do this for each of your thirteen candles.

Once each of your candles has a shadow aspect and a transformative idea carved into it, anoint each candle with your purification, sage, or sweetgrass oil. Hold the candle between your fingers with your nondominant hand and sweep the oil up from the bottom of the candle to the top. This will symbolically bring the shadow aspects up, through the transformational experience, to the positive nature of the light, from the subconscious into the conscious mind.

Place each candle in its candle holder and light it, focusing on the words that you carved into its surface. After all thirteen candles are lit, bask in their bright light, feeling the heat on your skin and knowing that as the candles burn your shadow aspects are being altered inside of you. Take some time to sit in the light of your candles. Meditate to see what messages the goddess Blodeuwedd has for you. When you feel ready, turn to each direction and thank the powers of the north, west, south, and east for aiding you in your magic. Twirl around three times in a counterclockwise direction with your arms extended, releasing the protective circle and sending it up into the universe, where it will be renewed.

Deposit the brownies and milk in a sacred manner, placing them inside at your doorway and leaving them for other darker energies who may try to enter your house. (If you have animals, be sure to secure the food so the animals will not eat it and become sick. Chocolate and animals do not always mix well.) Allow your thirteen spell candles to burn down naturally, working their magic as they become smaller and smaller. This could take several hours, so do not attempt this spell unless you have a completely free afternoon or evening. As the candles burn, make sure that they are on a safe, nonflammable surface, such as a kitchen counter, and are away from cabinets, walls, and curtains. If you have enough coasters, you could place the candles on a table as well. Use your own discretion and be safe: you don't want your house bursting into flames. The following day, dispose of the candle wax, brownies, and milk in a sacred manner, honoring them for their willingness to assist you in your spell. Huzzah! You have successfully turned darkness into light. Congratulations!

MEETING CYMIDEI CYMEINFOLL, WELSH GODDESS OF BIRTH AND WAR

Gaining Balance in Your Life

CYMIDEI CYMEINFOLL: GODDESS BETWEEN THE WORLDS

Cymidei Cymeinfoll (pronounced KEEM-uh-day KEEM-een-vol) is a goddess hidden behind the wondrous deeds and activities of more well-known goddesses. She has been forgotten through the mists of time, left to labor in the Otherworld by herself without honors or offerings or sacrifices. Yet she is as much a part of our existence today, in the modern world, as she was centuries ago, when civilization began. Life and death exist for all beings on our planet, past, present, and future, and Cymidei Cymeinfoll resides at this immortal crossroads. She walks among us in every newborn's cry and every coughing death rattle. She presides over birthing rooms and battlefields and, as such, intimately understands the passage between the worlds. With one foot on the earth and one foot in the Otherworld, Cymidei Cymeinfoll serves as the bridge we all must cross twice in our lives.

Cymidei bursts into *The Mabinogion*, the medieval Welsh epic that chronicles the tales of the gods and goddesses, with subdued vigor. Her tale is told secondhand, colored by the memories and perceptions of two warrior kings, Bendigeidfran (a.k.a. Bran, the Blessed), the king of the Island of the Mighty (Wales and England), and Matholwch, the king of the island of Ireland. Matholwch has arrived at Bran's court to woo and marry his sister, Branwen. Unfortunately, Branwen's half-brother, Efnisien, insults Matholwch by mutilating and killing his horses. Matholwch is incensed and declares the marriage negotiations over. Bran, ever the diplomat and conscious of the slight against his sister should Matholwch withdraw his suit, gifts the Irish king with rich treasures of gold and silver, even replacing the horseflesh from his own herd. Matholwch, however, will not be mollified until Bran offers him the Cauldron of Regeneration, which he quickly accepts.

The Cauldron of Regeneration is a huge asset during a time of war. When a slain warrior is thrown into the cauldron, he returns to life the following day, ready to continue to fight in the battle. He retains all of his vigor and fighting ability but not his voice: the reanimated warrior cannot speak a word. The lack of speech is important, because it shows that the warrior is not truly alive in all ways. He does not return from the Otherworld exactly the same; he has been changed by the experience, altered by his walk through the mists that separate this world from the next. *The Mabinogion* does not state whether the renewed warrior can function in life outside the bounds of war. The book simply asserts that the once-dead warrior "will be as well as he was at the best."[1] Since the phrase is mentioned in connection to war, it is assumed that the man will fight at his absolute best. Life after war is never mentioned, and perhaps for these warrior kings, it is of little interest.

Throughout the course of the night, Bran and Matholwch swap stories concerning the Cauldron of Regeneration and, in the telling, reveal much about the character of themselves and Cymidei Cymeinfoll.

Figure 3: Cymidei Cymeinfoll's Cauldron of Regeneration.

---

1. Jones and Jones, *Mabinogion,* 24.

Cymidei's story begins in Ireland, where the Lake of the Cauldron resides. One day, Matholwch is out hunting and, cresting a hill, he happens upon "a big man with yellow-red hair coming from the lake with a cauldron on his back."[2] Immediately following the man is an even bigger woman. These are Cymidei and her husband, Llasar Llaes Gyfnewid, described as being enormous, with a hard, mean look about them.[3] Llasar greets Matholwch with the declaration that his wife, Cymidei, will give birth to a fully formed warrior every six weeks. (Cymidei's phenomenal birth rate immediately identifies her as a being from the Otherworld, as does her emergence from the center of the lake.) Matholwch, ever calculating, realizes that Cymidei's sons and daughters would be very useful in swelling the size of his army, so he invites them to become members of his household. They graciously accept.

All is well between Matholwch and the family of Cymidei and Llasar for a year. But four months into the second year, unrest between the two families occurs. According to Matholwch, Cymidei's family begins to harass, insult, and molest the wealthy families under Matholwch's protection. The lords raise their voices against Cymidei and her family, claiming they are more trouble than they are worth and giving Matholwch an ultimatum: he must choose the leadership of his kingdom or the friendship of the family of Cymidei and Llasar. Naturally, Matholwch chooses his kingdom, and with much reluctance, forced by his council, he agrees to a nefarious plot against Cymidei, Llasar, and their family.[4]

In order to circumvent any possible bloodshed during the ousting of Cymidei and her family, the council decides to use subterfuge to rid itself of the Otherworldly family. (Naturally, with all of Cymidei's warrior children, a protracted war is out of the question.) The council agrees to create a house of iron. Using meat and drink (traditional signs of hospitality), they lure Cymidei and her family into the iron house and bar the doors. Matholwch and his council gather all of the blacksmiths in Ireland and pile huge mounds of charcoal around the house. Even the roof is covered in coal. When Cymi-

---

2. Ibid., 25.

3. These descriptions have led modern interpreters (including John Matthews in *The Elements of the Grail Tradition*) to believe that Cymidei and her husband are giants. While there are some references to giants in both Irish and Welsh mythological literature, Cymidei and Llasar are never named as "giants" in *The Mabinogion*. You, gentle reader, will have to make that decision for yourself.

4. Throughout *The Mabinogion*, Matholwch perfects the ability to perform heinous actions without apparent blame, seemingly "forced" by his council of lords. Since Matholwch tells the majority of Cymidei's story, it is thus tainted by his slippery personality and must be read with his character in mind.

dei, Llasar, and the warrior children appear drunk, the charcoal is lit and pumped to great heat by the bellows of all the blacksmiths. Matholwch and his lords seek to rid themselves of Cymidei's family by burning them alive. They hope that the Otherworldly family will be too besotted with drink to notice when the doors are slammed shut and the house grows uncomfortably hot. Unfortunately for the council, Llasar ascertains its plan and, despite the drink, is able to batter down one of the walls once it is weakened by the intense heat. Both Llasar and Cymidei survive, but all of their children die in the flames.[5]

It is interesting to note that at this point in the story, the Cauldron of Regeneration is not mentioned at all. It would seem plausible that, after the iron house cooled, Cymidei would be able to locate the bodies of her children and throw them into the cauldron. Yet she flees from Ireland, never returning to Matholwch's territory and the iron house. There is no indication in *The Mabinogion* that she ever seeks to reanimate the corpses of her children. Although Cymidei and Llasar possess the Cauldron of Regeneration, they never seek to use its magical properties for themselves. The cauldron, for them, is merely a symbol, an extension of the magic housed within the body of Cymidei. Cymidei is the cauldron, a cyclic goddess of birth and war (or death on a grand scale), Cymidei is the portal through which souls arrive and depart in this world. She is the true cauldron, the true transformative crucible through which we all must pass when we are born and when we die. Therefore, Cymidei knows that her children, dead at the treacherous hand of Matholwch, will return to her womb, altered and changed, bearing different demeanors and attributes, both physical and emotional. She does not throw them into the Cauldron of Regeneration, because she does not wish to hinder their journey through the Otherworld and back out through her womb. She wishes their souls to grow and change, and although she is undoubtedly despairing over their deaths, she does not want her children to remain static in their current bodies.

When the cauldron is viewed as an extension of Cymidei, it is not surprising that she would be pleased to give it to a wise and noble king. After the tumultuous iron house

---

5. An interesting connection can be made between Cymidei's interaction with Matholwch as a member of his household and Branwen's relations with him as his wife. Both are "put aside" by Matholwch after a year and sentenced to an unnecessary and horrible punishment by his "council." Also, the children of Cymidei and Branwen both burn to death through the intentional as well as unintentional actions of Matholwch. Matholwch is the catalyst that forces Cymidei and Branwen to reassess their lives and their very natures.

episode, Cymidei and Llasar flee Ireland with the Cauldron of Regeneration and present themselves before Bran, the Blessed, king of Britain. They offer the Cauldron to Bran, gifting it to him in exchange for safe passage and residence in his lands. When Bran relates this to Matholwch, Matholwch coyly asks, "In what manner, lord, didst thou receive them?"[6] And Bran tells the Irish king that he allows them to live everywhere and that they fortify and make prosperous much of the land. In other words, many years have gone by since the iron house incident, and Cymidei and her family have once again grown large and fruitful. Even without the physical representation of the cauldron, Cymidei is still a vessel of abundance and change, a bridge between this world and the next. Her magic is untarnished and intact, even with the cauldron in another's hands.

Cymidei's magic extends far beyond her own story and her own body. Since the cauldron, throughout Celtic mythology, is representative of rebirth, it serves as a physical reminder of the powerful goddess of birth and war, the Mother of Life and Death who stands with one foot in our world and one foot in the next. Therefore, as a symbol the cauldron encapsulates Cymidei Cymeinfoll and, although she is not mentioned by name, becomes her representative in the legends. She is the cauldron, and the cauldron is her, a universal symbol of a hidden goddess.

Another cauldron in Welsh mythology that holds magical properties is the Cauldron of Rebirth, which is used for potion-making by the goddess Cerridwyn. Like Cymidei, Cerridwyn has a large, strong husband, lives in a lake (albeit on an island in the middle of the lake), controls more magic than her physically strong mate, and, obviously, possesses a cauldron. In *The Tale of Gwion Bach*, Cerridwyn's cauldron brings spiritual as well as physical rebirth. For a year and a day, the goddess Cerridwyn mixes a potion that contains all of the wonder and wisdom of the world, condensing it down into three tiny drops. These drops are meant for her son, the dark and ugly Morfran, in order that he may be accepted by his peers. Unfortunately for Morfran, the drops happen to fall on Cerridwyn's young helper, Gwion Bach, instead of her son. Gwion Bach's tangle with the Cauldron of Rebirth results in his attaining the mystical properties of precognition, bardcraft, and shape-shifting. He too enters the Otherworld through the portal of the cauldron and returns a different man. In fact, he is actually birthed from Cerridwyn's

---

6. Jones and Jones, *Mabinogion*, 26.

womb as a different child altogether. (Sound familiar?) No longer called Gwion Bach, he takes the name Taliesin, which translates as "behold the radiant forehead."[7]

Taliesin eventually becomes known as a great Celtic bard whose knowledge and literary prowess surpass the tales of Merlin (who retreats into the Otherworld). The Otherworldly Celtic cauldron reemerges in Taliesin's poem "The Spoils of Annwn," found in the fourteenth-century *Book of Taliesin*. In this poem, Taliesin recounts the travails of a raiding party led by King Arthur as they enter the Underworld of the Lord of the Dead in order to steal the cauldron of Annwn. In this story, the cauldron is firmly fixed in the Otherworld and is no longer the doorway between worlds but rather a spiritual prize that one must locate and possess in order to realize its transformative powers. Yet the innate feminine essence of the cauldron, as evidenced in the cauldron of Cerridwyn and the cauldron of Cymidei Cymeinfoll, is still apparent in Taliesin's vivid description. The cauldron has "a dark ridge around its border and pearls,"[8] and "From the breath of nine maidens it was kindled."[9] Pearls are precious gems that are formed under the water, and as such, they are intimately connected to the divine feminine and the Goddess. The nine maidens are associated with the Goddess through the mystical number nine and through their femininity. Since the maidens "kindle" the cauldron, keeping it strong and true with their breath, they are a necessary element in energizing the power of the cauldron. Although the cauldron is housed in the Underworld, a place ruled by a male, it is in the keeping and care of females, for they are its depository of power. Like Cymidei, it is the innate feminine nature of the nine maidens that gives the cauldron its power and thus its allure.

The cauldron of Celtic mythology eventually morphs into the Grail of Arthurian legend, the mystical cup of Christ that eludes many an erstwhile knight. Like the cauldron, it is a much-sought-after item, as it is a physical link between this world and the next. The Grail symbolizes the purity and perfection of the spiritual realm, and of the spirit that resides in each one of us. It encapsulates the highest level of enlightenment that we can attain in our human form, and as such, it is difficult to locate and even harder to grasp. As a catalyst for change, the Grail "provides an object for personal search, for

---

7. Ford, *Mabinogi*, 165.

8. Higley, "Preiddeu Annwn," verse 16.

9. Ibid., verse 14.

growth and human development, for healing."[10] Through questing for the Grail, we undergo a "spiritual awakening,"[11] a true rebirth of the soul.

And thus we have arrived back at the beginning, with the regeneration of ourselves through the presence, whether literal or figurative, of the cauldron. Cymidei Cymeinfoll is the passage through time that never wavers or changes. However, our union with her alters us forever. Whether through physical reincarnation, transformative rebirth, or spiritual enlightenment, our journey into and out of the cauldron changes us beyond recognition. We are never quite the same after a visit with Cymidei, and although her name may be lost in the mists of the Otherworld, her power and magic remain true.

FINDING BALANCE: ENJOYING LIFE

Modern life is not peaceful. We are inundated with sounds and sights every single moment of our waking day. We put the radio on as we travel to work. We watch television to get our morning weather and our evening news. We hear cars and trucks rumble by our houses. We read our e-mail to connect with friends and family. When do we hear silence? When do we find the time to slow down and truly choose our own life? Many of us live our lives on hyperdrive, allowing outside influences to dictate our reality. We tell ourselves that we are simply "too busy" to look at our lives and make changes. So we continue on, as always, complaining about our hectic lives but refusing to take charge and do something about it.

How ridiculous! If we want balance, if we want happiness, we have to fight for it. Most of our lives are carved into deep ruts. Making a change—any change—alters that rut and creates tension, and oftentimes chaos. Nobody enjoys chaos. It's messy. It's unpredictable. Your rut disappears, forcing you to find a new road. Yet from chaos springs the seeds of new life, of new thought and activity. From the muck and mud, we can begin again, taking a long, hard look at our day-to-day activities and changing them for the better.

So balance is all about making choices that create a better, more fulfilling life. Look deeply at your life. Consider your daily activities, your choice of work, your range of friends. If you are unsatisfied with anything, make a conscious decision to change.

---

10. Matthews, *Elements of the Grail Tradition*, 3.

11. Ibid. 2.

Spending too much time on the Internet? Take up ballroom dancing or play chess in the park. Feeling unfulfilled at work? Consider a new career or, if that's not fiscally possible, work toward a new career by taking classes or volunteering at a nonprofit on the weekends. Tired of the same people in your life? Meet some new ones by speed-dating or attending that dreaded alumni outing. Life is not meant to be a drag. Change things around and create your own happiness, your own sense of balance.

THE PATHWORKING

In your journey to Cymidei Cymeinfoll, you will be forced to confront one of humanity's greatest fears: death. As a warrior and a mother, Cymidei is intimately connected to death, to the realm of the Otherworld. She crosses the threshold of the Otherworld every six weeks with the birth of a fully-formed adult warrior. Therefore, her peace and calm come from her acceptance of the possibility of death. She balances living and dying on a daily basis.

Experiencing death during a journey is never easy. It can dredge up old wounds and issues that we have successfully banished to our subconscious. The experience is frightening, as we truly accept our own mortality. Someday, we're all going to die. However, death within a meditative journey gives us much-needed perspective on our busy, day-to-day lives. If we wish for balance, we must understand the beauty of life and the stunning reality of death, not on a metaphysical or esoteric level but on a deep, soul-intimate level. The following meditation allows you to assess your life and decide what is most important. Within seconds, as your life force ebbs slowly away, you will make decisions based on your own happiness and your own understanding of the importance of life. These choices, in turn, will give you the freedom to balance your life, focusing on what will most fulfill you.

Despite the positive outcome of this meditation, experiencing death is difficult within a journey. Your pseudo death will happen in the great womb of the Mother, in the Lake of the Cauldron, Cymidei's home. Naturally, with water all around, the death will take the form of drowning. As you sink toward the bottom of the lake, continually remind yourself that you are floating in the nutrient-rich waters of the womb of the Goddess. Allow any and all fears to float away on the currents; do not cling to them. Instead, guide your mind toward those things that are most important to you and your life.

Should you begin to experience discomfort during the drowning portion of the meditation, such as shortness of breath or pain in your extremities, remove yourself immediately from the water and return to dry land. Remember, you have ultimate control over your journey. You can remove yourself from any unpleasant situation. Be sure to pack a protective talisman for the journey, either in material or psychic form. If you don't have a protective talisman that you traditionally use, hold a smoky quartz crystal or a household rock in your hand during the meditation. These will ground you to your location, giving you an easy way to return to the present. Simply focus on the rock in your hand and you will return to your warm, safe, comforting home. It may take several attempts before you can finish the entire meditation, especially if you already have a natural dislike of water or a fear of drowning. Take as much time as you need. Remember, the secret to being in balance is knowing when to move forward and when to take a break. Don't push yourself! You'll make it there eventually.

GUIDED MEDITATION: GAINING BALANCE IN YOUR LIFE

Take a deep breath, in through your nose and out through your mouth. Take another deep breath, filling your stomach, your diaphragm, and finally your lungs. Hold this breath for five seconds … 1-2-3-4-5 … and exhale, allowing the breath to exit your lungs first, then your diaphragm, and finally your stomach. Take one more deep breath, and as you breathe in, feel the energy of the dusky twilight enter you, supporting your fingers, your toes, your legs, and your shoulders, even the top of your head. Hold the breath for seven seconds … 1-2-3-4-5-6-7. As you exhale, feel all tension leave your fingers, your toes, your legs, and your shoulders, even the top of your head. Feel the cool, timeless earth under your body. Hear the gentle lapping of water against the shoreline. The sound enters your ears and flows through your body, melting away tension and strain. Continue breathing deeply, in through your nose and out through your mouth. Allow the earth to hold and support your body. Allow the water to wash away any remaining fear and anxiety. You have never felt so relaxed, so secure, so calm.

You are sitting on the edge of a large lake. Around you, rounded hills rise from the ground, deeply green and soft. The sun sinks below one of these hills, casting the world in a twilight gray, tinged by brilliant pink and soft blue. Birds call to each other across the gray waters of the soothing lake. Reeds waft around you in the soft, gentle breeze. It is quiet on the edge of the lake. You sigh, content.

Just as you begin to lie back and doze peacefully in the twilight, a deep groaning issues from the middle of the lake. Almost metallic in sound, it grinds fitfully against the serenity of your lakeside haven. Alarmed, you sit straight up, hidden by a fringe of greening weeds. From between the reeds and water-loving plants, you see a golden head emerge from the center of the lake. It is a man's face, large and thick with a fresh growth of russet beard and a bulbous nose. He rises out of the lake with lithe, catlike movements, his shoulders square and even, his legs as round as tree trunks. Despite the fact that a giant cauldron is strapped onto his back, he walks casually and with ease. He steps out of the water on the western bank, toward the setting sun, and does not even glance in your direction once.

As the golden man with the cauldron begins his ascent up one of the hills, a second groan emanates from the lake. This one is fuller and heavier than the first, without the high-pitched screeching of metal. It is guttural and coarse, reminiscent of childbirth or deadly battle. Your eyes leave the retreating back of the cauldron-bearer and flit to the center of the lake, where a woman's face emerges, shaded by dark red hair. As she climbs out of the water, you see that she is slightly larger than the golden-man. Her shoulders are wide, her legs strong yet flexible, and her belly inordinately large. She is unmistakably in the latter stages of pregnancy. She begins to follow the golden man but with one foot on the land and one foot in the water, she stops. Her head cocks to one side, as though she is listening to the wind. And then she turns her head and looks directly at you.

Her eyes root you in place. They swirl gray and white, with the restless motion of a windswept lake and the silent stillness of a cloudy day. You cannot move, nor do you want to. She calls to the golden man, never taking her eyes from yours, and says something in a language you do not understand. Her words echo off the hillsides, and you wonder if the land was formed from the pressure of her voice alone. The golden man glances in your direction, shrugs his shoulders, and, nodding, continues up and over the hill. You are alone along the side of the lake, and the woman is walking toward you.

You scramble to stand, but the woman motions you to sit as she settles onto the ground by your feet. She is undoubtedly the largest woman you have ever met. Your head barely comes up to her quite voluminous chest, and her shoulders blot out the rolling countryside. Her face is wide, with a pointed chin and large, slanted eyes framed by thick lashes. By comparison to her body, her mouth is delicate and soft, reminiscent of rose petals in late spring. The woman is dressed in a simple brown and green dress, covered with a stained apron. Inside the pockets of the apron, you spot a pair of scissors, a sheathed knife, and handfuls of fresh and dried herbs. Except for her size, this woman looks like every other country wife you have encountered.

"Good day," she says calmly, her hands folded neatly on her lap. "My name is Cymidei Cymeinfoll. This lake is my home." She looks at you expectantly. You look at the ground, trying to still your restless thoughts. Ever since this woman locked eyes with you, your mind has been in a whirl, unable to focus. You take a deep breath and force your mind to count the pebbles under your fingers. (pause) After you reach ten, you look up at the goddess and tell her your name and the location of your home.

"Ah," she smiles. "Very good." She looks out over the lake then, and you feel a sense of loss, as though you were dismissed from her conscious thinking. She sits, staring, for quite a while, as the twilight descends deeper and deeper into the darkness of night. You sit as well, and eventually your shoulders slump, releasing their tension, and your eyes unfocus. You begin to relax, truly, unbelievably, next to this giant woman from the lake.

"Life is a choice, you see," she says into the gloom. You can barely make out her hulking figure, even though it is right next to you. She has melted into the gray light, becoming one with her surroundings. She grabs your hand and holds it against her protruding belly. A strong kick reverberates against your skin. Something sharp and pointed scratches against the wall of her uterus. "We die to bring life into the world." Her loud sigh stirs the hair around your face. The grasp on your hand tightens painfully. "We allow others to die so that we may live." She squeezes, and you can feel the bones in your fingers grinding together. You gasp in pain, and she releases you. She touches your shoulder lightly, and you are suddenly down by the edge of the lake, having flown or floated there along the breeze. You glance at Cymidei in surprise, and she grins, one hand patting her belly.

"Stand on that rock," she says. You peer into the twilight, unable to see the rock until she laughs lightly and a golden sheen glitters around it. The rock is square, almost a foot high and almost two feet wide. You step up and stand on it with ease. You almost reach Cymidei's chin. She pats your hair and croons, "Very good," before motioning to another rock. This one is slightly smaller and closer to the water. You step down onto it and have no difficulty keeping your balance. You continue this exercise around the lake, stepping on slightly smaller and smaller rocks that Cymidei points out to you. She does not touch you but remains close enough that her rose-petal scent wafts over you when the breeze blows. (pause) Halfway around the lake, the rocks have become small enough that you can only stand on one foot at a time. (pause) The rocks grow increasingly smaller and smaller as you continue around the lake. (pause) By the time you reach the lakeside where you began, you are balancing on a pebble that is just slightly bigger than a grain of sand, right at the water's edge. You grin up at Cymidei, proud of your accomplishment. The ends of her mouth tug upward in a slight smile before she pushes you off the rock.

The force of her shove propels you into the lake. Your chest constricts from her powerful thrust. You have difficulty breathing, until you realize that you are floating on top of the water. Cymidei's push should have thrown you to the bottom of the lake, but you did not fall under the water. You lift your head in confusion and watch as Cymidei walks across the lake, her plain brown shoes slapping the water forcefully. She reaches your side and, with a bark of laughter, hauls you to your feet. You are standing on top of the water! You run and dance joyously around Cymidei, exploring this new feat, this new sensation. (pause) She smiles indulgently, and just as your body tingles with pleasure, just as water droplets mist every part of your body, just as the twilight hinges on the verge of darkness, Cymidei claps her hands, breaking the reverie, and plunges you down into the wintery darkness of the lake.

Water fills your eyes, your nose, and your mouth. A magical force pulls you downward. All is black. Your limbs grow heavy from lack of oxygen. Your head hurts. Your ears buzz with the pressure, and your eyes see stars. You are sure that you are about to die. Images flash before your eyes: people, places, events, and goals that hold the most importance to you. (long pause) Pay attention to these images, sounds, thoughts, and scents, as they hold the key to gaining balance in your life. (pause) These are the things that give your life meaning. (pause) Just as you feel your head start to spin, your chest begin to burn with the need for oxygen, and your mouth open to draw in a mouthful of water, strong arms drag you to the surface, and, choking and coughing, you breathe cool, nighttime air. Stars sparkle overhead. You float once again on the water of the lake, supported by Cymidei. She strokes your face softly, calming your fears and sweeping away the memories of near-death.

"Such is life," she whispers into your ear, cradling you ever closer to the side of the lake. "We balance on the knife-edge of death every minute of every day that we are alive. Life and death, birth and war, happiness and sadness are but shadow reflections of each other. To know the difference, one must know oneself. Know one's place. Know one's limitless possibilities." She lays you down on the bank of the lake, covering you in a thick woolen blanket. Darkness has descended, and all you can see are her changeable, swirling gray eyes. You focus on them until all of your world is encompassed in those eyes. "The choice is yours," her voice whispers along the breath of a breeze. "Your life is your own. That which you seek is yours, if only you reach for it." With a blink, the sky has lightened and you are back sitting amid the weeds, completely dry and composed, as Cymidei stands on the side of the lake, one foot on the land and one foot in the water. She has just emerged from the lake and turned her gray eyes on you. Her husband, the keeper of the cauldron, the golden-haired man, pauses in midstep, waiting for her to follow. Her eyes lock with yours, despite your cover of lakeside vegetation. She smiles gently, pats her belly, and, saying something to her husband, takes his hand in her own and lopes easily up the hillside into the light of the setting sun.

Now, take a deep breath, in through your nose and out through your mouth. Take another deep breath, filling your stomach, your diaphragm, and finally your lungs. Hold this breath for five seconds … 1-2-3-4-5 … and exhale, allowing the breath to exit your lungs first, then your diaphragm, and finally your stomach. Breathe deeply once more, and as you breathe in, feel the energy and the wonder of the world around you in your fingers, your toes, your legs, and your shoulders, even the top of your head. As you exhale, wiggle your fingers and toes. Shake your legs and move your shoulders up and down. Take another deep breath and, as you exhale, move your head from side to side. Feel the ground under your body touching every nerve ending and muscle. Hear the rustlings of the people around you. Notice the movements outside. Continue breathing. Stretch your arms out above your head. You are returning to the present, to the here and now. Continue stretching. Continue breathing. When you are ready, open your eyes, blink and focus, and sit up.

INVOCATION TO CYMIDEI CYMEINFOLL

Powerful one,
Straight and secure,
Rounded and restful,
Your power lies within your belly.
Life and death locked deep inside.

Darkness and light
Craft but one coin.
Birth and war
Balance on the knife-edge.
Happiness and sadness
Linger on mouth corners.

I need only decide
Up or down,
Right or left,
Inside or outside,
Above or below
To create my destiny.

Cymidei Cymeinfoll,
Warrior Mother,
You teach that choice is inevitable.
You show the power within my grasp,
Within my body, within my soul,
If only I reach for it.

Lend me your knowledge,
Great life-bringing Mother,
Great death-dealing Warrior,
And grant me the peace of balance.

MAGICAL ACTIVITIES

Written Word Magic: Message in a Bottle

Items Needed: A small bottle, a small piece of parchment paper, a colored pen, mugwort incense, mandrake (cut and sifted, not whole), three small onyx stones, and a lighter or matches

Moon Phase: Waning

Seasonal Cycle: Autumn

The essence of balance is in understanding what is necessary in your life and what is simply clutter. Clutter can take the form of physical objects, emotional trauma, old ideas, leftover attitudes, careless friends, or unfulfilling work and activities. By performing this spell, you will be discarding one of your personal forms of clutter in order to make room for positive change and future excitement. Obviously, you can cast this spell as many times as is necessary in order to clean out your life. However, I recommend removing only one item per waning moon. In other words, perform this spell only once every month. This spell can alter your life radically, so it is best to allow yourself time to adjust to the changes.

Before you perform this magic, take some time to focus on your daily activities and decide on an idea, object, or life choice that needs to be removed from your psyche. Keep this idea in your mind throughout the rest of the spell. Gather all of your items and place them within easy reach of your magical area. You should be able to sit down and touch each of the objects. Ground and center as you normally do, and focus on the life choice you wish to eliminate.

Once the idea or object is firmly in your mind, light the mugwort incense and waft it over each of the magical items you have gathered. Then allow the smoke to drift gently around your heart and over your head, waving your hand three times to direct the smoke to come closer to you. Place the incense back down and breathe deeply. Close your eyes and choose one or two words to represent the life choice about which you have been thinking. Write those words on the piece of parchment paper, using your colored pen. Hold the parchment paper over the incense so that the smoke curls around it, and then roll the paper up and put it in the bottle. Add the three onyx stones and mandrake, making sure the bottle is completely filled up with herbs and magical stones. Cap the bottle.

Place the bottle in the light of the waning moon for three days. During those three days, shake the bottle every so often and think about the idea, object, or attitude that you wish to remove from your life. On the fourth day, travel to a body of water (preferably a lake, but a river or the ocean will work as well) and empty the bottle into the water. As the contents sink beneath the waves and float away, know that you have altered your life, clearing space for new opportunities to emerge.

Elemental Magic (Water): Whisperings

    Items Needed: Spring water or water from a nearby lake, a bowl, a sage smudge stick, and a lighter or matches

    Moon Phase: Waxing

    Seasonal Cycle: Spring

Once you have been clearing away unwanted and unneeded clutter for several months, you can begin to fill those spaces in your life with new wishes and desires. This spell is simple and effective, connecting you to the element of water, the emotional center of our planet and ourselves. Do not be surprised if this spell unleashes a torrent of suppressed emotions in you. When working with water, upheavals can occur, because water forces us to delve into our innermost selves. If you suddenly find yourself yelling at the cat or crying during a television commercial, you'll know that the subtle power of water is working its way into your life. The key to working with water is to allow your life to simply "flow." Accept what comes your way with grace and dignity, consciously acknowledging the ebbs and flows. In this way, water will serve as a constant source of strength for you.

In order for this magic to manifest in your life, it is best to have cast the bottle spell above or a similar removal spell first. In this way, you will be making room for new ideas and influences to take root. If your life is too cluttered, it will be difficult to bring new opportunities into your life. Once you have removed some of your clutter, begin to consider what you would like to bring into your life. Decide on one idea. With that idea in your mind, light your sage and smudge the entire room in which you will be performing magic. Don't forget to pay special attention to your bowl, your water, and yourself.

Once you have cleansed the area with sage smoke, sit down with your bowl in front of you. Conjure up an image of the wish you want to manifest, and pour the water into the bowl. Place both hands on either side of the bowl and begin to hum softly while still thinking of your desire. You can hum a song, a chant, or a tuneless sound. The humming is meant to connect you with the water through the vibrations of your voice. It does not matter what you hum.

After several minutes, when the time feels right, place your face very close to the water. Breathe into the water with seven soft sighs, taking as much time as you want. Then, quietly croon your desire to the water. You can do this fast or slow, once or many times. It all depends on how you feel and how connected you are to the water. After you have told the water of your desire, return the water to its source by throwing it into a lake, river, stream, brook, or the ocean. If you don't have a body of water near you, pour the water into the ground, with the intent that it will seep down to the underground water system in your area. Now that water knows of your heart's desire, relax and prepare yourself for it to arrive.

Sympathetic Magic: Cauldron of Rebirth

Items Needed: Cauldron; mugwort incense; a lighter; one piece of pearl jewelry (necklace, earrings, tie clip, cuff links, ring, etc.); dried vervain or catnip; boiling water; a mug; warm water; a ribbon of any color; and a doll that looks like you. Note: Vervain should not be used by pregnant women. If you are pregnant, use catnip instead.

Moon Phase: New

Seasonal Cycle: Any, but especially the winter solstice

As you will be figuratively entering the Cauldron of Rebirth, I have included protective wardings and shields in this magic spell. You need to feel completely at peace during this spellwork, so be sure to set aside a time when you will not be interrupted. I recommend taking some time to find a look-alike doll or perhaps crafting your own if you have the time, talent, and inclination. The doll can be a simple Barbie doll with a haircut, a cloth doll with similar clothes, or a baby doll that reminds you of your youth. The doll can be big or small, but it should fit reasonably well inside the cauldron. If the doll is too big, you will not get the transformative feeling of entering into the Cauldron of Regeneration.

Set up all of your magical tools in the center of your sacred space. Ground and center as you normally do, and relax your entire body. If you'd like, play some ambient music that focuses on water sounds. Take as much time as you need, but try to sit and ground and center for at least five minutes. Once you feel completely relaxed, stand up and face north. Imagine a giant oak tree before you, its branches arching up over your head, its roots burrowing deep under your feet. Embrace the tree and feel its strength and security. When you are ready, say:

Mighty Oak,
I have called you here today
To protect and guide me
As I enter the Cauldron of Rebirth.

Walk to the east and envision a graceful birch tree joined with one or two of her sister trees, growing symbiotically together. See their delicate branches arching above you and entwining with the branches of the oak tree. Feel their roots reaching toward and grasping the roots of the oak tree under your feet. Embrace the tree and feel its delicate freshness and spirit. When you are ready, say:

Gentle Birch,
I have called you here today
To protect and guide me
As I enter the Cauldron of Rebirth.

Walk to the south and picture a stately chestnut tree. Its branches, thick and heavily laden with nuts, sweep upward, twining with those of the oak and birch trees. Its roots tunnel underground to join with those of the other trees. Embrace the tree and feel its vibrancy. When you are ready, say:

Fruitful Chestnut,
I have called you here today
To protect and guide me
As I enter the Cauldron of Rebirth.

Walk to the west and visualize a tall ash tree reaching up, straight and true. Its branches and roots join with those of the other trees, and you are surrounded by the warmth and protection of all four trees. When you feel ready, say:

Flexible Ash,
I have called you here today
To protect and guide me
As I enter the Cauldron of Rebirth.

Return to the center of your sacred space and feel the energy of the four trees. They form a sphere around you, encasing you in a natural web of protection. They allow only peace and calm to flow to you. With each tree, you have stepped farther and farther away from the mundane world and closer and closer to the Otherworld. You hover there, between time and space.

In your timeless cocoon, place the vervain or catnip in your mug and pour the boiling water over the herbs. Allow them to steep while you light the mugwort incense. Breathe in the dense scent of the incense and waft it around your cauldron, your doll, and your piece of pearl jewelry. Make sure that the incense is lit throughout the spell, as the mugwort will help you to lift the veils of the Otherworld and truly become one with the Cauldron of Rebirth.

Breathe deeply of the incense and begin to drink your mug of vervain or catnip tea. Both of these herbs are known for their shamanic and prophetic qualities, so they will also assist you in making the leap to the Otherworld and the realm of Cymidei Cymei-nfoll. Focus on the goddess and the cauldron as you drink your tea. Remember to keep breathing deeply of the incense, making sure it is still smoking.

After you have finished the tea, place the piece of pearl jewelry in the bottom of your cauldron. This jewelry symbolizes the new you that will emerge from the Cauldron of Regeneration. It represents your rebirth, which will involve new skills and goals, as well as new responsibilities. Pour the warm water over the piece of pearl jewelry until the cauldron is almost completely full of water. The water should feel warm to the touch and very comfortable, like stepping into the perfect bath.

With one hand in the water and the other holding your doll, close your eyes and envision the great Cauldron of Rebirth. Where does it appear to you? Is it in a forest? Next to a lake? Under the water? Floating in the sky? Wherever the cauldron appears, spend some time admiring it. What color is the cauldron? Is it decorated with any designs? Is anyone nearby the cauldron, perhaps Cymidei or Cerridwyn?

When the existence of the Cauldron of Rebirth is fixed in your mind, open your eyes and grasp your doll in both hands. Take a piece of your hair, an eyelash, or a nail clipping and attach it to the doll using the ribbon. Close your eyes again and breathe into the face of the doll, pushing your essence into the poppet. Do this as many times as you need, but I would recommend staying with the sacred numbers of three or seven. When you are ready, still holding your doll, chant:

You are me and I am you.
We are one.
(Chant your name three times.)

Touching the cauldron, chant:

Cymidei is the Cauldron and the Cauldron is Cymidei.
They are one.
Cymidei, Cymidei, Cymidei.

Lowering the doll into the cauldron, chant:

I enter the Cauldron of Rebirth.
The Cauldron enters me.
We are joined.
Rebirth, rebirth, rebirth.

Continue to chant "rebirth" over and over again very softly as you hold your doll in the cauldron. Allow the water to lap over your fingers so you can feel the connection. See the cauldron you envisioned earlier in the spell. Picture yourself stepping into it and relaxing in the warm waters of the womb of rebirth. Touch your forehead, your lips, your heart, and your belly with the water from the cauldron in front of you. Meditate in this position for as long as you like.

When you are ready, see yourself being reborn from the Cauldron of Rebirth, new and strong and whole. Remove the doll from the cauldron in front of you at the same time that you step out of your meditative cauldron. Assess yourself, physically, emotionally, mentally, and spiritually. What has changed about you? What feels different? When you have noted all of your alterations, remove the piece of pearl jewelry and put it on, saying:

> *This jewelry symbolizes my new form, my new self.*
> *May I always remember that I am born anew,*
> *From the raging waters of the Cauldron of Rebirth,*
> *From the peaceful womb of the Great Mother Goddess.*

Kiss your poppet and rise to bid farewell to the trees that sheltered you in the Otherworld. Beginning in the west, see each of the trees removing their branches and their roots from each other and retreating back into the Otherworld. As they do this, say:

> *Flexible Ash, Fruitful Chestnut, Gentle Birch, and Mighty Oak,*
> *You have protected and guided me*
> *Through the realm of the Otherworld.*

Turn to each direction, bow, and say:

> *I honor you.* (West)
> *I honor you.* (South)
> *I honor you.* (East)
> *I honor you.* (North)

Return to the center and say:

> *I have returned from the Otherworld, a new (wo)man.*
> *I am cleansed. I am renewed.*
> *I am reborn!*

MEETING CREIDDYLAD,
WELSH MAY DAY GODDESS
Learning to Love Yourself

CREIDDYLAD: THE CONSTANT GODDESS

Creiddylad (pronounced cree-THIL-ahd) is mentioned but a few times in Welsh mythology, but her power extends to the very depths of human desire. She is the eternal quest for peace, stability, and contentment. She is that which continues on despite alteration and change. Her story is rarely told nowadays, but its central theme, characters, and plot conjoin with many medieval British and Irish legends: Tristan and Isolde, Blodeuwedd and Lleu Llaw Gyffes, and Arthur and Guinevere, to name a few. Creiddylad is the force of love and devotion that continues despite hardship and despair. Yet she also teaches true understanding and acceptance of the self. For without love of self, one cannot truly love another. Full of passionate love, duels, secret deals, and kingly commands, Creiddylad's story brings eternal hope.

Creiddylad whispers into *The Mabinogion*, the Welsh medieval mythological epic, in the story of Culhwch and Olwen. In this story, Culhwch, a young lad, is enamored of a giant's daughter, Olwen, and requests the aid of King Arthur to win her hand. In the process of convincing Arthur, he names every personage of merit and worth in the Welsh kingdom in an effort to wrest a boon from his king. Creiddylad is among the ladies mentioned by young Culhwch. She is described as "daughter of Lludd Silver-hand (the maiden of most majesty that was ever in the Island of Britain and its three adjacent islands.)"[1]

It is interesting that the Welsh writers chose the word majesty to describe Creiddylad, as *beauty* or *purity* were more common descriptive terms for women in *The Mabinogion*. *Majesty* is linked to sovereignty and connection to the land, a concept that seems much bigger than necessary for this briefly mentioned woman. After all, Creiddylad never becomes a queen, never marries, and is never a bride to a human king. She remains a maiden her whole life, and as such, it would seem more likely that purity would be the value most associated with her. Creiddylad, however, is much more than simply the daughter of Lludd Silver-hand, faithful maiden. She is the object of affection for two Welsh warrior knights and the personification of a deeply held seasonal spiritual belief of the Briton peoples.

As is the case with most love triangles, Creiddylad's two suitors vie for her attention and her hand in marriage. *The Mabinogion* states that Creiddylad had a clear favorite, preferring Gwythr, son of Greidiawl, to Gwyn, son of Nudd. However, as with all great,

---

1. Jones and Jones, *Mabinogion*, 90.

tragic love stories, the maiden's choice is just the beginning of the story. "Creiddylad daughter of Lludd Silver-hand went with Gwythr son of Greidiawl; and before he had slept with her there came Gwyn son of Nudd and carried her off by force."[2] Creiddylad's marriage to Gwythr is interrupted by the appearance of Gwyn ap Nudd, who promptly abducts her. Since weddings in ancient Wales consisted of a feast and a consummation, Creiddylad was never fully married to Gwythr, and thus never his wife. It is unclear whether Creiddylad's marriage to Gwythr was sanctioned by her father or simply the passionate act of two youngsters in love. Either way, she chose to be with him, rather than Gwyn ap Nudd, as *The Mabinogion* states that she "went with Gwythr."[3] There is no indication of unhappiness or hesitation in Creiddylad's decision to marry Gwythr. On the other hand, Gwyn removes her by force from the wedding. Creiddylad, still a maiden, is wrested from her chosen beloved by man she views as less desirable.

Immediately, Gwythr gathers an army of warriors to fight Gwyn and win back Creiddylad. A massive battle ensues, with Gwyn emerging as the victor. He takes seven (a highly symbolic number in Celtic mythology, with ties to the Otherworld and the faery realm) esteemed noblemen as his captives, killing Nwython and cutting out his heart. After such butchery, Gwyn forces Nwython's son, Cyledyr the Wild, to eat his father's heart, whereupon the son goes completely mad. (Is it any wonder Creiddylad chose Gwythr over Gwyn?) Arthur hears of Gwyn's brutality and sets off to Gwyn's holdings in the north to settle the matter. Demanding that Gwyn attend him, Arthur forces him to free the noblemen, creating peace between the two suitors by decreeing that neither man shall have Creiddylad. Rather, Arthur declares, she shall live in her father's house, undisturbed by either Gwythr or Gwyn, a perpetual maiden. Every year until the end of time, the two suitors will fight for her on May Day. Whoever wins the battle on doomsday will have the right and privilege of marrying her. With Arthur's decision, Gwythr and Gwyn leave to prepare for the May 1st battle, and Creiddylad returns to her father's house.

Throughout the descriptions of battle, scenes of torture, and the restoration of peace, Creiddylad's father is conveniently absent from the story. He calmly sits by during the melee to save his daughter from Gwyn ap Nudd, which seems strange behavior for a nobleman whose daughter is abducted from her wedding. Lludd Silver-hand does

---

2. Ibid., 107.

3. Ibid.

not gather warriors or personally fight for his daughter's release. He is content to allow the two suitors to fight each other for the honor of his daughter's hand. Lludd's lack of involvement indicates that Creiddylad's story is more than it would appear to be. It is not an isolated legend in British literature; rather, it is one more story that fits a specific love-triangle pattern of heart-chosen lover, beautiful young noblewoman, and darkly driven suitor. Creiddylad's story is a metaphor for a traditional British mythic motif indicating the passing of time and the cycle of the seasons. The Gwythr ap Grei-diawl–Creiddylad–Gwyn ap Nudd love triangle is none other than the Oak King–May Queen–Holly King literary theme.

Figure 4: The Turning of the Wheel of the Year as viewed from the Holly King–Ivy/May Queen–Oak King mythos. Note the double hearts apparent in the natural vein structure of the ivy leaf.

The Oak King–May Queen–Holly King seasonal observances were part of the mythic world of our ancient agrarian ancestors. The oak tree, the tree of kings, was revered as one of the sacred trees by the Welsh Druids. It was a symbol of the chief's protection of his people and a "common emblem, both ancient and modern, of earthly and celestial kings."[4] Since lightning is attracted to oak trees, striking them with frequency, the oak came to be associated with the gods of the sky. The tree was believed to be a conduit between this world and the Otherworld. As a favorite of the sky gods, the oak tree soon came to represent the gods in the minds of the people, some even worshipping the tree as a deity itself. Since the oak tree flourishes in the light half of the year, sprouting leaves in spring and summer and dropping acorns in early autumn, it symbolizes the power and strength of the growing time, of a young, virile God, and of the entire cycle of sowing, reaping, and harvesting.

The holly tree, on the other hand, is a tree of death and resurrection rather than of growth and abundance. During the cold winter months, the leaves of the holly tree remain green and bright, and the berries glow with the red juice of life. Here is a tree that withstands the seasonal slumber of most plants and trees. For this reason, holly "has long been used as a symbol of the potent life force of nature."[5] It is a daily reminder during the depths of winter that life will spring anew. Sowing the seeds of hope, holly connects to the Otherworld, the realm of our ancestors, yet represents triumph over death. Since the plant looks very similar in the summer to how it looks in the winter, it is a symbol for immortality, reincarnation, and the continuance of the self after death.

The oak tree and the holly tree, then, correspond to different times of the year. The oak tree represents the bright, sunny greening half of the year, as the sun grows in strength (from winter solstice to summer solstice), while the holly tree symbolizes the descent into darkness as the days grow shorter and shorter (from summer solstice to winter solstice). As examples of the cyclic nature of the seasons, the oak tree and the holly tree were personified over the years as the Oak King and the Holly King, two Otherworldly beings or deities who battled each other on the solstices in order to "bring in" the new half of the year, an already foregone conclusion.

The May Queen is another symbolic personage in the seasonal vegetative cycle of the ancient Britons. She is honored at the May Day holiday, when plants are blooming

---

4. Gifford, *Wisdom of Trees*, 67.

5. Ibid., 81.

and animals are spawning their young. She is the ever-fertile maiden, fresh and pure but with the power to bring forth fruit. The lush vegetation of the blossoming land served as a symbol for the May Queen's abundance and warmth. In later years, the May Queen also came to be represented by the ivy plant, as that herb also represents the flourishing life force.[6] And as ivy, the May Queen infiltrated the typically male-dominated, Oak King–Holly King winter solstice or Christmas holiday. In the depth of winter, the ivy plant came to represent "woman," while the holly tree represented "man."[7] Pairing them up ensured a peaceful year ahead for married couples within the household.

In Creiddylad's myth, Gwythr son of Greidiawl takes on the role of the Oak King while Gwyn ap Nudd plays the part of the Holly King and Creiddylad, of course, is the beauteous May Queen. Gwythr, son of Greidiawl (whose name means "Victor, son of Fierce"), is known throughout Welsh mythology as a fair, just, and fertile man. His father, Greidiawl Gallofyd, is mentioned in the Welsh Triads as one of the three enemy-subduers of the Island of Britain.[8] Gwythr, himself, is named in the Welsh Triads as the father of one of the three Great Queens, all named Gwenhwyfar and all (conveniently) married to Arthur.[9] Later in the story of Culhwch and Olwen, Gwythr rescues a colony of ants from rampaging fire, for which he is rewarded. As Creiddylad's chosen lover, a man whose name and lineage indicate power and might, and a knight whose actions promote justice and fairness, Gwythr personifies the characteristics of the oak tree and the waxing, growing time of the year.

Gwyn ap Nudd, on the other hand, has many dark aspects to his personality. In *The Mabinogion*, it is written that the sacred boar Twrch Trwyth cannot be captured without the help of Gwyn ap Nudd, "in whom God has sent the spirit of the demons of Annwn, lest, this world be destroyed."[10] Annwn is the name of the Welsh Otherworld, where the spirit selves of the dead congregate and live. Immediately, Gwyn is connected to death and to the dark half of the year, when plants and trees rest and replenish. In Creiddylad's story, Arthur travels north to Gwyn's home, a fact backed up by the twelfth-century *Black Book of Carmarthen*, which places Gwyn in northern Wales. *The Black*

6. Mountfort, *Ogham*, 109.

7. Cunningham, *Cunningham's Encyclopedia of Magical Herbs*, 131.

8. Bromwich, *Welsh Triads*, triad 19.

9. Ibid., triad 56.

10. Jones and Jones, *Mabinogion*, 99.

Book of Carmarthen lists Gwyn's home as Caer Vandwy, which is the name of one of the Otherworldly castles of Annwn that Arthur attacks in the poem *The Spoils of Annwn* (*Preiddeu Annwn*).[11] Further evidence of his connection to death can be found in Welsh folktales. Gwyn (whose name means "Light" or "Blessed") possesses a black face and leads the Hounds of Annwn, the Cwn Annwfn, on the "Wild Hunt," a whirlwind ride of ghosts and specters through the countryside to pick up the souls of those who have died. In later years, Gwyn's role was diminished to the Faery King of the Tylwyth Teg, the collective name for the Welsh faeries. He is reputed to live in mounds under the ground, including Glastonbury Tor and *Glyn Nedd* ("vale of Neath"), which was originally named Glyn Nudd ("vale of Nudd") after him.[12] With his references to death, his abode in the land of Annwn, and his dark aspect, Gwyn ap Nudd personifies the characteristics of the holly tree and the waning time of the year.

Gwythr and Gwyn circle around each other all year, meeting annually for battle on May Day instead of the customary Oak King–Holly King battleground of the summer solstice. It is important to mention that the traditional fire festivals of the ancient Celts did not include the solstices. While these days were undoubtedly noticed, they were not considered mystic, sacred days of the gods. Instead, powerful temporal shifts occurred on Calan Mai (Beltane or May Day) and Calan Gaeaf (Samhain or Halloween). These days were outside of normal time and space, and as such are known as "liminal" times. Both May Day and the summer solstice focus on plant life, growth of vegetation, and fruitfulness of womb and earth. The essence of the celebrations is similar, and therefore the shift from the summer solstice to May Day can be understood from a Celtic point of view.

As Calan Mai dawns, Creiddylad becomes the beauteous May Queen, ever young, ever fair, harbinger of fertility and bringer of fruits and vegetables. Creiddylad, having been forced to return to her father's home until doomsday, never ages, never marries, and never moves beyond the time of her maidenhood. Since she is "the constant maiden,"[13] Creiddylad represents the fertile Goddess, ready to preserve humanity with her life-giving foods and abundant fertility. For Creiddylad is far more than just a young maiden awaiting a victorious suitor. She is the land, the stable and secure earth beneath our feet that Gwythr and Gwyn fight for dominion over. Creiddylad is the focal point,

---

11. Collins, "Arthurian Court List."

12. Evans, "Gwyn fab Nudd."

13. Bullfinch, *Age of Fable*.

the central axis around which her two lovers rotate. She is the heart, the quiet power that allows life to ebb and flow. Gwythr and Gwyn change and shift and evolve every year, playing out the same story time after time, but Creiddylad remains. She is forever beautiful, forever fruitful, and forever giving of herself to the living beings on the earth.

Although Creiddylad's story is short, it lasts forever, replayed time and again every May Day with the battle of Gwythr and Gwyn and recalled in numerous legends that have been passed down from ages past: Tristan–Isolde–King Marc, Gronw Bebyr–Blodeuwedd–Lleu Llaw Gyffes, Lancelot–Guinevere–King Arthur, Robin Hood–Maid Marian–Sheriff of Nottingham, Gwythr ap Greidiawl–Creiddylad–Gwyn ap Nudd. Creiddylad's story reminds us that love is eternal and crosses all age, time, and space. Creiddylad, constant goddess, giver of all, reminds us that love of self never wanes. Even as lovers leave and return and leave again, our sense of self, our truth, never flags. We are our own best friend, our own lover, and only with this knowledge can we, like the abundant land at Calan Mai, flourish and grow.

LOVING YOURSELF: BEAUTY WITHIN

As we grow up and live in a culture obsessed with outward appearances, is it any wonder that we constantly strive for outward perfection? Do we have the sculpted nails, the glamorous clothes, the stylish hair, the manicured lawn? Is it surprising that we constantly compare ourselves to the smiling faces and sculpted bodies flashing across our television sets and movie screens? Of course not. We are all a product of our culture and currently our culture is focused on outside appearances.

There is nothing wrong with wanting to look good, with working out at the gym, or with striving for a fashionista wardrobe or a golf-course lawn. The problem arises when we refuse to see the value of ourselves based upon the outward appearances of others. If we believe we have no worth due to our cheekbones, brand of jeans, dress size, or lawn ornaments, we lose the truth of ourselves. Every single person on this earth is unique. Each man, woman, and child is an individual, and all have merit and worth. All deserve respect, including you. So while it's easy to afford others a sense of worth, sometimes it's difficult to gift ourselves with that same ideal. We lose the innate love of ourselves that is so often found in very young children. If we have allowed others to steal this self-love away from us, we must take steps to reclaim it and bring it back into our lives.

This is easier to say than to do, but the task is not monumental. Remember, you are simply seeking to remember a sense of self that was second nature to you as a child. Begin small, with simple daily reminders. Choose a toothbrush or pair of pajamas that you absolutely love. Schedule a few moments during each day in which you don't have to do anything. Read a book. Peruse a magazine. Drink a cup of tea or coffee. As you begin to perform small tasks of love for yourself, add in bigger treats, like a massage once a month or a Broadway musical you've been dying to see. Before too long, you will begin to realize that your needs and wants are just as important as anyone else's. And these small gifts of love will help you to feel good about yourself, allowing your own inner power to shine forth brightly. People will begin to notice you, not for your coat or shoes or lawn, but for your inner beauty and your fire within.

THE PATHWORKING

Traveling to another time and another place is not always easy in everyday life. You have to take into consideration different languages, cultures, and time zones. It can leave you feeling drained and confused. Now imagine the disorientation in journeying to another time period, and you will have some idea of the mental stress that is sometimes felt during a past-life regression or a meditative journey into the past.

Your journey to Creiddylad will guide you to a small medieval village during a festival. You will experience a marketplace and many well-known medieval figures, such as the village baker, butcher, blacksmith, and gypsy. Children will frolic and play, and the sun will be shining. Despite the disease and inequality rampant in medieval Europe, this meditation will shelter you from the worst aspects of medieval life. Why? Simply because they do not serve our purpose of finding the value in ourselves and learning to love ourselves. It is important to note that the following journey is as much a myth as any storybook or Hollywood movie. It is not based on a specific village in a specific country. It is a compilation of all villages everywhere and reflects the modern conception of such experiences.

Despite the fact that your journey into the past is largely symbolic, it is important to note that you will be touching on truths inherent within medieval culture. These truths could manifest in unpleasant events or people. For this reason, I have built in a protective talisman and an avenue for return to the mundane world. If you get accosted on the street or hauled off into a dungeon, please utilize either device. The protective talisman will remind you of your power within your own journey, giving you the strength to change things if necessary. Your escape hatch or direct avenue for return is the horse you meet when you first enter the town. If you wish to leave the meditation and return to your own time and place, simply call the horse's name and she will guide you home safely. Enjoy this brief glimpse into the heart of medieval Europe, and accept the gifts and wonder of the goddess Creiddylad.

GUIDED MEDITATION: LEARNING TO LOVE YOURSELF

Take a deep breath, in through your nose and out through your mouth. Take another deep breath, filling your stomach, your diaphragm, and finally your lungs. Hold this breath for five seconds … 1-2-3-4-5 … and exhale, allowing the breath to exit your lungs first, then your diaphragm, and finally your stomach. Take one more deep breath, and as you breathe in, feel the energy of a spring breeze enter you, supporting your fingers, your toes, your legs, and your shoulders, even the top of your head. Hold the breath for seven seconds … 1-2-3-4-5-6-7. As you exhale, feel all tension leave your fingers, your toes, your legs, and your shoulders, even the top of your head. Feel soft, sweet air gently brush your skin. Hear it whisper through the greening leaves. The sound enters your ears and skims over your body, sweeping away tension and strain. Continue breathing deeply, in through your nose, out through your mouth. Allow the earth to hold and support your body. Allow the air to blow away any remaining fear and anxiety. You have never felt so relaxed, so secure, so calm.

You are walking into a small village that is bustling with activity. A sandy street stretches before you, flanked on either side by market stalls, wooden shops, and simple, rustic dwellings. There are no cars or streetlamps, no cell phones or fast food restaurants. You have stepped back in time to the Middle Ages. Take a few moments to gaze at your surroundings and orient yourself to this new time period. (pause) Look down at your clothing and see what you are wearing. Is it a tunic and leggings? A peasant skirt and apron? A fancy ermine-trimmed cape and leather boots? (pause) Slowly turn in a circle to acquaint yourself with this unusual clothing, making sure you feel comfortable moving around in your garments. When you are ready, continue your walk into the town.

The horses in the stable snort a greeting to you, instinctively knowing that you do not belong to this time. Reach into your pocket and give them a treat while patting their noses and murmuring softly. These horses will aid you in leaving this time period, should you grow anxious and wish to leave before the end of the meditation. As you give a lovely, gentle horse a treat, lean forward and listen for her name. (pause) Look into her eyes and whisper your name to her, knowing that you have created a bond between you, between animal and human. You finish giving the horses your treats and swing away from them, striding into town.

It is market day in the town, and there is activity everywhere. Jugglers and performers vie for the best places in the dusty square. Meat hawkers and fishmongers cry the benefits of their wares. Children run through the crowd in hasty packs, chasing wooden balls and clutching rag dolls. The warm scent of fresh bread wafts from the open-windows of the baker's, and the steely scrape of knives rings out from the butcher's. The blacksmith's shop, nestled under a grove of swooping tree branches, blasts heat and noise as he crafts new horseshoes, cooking implements, and weapons for wealthy patrons. There is noise, movement, and warmth everywhere you look. Housewives hurry forth with baskets under their arms, gathering food for the week and necessities for the upcoming months, taking time to chat and gossip in groups along the road. Their husbands gather at the pub, lounging at tables and chairs and standing around the entranceway, quaffing glasses of homemade beer. 'Tis a rollicking, fanciful, fun experience, and you immediately get caught up in the mirth and excitement all around you.

As you peruse the stalls of ribbons and tiny mirrors and buttons and cloth, you feel a tug on your sleeve and turn around. There, right before you, is a tiny, dark-haired girl. She wears a red bandana in her hair, and her dress is dirty and ripped in spots. The outer garment wraps around her diagonally and is very fanciful, with bright blue and yellow colors. Her chemise was once white but is now the color of pond scum; it protects up to her neck and down to her wrists. A tiny edge of the chemise peeks out from under her outer dress. Her feet are bare. She looks at you with large, brown eyes, deep and full of mystery, and hands you a gift. Then she scampers away, back to the voluminous folds of her mother's dress. Her mother is exotically attractive, and her eyes, like her daughter's, seek you out and hold your own eyes hypnotically. You instantly know that she senses the Otherworldliness of your arrival at the town. You smile and nod your head slightly, and she does the same. Then she turns her back on you and continues through the town. You glance down at the Gypsy's gift. (pause) Truly look at it from all angles. This gift is your talisman to enter the realms of the past—to explore your past lives and to seek the root of yourself. It is not given lightly and should be treasured for all time. (pause) Hold the talisman to your heart, vowing to honor it, and then slip it into your pocket.

Turning from the crowded stalls, you sense a vastness up ahead, a lull in the constant movement. You cannot see it, but the street traffic ebbs and flows around this stillness. You are pulled toward it, instinctively knowing that this is why you have arrived in this medieval town on market day. As you walk, guided by a faint pull in the middle of your chest, the people and animals miraculously move out of your way. You float through the village, pushed along by a sweet-smelling breeze that tickles your skin and lifts the ends of your hair. You are no longer moving under your own power, but rather are compelled forward by a strange, powerful force.

Next to the butcher's shop and in front of the blacksmith's is a large, open green. Covered in soft, new grass, it forms a circle. A puppet show entertains a chorus of laughing children near the road. Trees sway above the blacksmith's shop, close to a meandering brook that trickles merrily. In the middle of the green is a small, simple well with a bucket swinging in the spring breeze. And there beside the well stands the goddess Creiddylad. As the breeze blows around you, riffling banners and tangling hair, Creiddylad remains completely unaffected. Her curly blond hair does not move. Her simple white dress does not rustle in the breeze. The ivy crown atop her head stays securely fastened. It is as if she rests in a bubble of peace and quiet, unaffected by the elements around her. You approach her reverently.

"You have guessed who I am," Creiddylad says softly, smiling at you. She is taller than you supposed, and you have to crane your neck to look up at her. "Now, who are you?" she asks. You tell her your name and a little about yourself. (pause) "I am the May Queen," she intones, her voice growing deeper and fuller. "I am the beauty incarnate that men seek. They risk their lives for me and sacrifice much." A slender tear escapes down Creiddylad's cheek. You glance over her shoulder and see the shadows of two men in the trees, fighting each other. One is dark, dressed in navy blue with a cheeky grin and a few wisps of gray hair curling around his ears. The other is younger, with straight blond hair, and is dressed in a multihued tunic. They dance, swords locked and clashing, high above the unsuspecting villagers. You look around to see if anyone else sees them, but the children are focused on the puppet show and the adults are attending to their chores.

"They do not see," Creiddylad says to you, touching your shoulder and bringing your attention back to her captivating face. "The eternal struggle of Gwyn ap Nudd and Gwythr ap Greidiawl is beyond their knowledge. It happens before them every day of their lives, and yet …" She pauses and looks down at the ground, placing her hand on the gray stone well. "Look into the well," she commands, gesturing with her hand. You hesitate, licking your lips and glancing uneasily over your shoulder at the bustling marketplace. Creiddylad waits, patient and knowing. Finally, you step up to the well and look in. You see your reflection. A sense of disappointment washes over you.

"What do you see?" Creiddylad asks. You tell her you see your reflection. The goddess nods and, taking your hand, walks halfway around the well. "And what do you see now?" The village around you is empty, windows shuttered, brown leaves skittering across the ground. A single woman, sheltered in a warm, woolen shawl, scuttles from one building to another. The sun has gone, and the skies are dominated by gray clouds. The market festival has disappeared, replaced by a cool, dark autumn day. You glance behind you and see the blue-suited, dark-haired man jumping for joy amid the branches of the tree, a holly crown atop his head. In confusion, you look up at Creiddylad, who smiles benignly and gestures for you to follow. Hand in hand, you and Creiddylad complete the circuit around the well and return to your spot. Green leaves once again bud on the trees, and the children scamper and play outdoors. Bright sunlight shines down from a blue, cloudless sky. Birds chirp and tweet. In the tree across the clearing, the green-suited blond man smiles contentedly as he swings from thick tree branches, a crown of oak on his head. Despite the obvious spring day, the marketplace is gone. The jugglers, meat sellers, and roving carts have left this small, simple town for other village festivals.

Creiddylad covers your eyes with one of her hands, and she whispers to you, "True beauty comes from knowing yourself. Look again, little one, and see the beauty that radiates from within." She removes her hand, and you are once again staring into the depths of the well. You see your reflection, but it has changed somewhat. Gaze at it intently and know your own beauty, your path to remembering the depth of yourself. (pause)

When you have seen all there is to see, you feel a gentle tugging on the edge of your sleeve. It is the small Gypsy girl with a bowl in hand. She gestures toward the well and indicates she would like to get some water. You move out of her way and look around. Creiddylad has vanished, and the village is once again in the midst of a market day. There, in the trees high above the blacksmith's shop, you vaguely glimpse the movements of two shadow forms fighting for the hand of Creiddylad, as King Arthur commanded, until the end of time. The Gypsy girl flicks some of her water onto your head and shoulders, and as the drops reflect tiny rainbows in the air, you think about Creiddylad's gift of knowledge.

You smile, throw the girl a silver coin, and rejoin the rowdy excitement of the market day.

Now take a deep breath, in through your nose and out through your mouth. Take another deep breath, filling your stomach, your diaphragm, and finally your lungs. Hold this breath for five seconds ... 1-2-3-4-5 ... and exhale, allowing the breath to exit your lungs first, then your diaphragm, and finally your stomach. Breathe deeply once more, and as you breathe in, feel the energy and the wonder of the world around you in your fingers, your toes, your legs, and your shoulders, even the top of your head. As you exhale, wiggle your fingers and toes. Shake your legs and move your shoulders up and down. Take another deep breath and, as you exhale, move your head from side to side. Feel the ground under your body touching every nerve ending and muscle. Hear the rustlings of the people around you. Notice the movements outside. Continue breathing. Stretch your arms out above your head. You are returning to the present, to the here and now. Continue stretching. Continue breathing. When you are ready, open your eyes, blink and focus, and sit up.

INVOCATION TO CREIDDYLAD

Oh Creiddylad,
Lovely May Queen,
Source of love,
Beauty, pure and green.

Your inner flame
Warms the spring earth.
A testament
Of enduring worth.

No man, no child,
No hearth, no home,
Your life is full
Of you alone.

You cry to see
Our needless tears,

Slender, alone,
Becoming our fears.

But truth rise
From lakeside shore
And we wander,
Alone no more.

We find ourselves,
Our love divine,
Where it's always been,
On your vine.

MAGICAL ACTIVITIES

Faery Magic: Ribbons and Wings

Items Needed: Three seven-inch-long yellow ribbons; four seven-inch-long pink ribbons; a fine-point permanent marker; a small, handheld mirror; and gifts for the faeries, such as rose petals, elderberry wine, baked treats, etc.

Moon Phase: Waxing or full

Seasonal Cycle: Spring (especially around Calan Mai or May 1)

Although the fey folk are not mentioned in direct connection with Creiddylad, they still influence her story, her genealogy, and her essential characteristics. Like the faeries, Creiddylad is a perpetual youth. She does not age, become an elder, or gain the gray hair of wisdom or the wrinkles of knowledge. (Outward appearances are deceiving, however, for both the faeries and Creiddylad have learned much and can teach us many things.) Both the faeries and Creiddylad are connected to the festival of Calan Mai, one of the two days in the Celtic calendar outside the realm of known time and space. May 1 is a great time to contact the faeries and gain information and understanding from them. It is also the day featured prominently in Creiddylad's myth. As a May Queen, Creiddylad's link to the faeries corresponds to her appreciation of the earth and her innate sovereignty over the land. Lastly, the King of the Welsh faeries, the Tylwyth Teg, is none other than Creiddylad's dark suitor, Gwyn ap Nudd. Gwyn may actually be Creiddylad's brother, due to poor translations by medieval monks concerning their fathers' names,

Lludd and Nudd. (Both names are thought to correspond to a Romano-British deity known as Nodons.)[14] If so, Creiddylad is a faery goddess and her connection to the Celtic festival of Calan Mai is not a random coincidence.

Starting on a Friday (the day of love and relationships) during the waxing moon, choose an outside location that feels fey friendly and leave gifts for the faeries for an entire week. (Try to locate an area that has a tree or bush nearby.) These gifts should be environmentally safe and should represent your desire and wish to connect to the faeries in your area. Since the spell concerns self-love, you might consider choosing items that also have a connection to relationships and love in general. Rose petals, elderberry wine, corn cakes, and rose quartz are all excellent gifts for the faeries. Please do not leave any chocolate offerings for the faeries, as chocolate can be harmful to some animals. The faeries would not want to be the cause of any animal's discomfort.

After a week of leaving gifts, return to your faery site on Friday with your ribbons, marker, mirror, and one final offering. Sitting down within your faery area, take each ribbon and write one positive characteristic about yourself. Don't limit yourself to only your physical appearance. Remember all of the great qualities that you exhibit at work, within your family, and with your friends. Maybe you're a great listener or can solve problems quickly. Perhaps you think fast under pressure or remain calm during a crisis. Do you have a strong threshold for pain or a genius for comic timing? Can you make people laugh or see the truth of a situation? Whatever your unique attributes, write them down, one on each ribbon.

Take each ribbon and, looking in the mirror, say the positive trait out loud while looking into your eyes. After you have said the characteristic, tie the ribbon onto a nearby tree or bush, connecting it to the faeries of the land. After all of the ribbons have been tied onto the tree or bush, leave your last gift for the faeries. If you want, you can meditate for a while in order to gain messages from the faeries or from Creiddylad. When you feel ready, blow a kiss to the faeries on your site and leave the area, knowing you have honored your own unique gifts to the world.

Natural Magic: Perpetual Wild Wood

Items Needed: Two acorns, three holly leaves, cornmeal, a cloth sack or old pillowcase, gold spray paint, vegetable glycerin, a glass or enamel container, hot water,

---

14. Evans, "Nudd/Lludd/Nodons."

a hammer, green food coloring, a surface sealer, a hot-glue gun (optional), and extra glue sticks (optional)

Moon Phase: Any

Seasonal Cycle: Late summer or early autumn

Creiddylad's story beautifully describes the turn of the seasons, the Wheel of the Year, the ebb and flow of time. The following spell intimately connects you to the passage of the year as influenced by Gwythr, the Oak King, and Gwyn, the Holly King. By communing with nature and crafting a lasting emblem of your time outside, you are becoming one with Creiddylad's myth. This spell will help you to move beyond merely reading the story of Creiddylad by experiencing it firsthand.

On a sunny, bright autumn day, go outside to collect your acorns and holly leaves. Do not choose the first ones you stumble across. This spell is meant to help you create a heart bond with the natural world and thus with Creiddylad, Gwythr, and Gwyn. Take your time and ramble through the countryside. Each time you find one of your items, honor it by stating why you are attracted to it, place it in your sack or pillowcase, and scatter some cornmeal on the ground as a gift back to the land.

Once you have found your holly leaves and acorns, return home and mix two parts hot tap water with one part vegetable glycerin in your glass or enamel container, making sure the finished mixture is at least two inches deep. Add a lot of green food coloring, in order to preserve the green color of the holly. Open up the bottom edge of the holly stems by hitting them a few times with the hammer, and then immerse the holly leaves in the mixture. Allow them to sit for four to five days before removing them from the mixture. Dry them off and apply a surface sealer specifically designed for "fixing" dried flowers or leaves. (Your local craft store should have it in stock.)

While you are waiting for the holly to be preserved, spray your acorns with the gold spray paint. For best results, apply several layers, allowing the paint to dry between applications. If the acorn caps fall off, glue them back on using the hot-glue gun. Once the acorns and holly are preserved and colored, set them in sunlight for three days, allowing them to bask in the warm autumn days.

On a Sunday when the sun is shining, gather your acorns and holly leaves and hold them in your hands. Stand facing the sun, allowing your body to be bathed in light. Hold your hands before you, clasping them together while still holding the leaves and acorns. (The holly and acorns will be in darkness.) Take several deep breaths and remember your walk in the woods when you gathered these items. Try to picture the vegetation, the trees, and the movements of the small animals. Hear the bird songs and the crunch of the ground under your feet. Feel the soft (or wild) wind and the warmth of the sun on your neck and shoulders. Recall all of the details of that time alone with nature.

When you feel ready, open your hands so that the holly leaves and oak acorns can once again soak up the sun. Open your eyes at the same time and know that you are intimately connected to nature. Through this spell, you have plumbed the depths of the story of Creiddylad, Gwythr, and Gwyn and have emerged with a newfound respect and intimacy for the land around you, for the seasonal cycles, and for the importance of the light and dark halves of the year.

Meditation/Creative Visualization: The Battle Within

Items Needed: Soft, meditative music; incense that represents May flowers in your area (possibly lily of the valley); two brown candles with holders; two green candles with holders; your perpetual wild wood (if you crafted it already); and a lighter or matches

Moon Phase: Waning or new

Seasonal Cycle: Spring (especially May)

As this spell works with the seasonal energies of Gwythr ap Greidiawl and Gwyn ap Nudd, I have included an invocation to the directions, as they are representative of the light and dark halves of the year. You do not need to invoke the directions, but the phrases will help to put you in the right frame of mind for the creative visualization. Creative visualization is often the most difficult form of magic, because it uses so few magical items and tools. There are no colorful candles, fragrant herbs, scented oils, or secret chants through which to focus your energy. Creative visualization works only with your mind and your intent; thus, it is often thought to be the purest form of magic, the most direct route to the divine. Some people find creative visualization to be very difficult. During the spell, if your concentration wanes and you begin to think about your groceries or job, simply take several deep breaths and focus on your breathing. When your grocery list and your job recede into the background, you can once again focus on your spellwork. You might find that it will take several tries to complete this spell. Don't worry about it. Magic happens when it is most needed. With preparation and intent, you will complete this spell, crowning yourself with the power and majesty of the oak, holly, and ivy.

Find a time and place where you will not be disturbed for at least one hour. Unplug the telephone and place a "Do Not Disturb" or "Shh … Meditation in Progress" sign on the door. Put your green candles at the east and south directions and your brown candles in the north and west, all within easy reach of your sacred space. Start your incense and your music, and then sit down in a comfortable position, facing east. You may want to wrap yourself in a blanket or quilt and find a soft, comfortable pillow on which to sit. Some people prefer to lie down during visualization, but that may make you too relaxed, causing you to fall asleep. Once you have found a comfortable position, take some time to breathe deeply and ground and center. This will help calm your mind, bringing your brain-wave patterns from the very active alpha waves down to the more relaxed theta waves. Relaxing the mind will help you to access your intuition, uncover your subconscious, and listen to the will of the divine.

Open your eyes to a soft focus and, remaining sitting, light the green east candle, saying:

Springtime bright
Bunnies alight
Birds in flight
On a warm night.

When the fragrant, youthful energies of spring fill the room, lean toward the south candle, light it, and say:

Summer glow
Garden grow
Sweet sap flow
Ages ago.

Welcome the warm, passionate energies of summer and, when you are ready, reach for the west candle and light it, saying:

Autumn dim
Salmon swim
Cauldrons brim
Time of grim.

Feel the eerie, cooling breezes of autumn throughout your sacred space. As they swirl around you, light the north candle and say:

Winter dark
Hearthfire spark
Quest embark
Earth's time stark.

Allow the fragile, barren energy of winter to seep into your room. When all four seasons have been honored and remembered, close your eyes and take four deep breaths, one for each season. With your mind's eye, see the seasonal energies moving and mingling within your sacred space. These are the energies with which you will be working during this spell. Make sure you feel comfortable with all of them before continuing with the rest of the spellwork.

With your eyes closed, envision two men fighting against a gray-blue backdrop. These are Gwyn ap Nudd and Gwythr ap Greidiawl, following the cycle of the seasons. Allow the forms of these men to shape themselves as they will. They may take the appearance of the descriptions from the earlier meditation, or they may look completely different. (They may even take the form of animals or faeries or Otherworldly beings.) Whatever form Gwyn and Gwythr assume, know they are the energies of the conflicting seasons seeking to gain control over the other for the fair Creiddylad.

Once the two men have been established in your mind, look around for Creiddylad. She will probably be located near Gwyn and Gwythr. She might even be inside the circle of their fighting. Creiddylad embodies the power of the Goddess, of the earth, and of the very land itself. She is the "center" around which time circles. She is the calm, peaceful eye of the storm. She does not change but anchors the world and the universe by her very presence. Once you have located Creiddylad, take some time to drink in her energy. Pay attention to her appearance and her demeanor. When you feel ready, walk to Creiddylad's side and stand next to her.

The battle between Gwyn ap Nudd and Gwythr ap Greidiawl continues around you. It is frightening but exhilarating at the same time. Creiddylad places a hand on your shoulder to tell you that you are safe within her protection. You realize, as you stand there, that you need to embrace the battle in order to gain the peace and knowledge of this stable, unwavering goddess. You take a deep breath and focus on Gwyn. See aspects of your shadow side in the folds of his dark-aspected clothes. Relax and breathe. When you are ready, turn and look at Gwythr. Your many positive traits hide in the wrinkles of his brightly colored clothes. Relax and breathe, drinking in both the shadow side and the light side of your personality.

Suddenly, without warning, the two men stop fighting and turn toward you. They walk forward, Gwyn reaching you first. He places a holly crown on your head. "Of all the plants, holly wears the crown," he says, and leaning toward you, he breathes into your left ear.

When Gwythr arrives, he puts a wreath of oak on your head. "The mighty oak is the King of the Trees," he whispers, breathing into your right ear.

Both Gwyn and Gwythr step back, leaving room for Creiddylad. She places a ring of ivy on your head. "The ivy binds the two," she intones, kissing the top of your head. You know that this visualization has helped you to integrate both aspects of yourself, your light and dark halves, in order to step closer to the true majesty and complete self-love of Creiddylad. The goddess smiles at you and pushes you away from the never-ending seasonal tableau of Gwythr and Gwyn. You bow to her respectfully and begin to walk away from the trio. As you do, you hear the sounds of battle once again behind you.

Taking three deep breaths, you begin to acclimate yourself to this world yet again. You hear the sounds of your house or apartment building. You smell the scents of the candles and the incense. You focus once again on the music. Open your eyes to a soft focus and re-enter this time and space, knowing that you have performed a powerful spell.

Turn to the directions, snuffing out the candles and saying:

Hail the bright Spring!
Hail the glowing Summer!
Hail the dim Autumn!
Hail the dark Winter!

There is no need to bid farewell to the seasons, because they are a part of our cyclical world and a part of the ebb and flow of our lives.

If you wish, write down your creative visualization in your journal or Book of Shadows. At a later time, you can enhance the integration of your shadow and bright halves by creating a holly, oak, and ivy head wreath out of silk flowers. It is not necessary, but it will serve as a physical reminder of the powerful magic you have just created.

LESSONS FROM
THE IRISH

MEETING AIRMID, IRISH GODDESS OF HEALING AND HERBCRAFT
Accessing Your Healing Ability

AIRMID: GODDESS OF CYCLES

Unlike many Celtic Irish goddesses, Airmid (pronounced AIR-mit) is content to wait. She does not force her opinion upon others. She does not push to get things done. Airmid knows that life takes time, that growth and healing do not happen quickly. As a goddess of healing, especially herbal healing, her personality and mantra preach patience. After all, even a goddess must bow to the temperamental mood swings of the gracious Earth Mother.

Airmid grew up in a family of healers. Her father, Dian Cecht, is the god of healing of the Tuatha de Danann, the mythical race of gods known as the "children of the goddess Danu." Two of six children born to Dian Cecht, Airmid and her brother Miach are gifted with their father's healing touch. Her sister Etan is gifted with the craft of poetry and marries Oghma, the god who creates the Irish tree alphabet and oracle, the Ogam. Three other brothers, Cian, Cu, and Cethe, serve as warriors for the high king of Tara, King Nuada. Airmid's mother is the abundant mother goddess of the Tuatha de Danann, Danu the Earth Mother, the Waters of Life.

As with many Irish legends, the story of Airmid begins in the midst of battle. As the Tuatha de Danann strive to control all of the land of Ireland, battles commence with the Formorians, an earlier tribe of gods (or demons, depending on your point of view) who have settled in Ireland. In the First Battle of Mag Tuired between the two opposing godlike forces, King Nuada loses a hand, leaving him disfigured and thus ineligible to rule Ireland. (Celtic rulers had to be fit both mentally and physically, as the physical condition of the body indicated the health of less obvious features, such as the mind and the spirit.)

The half-Formorian, half-Danann prince Bres takes over the kingship of Tara, but his stingy, parsimonious ways become his downfall and he is forcibly removed by the Danann lords. (However, he lives still and eventually convinces the Formorians to fight against the Tuatha de Danann once again in *The Second Battle of Mag Tuired*.) Without a leader and truly wishing that King Nuada was eligible to rule, Dian Cecht, the healer of the Danann lords, steps forward with a plan: he will heal Nuada and restore him to the Irish throne. Dian Cecht asks Creidne, the god of bronzecraft and intricate metalwork, to craft a hand made from silver. Through his magical healing skill, Dian Cecht brings the hand to life so that it moves and works like a natural hand. Once it is attached to Nuada's arm, he is crowned king once again.[1]

The glory of Dian Cecht, as the healer of the king, shines brightly until his son Miach and his daughter Airmid arrive at the gates of Tara. They offer an alternative healing cure for the king's hand and are invited in to voice their proposal. They claim that through herbs and incantations, they can heal the withered, wrinkled, dry stump that was cleaved off of Nuada's body. Once whole, this newly wrought hand could be reattached to Nuada's arm. Dian Cecht, furious at possibly being overshadowed by his children, decries their plan in front of the whole Hall of Tara. However, Nuada gives them permission to work their craft.

Miach collects the hacked-off appendage and begins his work, sprinkling the hand with herbs and reciting incantations. He works his magic for nine days, dividing the healing into three parts, each part three days in length. For the first three days, he wears the hand against his body, and wondrously, when he removes it, the hand is covered with new skin. Then Miach holds the hand against his chest for three days. When it emerges from beneath his shirt, the hand has new veins and tendons, having gained strength and power. For the last three days, Miach throws "white wisps"[2] of bulrushes that have been blackened in a fire onto the newly formed hand. These ashes must work to seal in the magical healing process, having combined the intense heat of fire, symbolized by the burning plants, with the peaceful calm of water, symbolized by the aquatic nature of the bulrush. (This duality mirrors Miach's brash, fiery nature and Airmid's placid, introspective personality.) And so Miach crafts a healing that relies on the magical nature of his healthy body, incantations, and herbal craft, believing it will restore King Nuada's hand. Being an accomplished healer, Miach is completely right.

Upon presenting the unblemished, perfectly whole hand to the king, Miach is met with a flurry of praise and the biting sting of a sword blade. Furious at being overshadowed by his son, Dian Cecht challenges Miach to heal several wounds on himself, just inflicted by his father! Three times Dian Cecht slices into the skull of his son, and three times Miach heals himself. On the fourth attack, Dian Cecht cuts right to the very center of the brain,

---

1. Gray, "Second Battle of Mag Tuired," verse 11.

2. Ibid., verse 33.

actually removing it. Miach cannot heal such a grievous wound, and he dies, at the foot of the king by the hand of his father.[3]

Throughout Miach's magical healing and his ordeal with his father, Airmid disappears from the story. She does not aid her brother in reshaping King Nuada's hand. She does not help her brother when he is attacked by their father, Dian Cecht. Perhaps she withdraws out of respect for her father's feelings, or perhaps out of fear for her father's actions. Her delay may stem from her brother's arrogant, showy attitude and healing techniques or from her quiet, serene demeanor and her unwillingness to take sides in a family dispute. Perhaps she loved her family so greatly that she could not choose one family member over the other. Or perhaps Airmid did not have access yet to her own healing power, as it was hiding deep inside herself.

Whatever the reason, Airmid's healing magic was unavailable to her brother until after it was too late. Once his brain or head was severed from the rest of his body, his soul flew away and could not be recovered. (The ancient Celts believed that the soul resided in the head, hence the practice of taking the heads of slain enemies and putting them on pikes.)

After the death of his son, Dian Cecht buries his body near the Hill of Tara and allows his daughter to visit as often as she wishes. Airmid travels every day to her brother's grave, showing her love and devotion through her actions and tears. Angry at her father and distraught over her brother's death, Airmid spends an entire year[4] visiting his grave, spending long hours at the site and ignoring her other responsibilities and duties. Airmid delves into a period of sickened grief, focusing entirely on her brother's death. Through this anguish and, undoubtedly, depression, she accesses a part of herself that she has never experienced before in her young life. The death of her brother forces Airmid to delve into the very depths of her soul, gaining her own wisdom and her own insight. She steps out of the shadow of her magical brother and controlling father and (in integrating the shadow) becomes powerful in her own right.

---

3. Ibid., verse 34.

4. *The Second Battle of Mag Tuired* never states the length of time that Airmid visits her brother's grave. However, since 365 herbs grow from his burial site, one modern interpretation of the legend claims that she visited for the length of a year (365 days) and that on each day a new herb appeared. Another modern interpretation states that she visited for the span of a year and that on the following day (the 366th day) a blanket of herbs covered the burial mound of her brother. Neither theory can be supported by ancient lore.

On the anniversary of her brother's death, Airmid notices several beautiful green shoots growing from the grave. Paying close attention, she realizes that they are various healing herbs—365 healing herbs, to be precise, one for each joint and sinew of her brother's body. She leaves the grave and returns the next day, ready to learn the remedies of the herbs. On this day, a year and a day from Miach's death, Airmid gathers the herbs, laying them out on her apron or her cloak in a pattern that indicates their healing properties. There is no mention in ancient sources of how Airmid gained the knowledge of the herbs. Some scholars have speculated that the way the herbs were growing on the earthen mound indicated their usefulness. Others believe that the herbs actually spoke to Airmid, telling her their healing powers. Perhaps her brother visited her in a dream or transferred all of his considerable herbal knowledge to her in her sleep. Or perhaps Airmid already knew, intuitively, the properties of the herbs, and her brother's death brought this inner knowledge into her conscious mind. Miach's death, then, becomes the catalyst for the birth of Airmid, allowing her to access the dark realms of her psyche.

As fate would have it, Airmid's gift to the world of herbal knowledge is fleeting in nature. Her father, suspicious of her actions, follows her to Miach's grave on the day she gathers the herbs. Once again fearing to be outshone by his child, Dian Cecht mixes up the herbs that Airmid has so painstakingly arranged: the knowledge, once again, remains hidden. As Dian Cecht exclaims in *The Second Battle of Mag Tuired*, "Though Miach no longer lives, Airmid shall remain."[5] In order to know the healing within the herbs, individuals cannot rely on the bright, obvious answers provided by Miach. Instead, they must travel within the darkness of the self in order to find the inner knowledge, just as Airmid gazed within to originally understand the meanings of the herbs.

The inner depth of the magic and knowledge of Airmid shows itself in another section of *The Battle of Mag Tuired*. As the Dananns make ready for their battle with the Formorians, Dian Cecht, Airmid, Miach, and another son, named Octriuil, chant over the Well of Slaine, creating a magical well that will bring dead men back to life and heal all wounds.[6] Although Irish mythology rarely follows a simple chronological timeline, the mention of Miach is a glaring admission into the story. After all, just eighty-nine stanzas ago, he had been killed by his father! Wells, as wellsprings of healing, regeneration, and inspiration,

---

5. Gray, "Second Battle of Mag Tuired," verse 35.

6. Ibid., verse 123.

were associated with the Underworld in the ancient past. They were seen as a physical link to the dead, to the spirits, to the gods and goddesses, and to past ancestors. Wells were locations in the physical landscape that allowed the powers of the Underworld to rise and aid mortals on earth.[7] Miach's inclusion in the creation of the Well of Slaine may indicate his spirit's willingness to rise from the depths of the Underworld to aid his family. Adopting the intuitive healing powers of Airmid, Miach becomes a symbol of dormant knowledge and energy that rests in the darkness below, and Airmid becomes the conduit through which that energy flows.

Intimately connected to the growing cycles of the earth, Airmid knows the beauty of life after death. Her brother's herbal knowledge and powerful incantations live on through her, as she remains an immortal goddess, forever linked to the Underworld, to the knowledge within. Airmid understands the power of illuminated darkness and lives with the sadness such wisdom often brings. Her power arrives on the edge of her brother's death. Only by withdrawing within and mourning his loss does Airmid tap into a hidden wisdom within herself. As long as she lives, as long as green plants sprout, as long as people welcome the challenge of herbal healing, her brother's memory remains intact, his knowledge in the forefront and her knowledge in the darkest recesses of the heart and soul.

HEALING ABILITY: THE MYSTERY

Healing comes in all shapes and sizes. You can heal through herbs or crystals, with acupuncture needles or tuning forks, by being a channel of divine energy, or by simply listening. Healing happens all around us, in different ways and through varying modalities. A massage can be a healing experience, as can a drive in the countryside, a bowl of fruit, a yoga class, or a picnic by the lake. Open your mind to the potential of healing and you will see that healing is not as clear-cut as Western medicine would have us believe. Healing is a mystery, a process that happens within the body and is hidden away from the light of the world. It concerns all aspects of the self—the emotional and spiritual as well as the physical. And it is not always easily explained, as the labyrinthine passages of the mind change and alter the physical form and function of the body.

---

7. Church of Y Tylwyth Teg, "Water and the Sacred Well" and "The Celts and Sacred Wells."

Therefore, the healer must understand the secret of the healing process: that he or she is the facilitator of positive change, not the source of it. Wellness comes from the center of each individual. A healer can tap into that wellness, but it is up to the patient to accept and embrace it. The herbs, crystals, acupuncture needles, and divine energy are ways of opening to the wellness. However, if the patient has no wish (whether consciously or subconsciously) to get better, the healer will be unable to help.

Healing is our link to the subconscious past, an access road into the knowledge and ways of our ancestors. Treat whatever healing ability you have with respect and reverence. You are part of an endless cycle, a chain of wisdom that reaches deep into the heart of the collective unconscious, and thus deep into the heart of yourself. Your healing may be unconventional. It may be specific only unto you. Maybe you suggest that patients hug trees or collect seashells or eat specific foods. Perhaps you bring coffee to people in a crisis or use your telephone to offer a sympathetic ear. Whatever form your healing takes, honor it and love yourself for giving this energy to the world.

THE PATHWORKING

Visiting a barrow mound (or burial site) is neither easy nor for the weak of heart. It is a place filled with the energy of sorrow and mourning. Yet Airmid learns at such a place that life springs from death and that enlightenment comes from the depths of one's being. Therefore, she will be guiding you through your own spiritual journey into yourself, to access the healer within.

The goddess will meet you at the center of her brother's burial mound and guide you in collecting and sorting the plants found upon it. Take your time while you gather the herbs, for they may talk to you. Plants do not always talk in the same way as humans, or even gods and goddesses. Often, they give off energy signatures that activate emotional or physical responses in our own bodies. You might feel a tingling in a certain area of your body or a lethargic or euphoric feeling in your head when touching a specific herb. Disconnected images, sounds, or snippets of songs may flash before your eyes or resound in your ears.

If this occurs, try not to question the validity or overanalyze the meaning of the message. Plants tend to be rather straightforward and do not usually send convoluted or confusing messages. "What you see is what you get" with most of the members of the plant kingdom. However, if you are truly unsure of a plant's message, simply ask for clarification. The plant may stop singing you a song and instead show you pictures that express its message and meaning, or you might hear a thought wafting and curling, like flower petals on a spring breeze, through the back recesses of your mind. The limited verbal skill of the plant makes you the detective of your own meditation. Pay attention, stay alert, and be prepared for anything!

GUIDED MEDITATION: ACCESSING YOUR HEALING ABILITY

Take a deep breath, in through your nose and out through your mouth. Take another deep breath, filling your stomach, your diaphragm, and finally your lungs. Hold this breath for five seconds … 1-2-3-4-5 … and exhale, allowing the breath to exit your lungs first, then your diaphragm, and finally your stomach. One more deep breath, and as you breathe in, feel the energy of the soft, boggy ground around you supporting your fingers, your toes, your legs, and your shoulders, even the top of your head. Hold the breath for seven seconds … 1-2-3-4-5-6-7. As you exhale, feel all tension leave your fingers, your toes, your legs, and your shoulders, even the top of your head. Continue breathing deeply, in through your nose, out through your mouth. Feel the dewy grass under the soles of your feet, soft and springy. The air is heavy with the moisture of rain. Low clouds form in the sky, banding together to form one bright mass of never-ending gray and white. The sun is wrapped in wreaths of clouds that descend to the earth in wisps of fog and mist. They swirl around you, removing any tension, any stress, any worry. In this mystical, shifting world, you have never felt so relaxed, so secure, so calm.

You follow an indentation in the muted green grass before you. It is not quite a path, yet it looks to be well-worn, sparser than the surrounding ocean of green. The grass encompasses your entire vision; no matter which way you look, fields and meadows of grass and tiny yellow and white flowers flow before you. The mist shrouds the distance, wafting up from the ground as you continue to walk. Although you cannot see ahead of you, you are not afraid. Reaching into your pocket, you grasp your protective talisman and know that you are safe, even in the wilds of the Otherworld.

Ahead of you, the mist begins to shift slightly. Forms and figures dance and melt inside the mist, giving you tantalizing glimpses of people and things. Pay attention to these glimpses. They are messages from the goddess Airmid and are meant for you and you alone. They will help you in accessing the healing power that is deep within yourself. (pause)

As the glimpses become less and less frequent, you become aware of a growing golden light. It catches at the edges of the mist, dissipating the silken strands until only a few remain. The meadow stretches out before you in all its glory and splendor. Birds sing in the branches of elder and willow trees. A burbling brook meanders gracefully across the field. Wind catches your hair and shirt, flinging them with the wild, carefree abandon of a child. You smile and twirl in a circle, wishing to capture the beauty of this place and hold it in your heart. The mists have cleared, and you are whole and safe within this living, breathing environment, within your own skin.

"So it is when the dark shroud falls away and we allow the light to enter." The voice is quiet but deep, with a heavy backbeat like the pounding of a drum. It reverberates through your entire being, taking up residence in the core of your soul. You shiver and look around for the source.

"So it was when I found my power. A sweet singing in the veins that cannot compare to any life before." The words emanate from a woman a few feet ahead of you. She is sitting by a burial mound and toying with the grassy shoots that spring from the moldy earth. She is young, with an open, square face that is covered across the nose with freckles. Her hair is deep mahogany in color and wisps unexpectedly around her high cheekbones and slender neck. She wears a green cloak, which covers a simple homespun dress and much-mended shift. You walk toward her. She motions you to sit down next to her.

"I am Airmid," she says, her voice steady and true. "This is my brother…Miach's…mound." Her voice catches slightly, trembling like a raindrop on a blade of grass. She averts her eyes, sweeping dark eyelashes down to avoid your penetrating gaze. You wait. When she glances up again, you can see unshed tears hiding behind her dark eyes.

"It was here, many years ago, that I first came to experience the depths of my soul. To mourn my brother and acknowledge my sorrow." Airmid's eyes bore into your own, eyes with wisdom and pain that belie her youthful appearance. Here is a woman old beyond her years. She reaches out a weather-beaten hand and covers one of your own. "Tell me of your sorrow," Airmid requests, squeezing your hand. You tell her of a time when you felt deep pain, sorrow, or sadness. (pause)

Airmid nods in understanding. "So it was when my brother died," she says. She reaches down into the rich, moist earth of the mound and pulls out a single herbal plant. Its roots dangle in the air, white and spotted with dirt. Airmid continues, "Then I realized that acknowledging and experiencing my darkness allowed me access to a buried wellspring of knowledge deep inside myself. This knowledge had always been accessible to me, but I was blind to it, unable or unwilling to touch the intuitive wisdom within my heart and soul." She holds your hand, cupping the fragile plant between your palm and hers. You feel something from the plant. Focus your attention on it and receive its message. (pause)

"You have felt the first stirrings of new life," Airmid says, her voice becoming fuller and richer as you listen. It sounds like rolling thunder across the hills or a herd of stampeding wild horses or the steady tattoo of raindrops on a deep mountain lake. You look around and Airmid has disappeared, yet her voice remains on the wind and her presence remains in the earth. "Gather the herbs on my brother's mound," Airmid instructs. "But do so with your mind, and spirit, and heart, not just your hands. Remember your dark time. What did you learn from it? How have you changed? How are you stronger or surer of yourself? And when you have gained your own knowledge, listen to what the last plant has to tell you, for he speaks with my voice." Airmid's last words drift into the sky, and you are alone on Miach's burial mound. Take time now to gather the herbs and listen to your inner voice. Then hear the healing guidance that Airmid has for you. (long pause)

After you gather the herbs and receive Airmid's guidance, the goddess appears before you, her green cloak spreading out behind her with the gusting wind. She smiles at you and, with a flick of her fingers, replants all of the herbs you have just uprooted. She smiles. "Such is the cycle of life," she says. Airmid leans over and hugs you soundly. Her green cloak wraps around you, enveloping you in darkness and warmth, giving you peace, showing you the way home.

Now take a deep breath, in through your nose and out through your mouth. Take another deep breath, filling your stomach, your diaphragm, and finally your lungs. Hold this breath for five seconds... 1-2-3-4-5... and exhale, allowing the breath to exit your lungs first, then your diaphragm and finally your stomach. Breathe deeply once more and as you breathe in, feel the energy and the wonder of the world around you in your fingers, your toes, your legs, and your shoulders, even the top of your head. As you exhale, wiggle your fingers and toes. Shake your legs and move your shoulders up and down. Take another deep breath and, as you exhale, move your head from side to side. Feel the ground under your body touching every nerve ending and muscle. Hear the rustlings of the people around you. Notice the movements outside. Continue breathing. Stretch your arms out above your head. You are returning to the present, to the here and now. Continue stretching. Continue breathing. When you are ready, open your eyes, blink and focus, and sit up.

INVOCATION TO AIRMID

Oh Airmid,
Gentle, sweet,
Fierce and dark,
You dove into the depths
and found your power.

Through the strength of
the lion,
the snake,
the flower,
you gained your self,
healing,
sensing,
controlling,
T h e F a t e

Of countless others
—Dian Cecht—Miach—the Danann warriors—
And yourself.

Oh great giver, Airmid,
help me to honor my gifts
so I may appreciate
the life around me,
so I may appreciate
the life within.

MAGICAL ACTIVITIES

Physical Magic: Create Affirmation-infused Rose Water

Items Needed: Two large, fragrant red roses; a small cooking pot; water; and a spray bottle

Moon Phase: Waxing

Seasonal Cycle: Spring or early summer (when roses are in bloom)

Rose water is probably the easiest herbal recipe to make, and still it allows you access to the earthy, tangible world of plants. Healing on an emotional and spiritual level, rose water helps with issues of self-esteem and self-love, allowing you to blossom into self-truth and action. (Much like Airmid, who conquers her self-imposed quiet nature and blooms into a skilled and knowledgeable healer.) Rose water works by opening up the heart chakra and will affect most people in the immediate vicinity of the spray. (This is especially useful at work if you have a lot of cranky, negative people nearby.)

Rose water has a light, musky aroma that does not linger very long and is not obvious or heavy. It makes an excellent room spray, serving to lighten the mood and energy of the room. Try spraying it around your house before company arrives and see how positive and cheerful everyone behaves. Since roses are especially dear to faeries, rose water can be used to attract the attention of the faery realm or to honor any faeries in your home. It can also be used to consecrate or bless objects or cleanse them of any negativity. In short, rose water can be used for just about anything. Its uses are limited only by your imagination.

To create your affirmation-infused rose water, purchase two large, fragrant red roses. You can truly use any color of rose, but I have had the best luck with red roses. Put one cup of water into a small pan and pluck off the rose petals, placing them into the water. State an intention while plucking off each rose petal, keeping an overall goal in mind. Each petal and affirmation should strengthen and bolster your goal. Try to keep your goal in the rose's traditional realm of influence, focusing on bringing positive attitudes and traits up from the deep wellspring of your soul. You can repeat the same affirmation over and over again or state as many as you can think up. The choice is up to you!

Once all of the petals are in the water, put the pan over low heat. Heat the water slowly, making sure it does not boil. Turn the heat down if you begin to see tiny bubbles along the edges of the pan. Check frequently, and when the petals are translucent and see-through, remove the water from the heat. (This should take no longer than ten or fifteen minutes at most.) Strain the rose petals out of the water. Allow to cool, and then pour the beautiful ruby-pink water into a spray bottle and store in the refrigerator. Your rose water is complete. Enjoy!

Crystal Magic: Charge a Crystal for a Specific Purpose

Items Needed: A crystal or gemstone of your choice, a smudge stick (optional), sea water (optional), and sea salt (optional)

Moon Phase: Waxing or full

Seasonal Cycle: Any

Many people use the energetic properties of crystals and gemstones to enliven their homes or heal their bodies and spirits. Yet not everyone realizes that the energy of crystals can be harnessed to change and alter lives through spellwork. The process is relatively easy and straightforward, but it does take some research in order to be able to identify crystals and gemstones and their metaphysical and physical properties.

First you need to decide what goal you would like to manifest with the help of a crystal. Take some time to really narrow down your focus while still allowing the universe to work in all its mysterious ways. For instance, if you wish to bulk up your bank account, you could state your objective as "Bringing monetary abundance" instead of "Winning the lottery."

Once your objective is fixed in your mind, research the crystals and gemstones that will naturally help you in this endeavor. Your local New Age store should be able to help you. Many of them state the uses of crystals and gemstones directly on their in-store displays. Others will be able to make suggestions or (if your goal is truly a private affair that you don't want to share) offer books that you can look through for free. After you have chosen the type of crystal that will help you, allow your hand to skim over the store's selection. All stones have a different "feeling" to them, even if they are the same type of crystal or gemstone. Choose the stone that "feels" the best to you. Your hand might tingle or feel a pulse from a particular stone. Buy that one, regardless of size or clarity.

When you get home, cleanse your crystal by running it under tap water, placing it in a dish of sea salt or sea water, or smudging it with sage. (Note: Not all crystals react well to water. Some disintegrate or leak toxins into the water. Do your research before submerging any crystal in water.) Once your crystal is cleansed, tell it your plans and your goal, making sure that it wants to lend its energy to your magical spell. I know this sounds silly and you probably will feel weird talking to a stone, but crystals and gemstones do have personalities. Animists believe that all organic things are alive and should be honored for their life spark. So whether you want to talk to your stone or simply connect to it through your heart, make sure that your crystal is amenable to your magical purpose.

If your stone doesn't jump out of your hand or send you any other kind of negative impression, it is probably happy to help you. Hold your stone or crystal between your hands. Take several deep breaths and ground and center. Once you feel completely relaxed and carefree, allow the energy of the earth and sky, which is mixed with your own innate energy, to flow from your hands and into the stone. Visualize the crystal as bathed in your light energy. Just as the energy crescendoes, whisper your magical goal to your crystal while visualizing it in your head. The crystal will absorb your wish and focus its energy to manifest your will. Sit awhile with your crystal or stone and then set it in a place where you will see it every day.

If you want the crystal to work on your goal over a long period of time, recharge your crystal in the same way every full or new moon. If you feel your wish has been created and you want to release the charge on the crystal or stone, simply cleanse the crystal again. This will remove your energy from the crystal or gemstone and bring the object back into a pure state.

Herbal Magic: Celebrate the Healer Within

Items Needed: Several handfuls of each of the following herbs: rose petals (fresh), rosemary (fresh or dried), thyme (dried), and vervain (fresh); a sheet of beeswax (found in candle sections of craft stores); a bowl of water; a bowl of olive oil; a charcoal disc and a burner or bowl of sand to place it on; a taper candle holder, preferably gold or brass; a lighter or book of matches; a towel; a circlet of flowers (handmade or bought); an indigo bag or sack no bigger than a pillowcase; two small plastic or glass jars; four small plastic or paper bags; and a pillow (optional)

Moon Phase: Waxing or full

Seasonal Cycle: Summer

Having journeyed to the realm of Airmid and looked deep inside yourself, you have touched your own inner healing ability. You have understood the traits and characteristics of a true healer and have realized that you possess many of them. Whether you heal through traditional methods, through alternative energetic methods, or through simply being yourself, the time has come to accept your healing instincts and give respect and honor to them. Comparing yourself to other healers only hinders your exploration into your true self, so stop judging your healing ability. Keeping your heart open and working from a place of love automatically makes you a healer. Remember that, always.

Choose to perform this spell in a very comfortable, relaxing place, either inside or outside. You should feel completely at ease and free from worry or anxiety. This magic can be performed at any time during the day or night, whenever you can be by yourself, without interruptions, for an hour or so. Place all of your sacred items in the center of your sacred space, except the herbs. These will represent the powers of the elements and should be placed on the periphery of your circle: thyme in the east, rosemary in the south, rose in the west, and vervain in the north. Sit in the center of your sacred space (on a pillow, if you wish) and breathe deeply. Ground and center as you usually do and focus on the greening life of the world around you. Think of all the myriad plants in the world, including those around your yard or in the park. Feel their song in your heart. Hear their wisdom in your mind. Know their truth.

When you have established a connection to the plant world, stand up, hold your indigo bag, and walk to the east. Pick up the thyme, smell it, and hold it out before you, saying:

Thyme, ancient herb of purification,
Hear me now as I call to you!
Sacred herb of the Greeks,
Bringer of restful sleep, prophecies, and energy,
Grant me your strength and love
As I celebrate my own inner healer.

Walk around your sacred space in a circular fashion, sprinkling thyme as you go. When you return to the east, hold the thyme out once again, and then tuck it into your indigo bag. (If any of your herbs are loose, be sure to place them in separate small paper or plastic bags first.) Walk to the south. Pick up the rosemary, smell it, and hold it out before you as you call:

Rosemary, ancient herb of cleansing,
Hear me now as I call to you!
Mystical herb of the elves,
Bringer of health, youthfulness, and vitality,
Grant me your light and love
As I celebrate my own inner healer.

Walk around your sacred space in a circular fashion, sprinkling rosemary as you go. When you return to the south, hold the rosemary out once again, and then tuck it into your indigo bag. Walk to the west. Pick up the rose petals, smell them, and hold them out before you as you say:

Rose, ancient herb of love,
Hear me now as I call to you!
Stolen herb of emotions,
Bringer of protection, peace, and romance,
Grant me your sweetness and love
As I celebrate my own inner healer.

Walk around your sacred space in a circular fashion, sprinkling rose petals as you go. When you return to the west, hold the rose petals out before you, and then tuck them into your indigo bag. Walk to the north. Pick up the vervain, smell it, and hold it out before you, calling:

Vervain, ancient herb of charm,
Hear me now as I call to you!
Honored herb of the Druids,
Bringer of healing, prosperity, and knowledge,
Grant me your truth and love
As I celebrate my own inner healer.

Walk around your sacred space in a circular fashion, sprinkling vervain as you go. When you return to the north, hold the vervain out before you, and then tuck it into your indigo bag. Return to the center of your sacred space.

Considering the purifying properties of the healer, place the charcoal disc on its burner or in the bowl with sand. Light it and watch the sparks jump across its surface. When the disc starts to show gray along the edges, take a handful of thyme and hold it between your two hands. Think of all the ways you have purified your life, moving out the old energies so that new energies can take root. State three instances of purification out loud as you drop the thyme onto the charcoal disc; allow the smoke to envelop your hands, your face, and your heart. Breathe in as much of the smoke as you can, knowing that you are purifying yourself within as well as without. (Feel free to add thyme to the charcoal disc throughout the rest of the ritual.)

As the smoke begins to thin, contemplate the cleansing characteristics of the healer. Take the sheet of beeswax and move it over the burning and smoldering charcoal disc. The heat will soften the beeswax, making it more malleable. Once it is soft to the touch (but not melting), place the beeswax in front of you and hold a handful of rosemary between your two hands. Think of how you clear away negativity in your life and in the lives of your family members and friends. State three instances of clearing negativity out loud as you place the rosemary along one edge of the beeswax. Continue thinking of these three examples as you add a length of string (provided in the beeswax-candle craft package) to the herbs. Starting with the edge that has the herbs, begin to roll the beeswax tightly, creating a rudimentary candle. Take the finished candle and warm it up over the charcoal disc once again. Pay special attention to the unfinished edge, heating the wax so that you can close the candle by melting the edge to the main section of the candle. Place the candle in the tapered candle holder and light it. The herbs will blaze faster and hotter than the wax, so do not leave it unattended. For this reason, you might also want to place a small plate under the candle holder.

After staring into the flame of the candle for a few minutes, ponder the loving attributes of the healer. Take the bowl of water and move it in front of you. Make sure that you can see the flame from the candle, the smoke from the incense, and your own face in the water's reflection. Hold a handful of soft, silky rose petals between your two hands. Gaze into the water and unfocus your eyes. Feel the texture of the flowers under your fingertips and remember all of the ways you bring love to the world. When your eyes begin to feel strained, state three examples of your loving nature out loud and drop the rose petals into the water. Wash your hands and face in the rose-petal water, knowing that you are experiencing the essence of pure love.

Once you've dried your hands and face on your towel, reflect on the charming traits of the healer—the ability for people to believe in you and trust your skills. Move the bowl of oil so that it rests directly in front of you. Place the fresh vervain between your two hands, with the fingertips pointed down. Instead of holding the herb near your heart, hold it in front of your stomach and lower abdomen, making sure your finger-tips just barely touch the oil. Focus on all of the times you have opened the minds and hearts of other people. Consider all of the times you convinced them of a good idea or helped them heal themselves with some thoughtful suggestions. When your hands start to feel uncomfortable, state three examples of your charming nature out loud. Open your hands so that they resemble the wings of a butterfly, and drop the vervain in the oil. Swirl the vervain in the oil clockwise three times, and then anoint yourself on the forehead or third eye with the oil.

Clasping the flower circlet in both hands, pass it over the smoke of the thyme and the fire of the rosemary beeswax candle. Anoint it with the rose water and the vervain oil. As you bless your flower wreath, say:

> *By the power of the smoking thyme,*
> *By the power of the fiery rosemary,*
> *By the power of the watery rose,*
> *By the power of the earthy vervain,*
> *I celebrate my inner healer.*

Place the flower wreath on your head with these words:

> *I am healer.*
> *I am healed.*
> *I am healer.*
> *I have healed.*
> *I am healer.*
> *I heal!*

Take a few moments to realize the immensity of those words. Then, facing north, hold up the vervain oil, saying:

> *Charming plant of the Druids and their beauteous daughters,*
> *Truthful and bountiful vervain,*
> *I thank you for your presence in my circle this day/evening,*
> *As I celebrate my true inner healer!*
> *Your lessons stay with me, in my soul, in my heart,*
> *and in this blessed oil!*

Pour the vervain oil into one of the small jars. Then pick up the rose water and, turning to the west, say:

> *Loving plant of endless, romantic, and lustful love,*
> *Sweet and caring rose,*
> *I thank you for your presence in my circle this day/evening,*
> *As I celebrate my loving inner healer!*
> *Your lessons stay with me, in my soul, in my heart,*
> *and in this blessed water!*

Pour the rose water into one of the small jars. Then pick up the rosemary beeswax candle and, turning to the south, say:

> *Cleansing plant of the shining elves in their secret homes,*
> *Light and sacred rosemary,*
> *I thank you for your presence in my circle this day/evening,*
> *As I celebrate my mystical inner healer!*
> *Your lessons stay with me, in my soul, in my heart,*
> *and in this blessed candle!*

Place the rosemary beeswax candle in the center of your circle. Allow it to continue burning until it goes out naturally. Pick up the dried thyme incense and, turning to the east, say:

> *Purifying plant of Greek temples and priestesses,*
> *Strong and noble thyme,*
> *I thank you for your presence in my circle this day/evening,*
> *As I celebrate my ancestral inner healer!*
> *Your lessons stay with me, in my soul, in my heart,*
> *and in this blessed incense!*

If you have not already done so, pour the thyme incense into a small plastic or paper bag. Speak your gratitude to the directions, the elementals, and the herbs. Speak from your heart and know that all respect is accepted and loved by the universe. You have now acknowledged and celebrated your inner healer. Your life will never be exactly the same again.

MEETING CESSAIR,
FOUNDING GODDESS OF IRELAND
Taking Risks

CESSAIR: DAUGHTER OF THE LAND

Cessair (pronounced KAH-seer) is a goddess of manifestation and action. Presented with an untenable circumstance (the destruction of her homeland), she formulates a plan and strides out into the unknown world to carve a new destiny, a new future, a new land and people. Ever practical, yet still deeply respectful of the sacred in life, Cessair is not afraid of change. She embraces risk taking, knowing that only by expanding our horizons can we grow and evolve into our powerful true selves. Trying something new and unexpected creates chaos in our lives, which manifests in exciting, revolutionary transformation. It is this movement, the process of leaving behind the old for the new, that embodies life. Cessair understands this truth and brings her wisdom to us as we sail upon the tumultuous seas of existence on this planet.

Cessair is mainly mentioned in Irish mythology in the ancient text *Lebor Gabala Erenn*, the Book of Invasions or Conquests, which is a collection of poems and narratives compiled by an anonymous scholar in the eleventh century. (The *Lebor Gabala Erenn* is but one section in the Book of Leinster, which was collected at a later date, around 1160 AD, and is now housed in Trinity College in Dublin, Ireland.) The Book of Invasions is a mythological account of the founding of Ireland. It outlines the various races that came to live in Ireland, chronicling their arrival, subsequent issues and predicaments, and (in most cases) their departure through death or abandonment. It is not meant to be a factual history of the founding of Ireland. Rather, the *Lebor Gabala Erenn* serves as a tenuous link to the minds and hearts of the people of ancient Ireland. This story, the Book of Invasions, holds truths that extend far beyond our narrow understanding of linear history. As such, it is meant to be studied and read in the context of the land, for the actual earth of Ireland is as much a character in this mythological cycle as any Danann prince or foreign warrior king.

Cessair is the main character in the first of the seven invasion myths recorded in the *Lebor Gabala Erenn*. She is of the first peoples to set foot on the land of Ireland. Her story begins in the east, several years before the biblical flood that changed the world. Cessair is the daughter of Bith and the granddaughter of Noe or Noah, who built the ark according to Yahweh's commands in order to preserve life after the floodwaters receded. Unfortunately for Cessair and Bith, they were not allowed aboard Noah's ark. In the text, as collected in the Book of Leinster, Noah gives no reason for not allowing his son and granddaughter onto the ark. Yet he does give them an idea of how to live through the Flood. "Rise, said he [and go] to the western edge of the world; perchance the Flood may not reach it."[1] The *Lebor Gabala Erenn* states that Cessair took her grandfather's advice and led three ships to Ireland, but only one survived. The other two wrecked on the rocky shores of Erin.[2]

In the account of Ireland's founding told by Geoffrey Keating in his book *The History of Ireland*, which was completed around 1634 AD, Noah still gives no reasoning for not allowing his family aboard the ark, and now he offers no viable alternative either. In short, he leaves Bith and Cessair to the fate of the waves. Bith, Fintan (a mystical poet, known as the "White Ancient," who lives for thousands of years after the flood), and Cessair take counsel together and Cessair tells them that if they listen to her, she will save them. The men agree, and Cessair tells of her plan to turn away from the god of Noah by creating an idol and worshipping another deity. Bith and Fintan perform this task, and the idol tells them to build a ship and "put to sea,"[3] but unfortunately the god[4] does not know the exact timing of the flood, so the Cessairians spend the next seven years and three months living on the ship before eventually reaching Ireland.

Both accounts agree that fifty women and three men survived the voyage from the east and landed on Ireland's shores at Dun na mbarc (or Dun na mRarc), which is now known as Donemark, on Bantry Bay in County Cork. Keating goes on further to elaborate their settling at Bun Suaimhne, at the junction of the Suir, Nore, and Barrow rivers.[5] These three rivers exist in Ireland today, in the southeast section of the country, covering massive distances and draining sections of five counties. They enter the sea near Waterford City and Hook Head. Together, they are known as the Three Sisters.

As the *Lebor Gabala Erenn* and *The History of Ireland* relate the arrival of Cessair and her people from the east, it is important to note the many feminine attributes in the story. First, the people are led by a woman—a woman who is shut out of the religion of the patriarchal god of the Israelites and destined to die. Unlike the quiet and reserved women in the east who worshipped Yahweh, Cessair does not merely accept her fate and agree to drown in an ocean of regretful tears. Instead, she wrests the situation from the

---

1. Best, Bergin, and O'Brien, "Lebor Gabala Erenn," verse 27.

2. Ibid., verse 28.

3. Keating, *History of Ireland*, 143.

4. Keating uses the pronoun he.

5. Keating, *History of Ireland*, 145.

hands of two very capable men and, casting about for inspiration, suggests a plausible, if unorthodox, plan: leaving the religion of Yahweh for that of another deity. To the men of Yahweh, creating and eventually turning to an idol for help was in direct violation of their god's edicts, as written in the biblical Commandments three, four, and five. The Bible is full of admonishments against idol worship, which proves that it still existed. (Otherwise, the writers of the Bible would have admonished something else!) Numerous ancient idols have been found throughout the Middle East, and one of the most prominent kinds has been ascribed to the goddess Asherah, named Ashtaroth in the Bible.

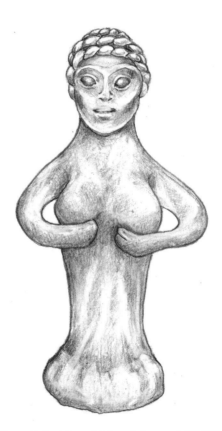

Figure 5: A statue of Asherah from c. 1400 BCE,
which is currently housed in the Israel Museum in Tel Aviv.

Asherah was the "Great Mother Goddess" of the Canaanites. Small house shrines were often dedicated to her, and communities would celebrate her fertility by erecting large, phallic poles or trees. The sacred groves and hill shrines were called "aserah" after her, and it is these locations that were condemned by many of the biblical prophets.[6] The Bible proclaims: "Then you will know that I am the Lord, when their slain are among their idols around their altars, on every high hill, on all the tops of the mountains, under every green tree and under every leafy oak—the places where they offered soothing aroma to all their idols."[7] Indeed, not only her sacred sites but also her name was well-known to the worshippers of Yahweh. In Judges 10:6, "the sons of Israel again did evil in the sight of the Lord, served the Baals and Ashtaroth" and in the Book of 1 Samuel, the goddess Ashtaroth and the god Baal are mentioned at least three more times.[8]

Like all mothers, the Great Mother Goddess Asherah had diverse interests and skills, and her people called on her for a variety of needs. As a mother of seventy children, she was honored for her fertility. Yet as a deity of a seafaring people, she was also the goddess turned to for good travel and calm seas. One of her many titles is Lady Asherah of the Sea, and her full title, as found in the ancient Syrian city of Ugarit, is Rabat Athiratu Yami, meaning "Great Lady She Who Treads on the Sea." In Phoenicia and Carthage, under the name of Tanith, she is often shown with dolphins or fish.[9] As a mother goddess known to the Israelites, connected to idols and shrines, and well-known for her association with the sea, it is not inconceivable to suggest that the idol Cessair crafted was a representation of the goddess Asherah.

No matter what idol was crafted, a strong feminine energy surges through the story of Cessair and her people. Not only are they led by a woman, but their company consists mainly of women and they land at a place known as the Three Sisters, where three rivers intersect. The number three is often seen as an especially sacred number to the Irish Celts, who divided their world into "sea, land, and sky" and whose deities, such as Brigid and Morrighan, presented a triple nature. In fact, the rivers known as the Three Sisters could be aspects of the goddesses of the very land of Ireland: Eriu, Banba, and Fotla. The modern name Ireland is itself named after the goddess Eriu, and Keating in

---

6. Jordan, *Encyclopedia of Gods*, 27.

7. Ezekiel 6:13 (*New American Standard Bible*).

8. Judges 10:6, Book of 1 Samuel 7:4, Book of 1 Samuel 12:10, Book of 1 Samuel 31:10 (*New American Standard Bible*).

9. Biti-Anat, "Major Deities."

The History of Ireland recalls a tale wherein Banba is the first female to lead a party to Ireland's shores. It is her name, in many of the ancient tales, that is synonymous with the land itself.

After Cessair's people have settled themselves at Bun Suaimhne, the difficult task of creating a community begins. Fintan, Bith, and a resourceful pilot named Ladra are the only men in Cessair's company, and "for peace and for reason,"[10] the women break up into three household groups, containing one man and either seventeen or sixteen women. The extra woman (perhaps Cessair herself, as she is a member of his household) was given to Fintan, presumably because he was neither "war-like,"[11] like Bith, nor "bold,"[12] like Ladra. Unfortunately for the Cessairians, they arrive on Ireland's shores only forty days before the Flood sweeps from the east and engulfs the west, including Ireland. All of the members of Cessair's party die, except for the resourceful and magical Fintan, who lives for thousands more years in various shapes and forms. Ladra is the first man to be buried in Ireland, and Ard Ladrand is named after him. Sliab Betha is named for Cessair's father, Bith, who died in the mountains, trying to climb higher than the encroaching sea. Cessair, on the other hand, fled to a nook, called Cul Cessrach, where she and her fifty maidens died. Her burial site is often attributed to one of the cairns on Knockmaa Hill in Connacht.

Despite the unfortunate conclusion of Cessair's attempt to escape the Flood, her story resonates with power and passion. In order to save her life and the lives of her loved ones, Cessair risks everything. She ignores the edicts of her grandfather's god and creates an idol. She wrests the position of leader from her father and an accomplished magician in a society in which men hold authority over women. She leads her people across the globe on what probably felt like an endless search for safe land, leaving her own country and her own customs behind. In the face of adversity, Cessair reshapes her sense of self. She becomes greater than she ever thought possible. Cessair teaches us that only by giving up that which we think is necessary can we expand our horizons and grow toward the wisdom and mystery of the Goddess. In the end, Cessair, surrounded by her fifty maidens, is welcomed into the loving embrace of the Goddess as a complete

---

10. Best, Bergin, and O'Brien, " Lebor Gabala Erenn" verse 29.

11. Ibid., verse 36.

12. Ibid., verse 29.

woman, fully aware of her innate abilities, skills, and characteristics. She has found her true self.

TAKING RISKS: MOVING FORWARD

It is difficult to take a risk, to step outside of the comfortable and try something new. All that you have known is left behind, and you are forced, by sheer uncertainty, to face yourself. You, after all, are the only thing left that resonates with even a modicum of familiarity. Therefore, risk taking involves not only striking out and exploring new ventures but also delving within and understanding the true self.

The dual nature of risk taking creates a maelstrom of emotions: fear, uncertainty, courage, strength, introspection, and extroversion. This is why taking a risk is so difficult. If it simply involved trying something new, it would be hard but not particularly complex. You would simply take a deep breath and plow forward, accepting the situation as it presented itself. However, that other aspect of risk taking, the inner lesson of self, is what creates the turmoil. In new and uncomfortable situations, we are forced to view the truth of ourselves. We see how we handle crisis, conflict, love, and happiness. We can locate the core essence of ourselves, understanding the reasoning behind our actions. Do we react from our true selves or from past lessons and life experiences? Are we shining with the brilliance of our pure goddesshood, or are we masked with pain left over from what we had hoped were forgotten experiences?

Moving out of the ordinary gives us the space to really look at the reality of ourselves and our lives and, if necessary, make appropriate changes. It opens up our minds and hearts, forcing us to see with fresh eyes our old lives and habits. With this new knowledge, we can then move forward, past the new experience, taking our newfound wisdom back into our familiar surroundings and making them not so secure and comfortable. It is here, at the crossroads of the old and the new, that we find our inner power, the strength to fight old demons, the determination to create the best life possible, and the resolve to become all that we are capable of being. By striking out into the unknown, we gain a clear understanding of exactly where we are and what could be changed to create a better life for ourselves, our family, and our friends. So taking risks, while scary and often painful, precipitates a life change of monumental proportions. Don't just stay in your safe environment! Move out and look within in order to craft the life you were meant to live. Don't be afraid! Your destiny is waiting right around the corner.

THE PATHWORKING

Cessair's meditation, like the goddess herself, is designed to open up your mind and heart to accepting changes. It is not an especially difficult meditation. It does not ask you to confront past issues or face uncomfortable situations. Instead, it requires you to truly look into yourself and ascertain whether you are ready for this commitment. Once you have drunk from the waters of the Three Sisters' crossroads, there is no going back. You will be forging ahead on a new adventure in life, taking a risk by choosing change rather than comfort.

The decision to transform your life should not be made quickly. It is best to look at your whole situation before making the decision. If you are starting a new job, getting over a past relationship, or moving to a new home, you might find that this is not the best time to revolutionize your way of thinking. However, you might resolve that, due to these outward circumstances, now is the perfect time to alter your inner vision and sense of self. Whatever your choice, follow your instinct. When it is time for Cessair to enter your life, you will know it. Don't force the issue.

Whether you decide to change your life view or stay rooted in the familiar, you will benefit from getting to know the goddess Cessair. She is a wonderfully giving goddess with a quirky sense of humor and a sweet, calming demeanor. Feel free to travel to her realm during the following meditation, even if you don't wish to partake of the waters from the Three Sisters. The meditation prompts you to skip a few paragraphs if you don't want to drink the waters but still wish to meet Cessair. I encourage you to visit with this goddess whether you are ready for a life change or not. Her essence is powerful and meaningful. Also, do not judge yourself if you choose not to drink the waters. Cessair does not judge you but welcomes you as you are. Trust your own inner voice and accept yourself in this time and space. Love yourself as the Goddess loves you.

GUIDED MEDITATION: CROSSROADS AT THE THREE SISTERS

Take a deep breath, in through your nose and out through your mouth. Take another deep breath, filling your stomach, your diaphragm, and finally your lungs. Hold this breath for five seconds … 1-2-3-4-5 … and exhale, allowing the breath to exit your lungs first, then your diaphragm, and finally your stomach. Take one more deep breath, and as you breathe in, feel the energy of the rushing river water guiding and supporting your fingers, your toes, your legs, and your shoulders, even the top of your head. Hold the breath for seven seconds… 1-2-3-4-5-6-7. As you exhale, feel all tension leave your fingers, your toes, your legs, and your shoulders, even the top of your head. Continue breathing deeply, in through your nose and out through your mouth. Feel the gentle mist touching and dripping on the exposed parts of your body: your head, your face, and your hands. The air is heavy with the moisture of rain. Allow the tiny water droplets to massage your weary body, removing any tension, any stress, any worry. You sigh, and the massage moves inward to your soul and your spirit. You breathe deeply and have never felt so relaxed, so secure, so calm.

You are walking across a large grassy meadow in the early hours of dawn. A light mist settles over the land, coating everything in tiny raindrops. The glooming clouds make the light seem hazy, and the outlines of trees and shrubs waver in the distance. An outcropping of round huts blossoms on the horizon. They look to have sprung directly from the earth itself, brown and weathered with moss creeping up their sides. Behind you, you hear the incessant sigh of the ocean as it caresses the rocky seashore. The stream at your feet bubbles quietly with repressed power, rushing for the shoreline and sliding easily into the wide sea. All else is quiet. All else is still. There is no crackling fire, no chattering bird, no lonely dog howl. All is silence, save the softly falling mist and the burbling brook and the hushed sigh of the ocean waves.

In the gray light, you turn away from the scattering of huts to an open plain between two heavily forested woodlands. You contemplate your footsteps as you deliberately avoid clumps of clover, patches of wildflowers, and thickets of hawthorn. You weave across the meadow, watching the mist and loosely following the stream. You feel the silence, hearing only your own measured breathing. Suddenly, without warning, the stream branches off into three streams, and you have arrived at the crossroads of the Three Sisters.

Early-morning fog rises from the streams, cloaking them in wispy tendrils of white and gray. The mist swirls around the meeting point of the three rivers, hiding their origins, but you can hear their swiftly moving currents and feel their active energy. There is power in this place. Take a few moments to breathe it in. (pause) When you open your eyes again, you see a woman striding out of the fog toward you. It is Cessair.

She wears indigo blue leggings that hug her calves and ankles. Her feet sport sturdy sandals that lace up her legs and from a distance look like knee-length boots. A pink, beige, and ivory tunic flows around her upper body, sliding with her movements, loose and free. Her face is round, welcoming, if a bit pale, and her hair is a mass of curls around her face, tamed, though not very efficiently, by a leather thong at the base of her neck. With the slight breeze and the misting rain, she is movement and stillness at the same time. She holds her hand up to you in a sign of universal greeting. You walk closer to her, toward the apex of the rivers' crossroads.

As you approach the goddess, Cessair nods to you. You bow down before her, kneeling in the damp morning dew and touching your forehead to the rain-slick meadow grass. She smirks with just a touch of embarrassment and, placing a hand on your shoulder, guides you to a standing position. "You know who I am," she says, with a slightly raised eyebrow, "but you have me at a disadvantage, for I know not your name." You quickly amend the oversight and introduce yourself. Feel free to tell Cessair a little about yourself and your family and friends. (pause) When you are done, Cessair smiles, and with a small movement, she invites you to walk beside her, closer to the junction of the Three Sisters.

"The water is the lifeblood of this land," Cessair says quietly. "The lifeblood of any land, for without water we cannot survive." She looks at you from under her eyelashes, and her mouth forms a grim line. "Yet water will be the death of me and my people." A tiny spark of humor lights in her eyes, as if she understands and appreciates the irony of her situation. Cessair kneels down and cups the water of the joined rivers in one hand. She brings it to her lips and drinks fully. It drips down her chin and through her closed fingers. She wipes it with the back of her flowing sleeve. Cessair continues, "The water opened up new avenues for me, new ways of thinking and acting. I became more of myself due to the emergence of water in my life. I honored a goddess, led a people, founded a land, and changed myself forever. May the same happen for you."

She turns and pulls a rough leather bag from her shoulder. It is worn and patched with lifetimes of care and worry, adventures and explorations into the unknown. From its depths, Cessair pulls a simple wooden cup. She hands it to you. Take some time to look at the cup. What color is it? Are there carvings or markings on it? What kind of wood does it feel like? Discover the essence of the cup, its true meaning and worth. (pause)

When you are ready, kneel down next to Cessair at the crossroads of the Three Sisters. Here, at this meeting point, where the waters of three rivers join into one, you touch the truth of risk taking. You move beyond your current self to someone who is whole, someone truly complete and comfortable with him or herself. By drinking the water, you welcome the chaos and uncertainty of moving outside your comfortable existence. You challenge your life, seeking to make it better, a pure representation of your Goddess-given powers within. Taking a deep breath, you plunge the cup into the rushing current and bring out a full cup of sweet water. You glance at Cessair, who is calmly sitting with her eyes downcast and her hands folded in her lap. Her presence is palpable—supportive but not intrusive. This is your moment, and the goddess will not interfere, whatever your decision. Do you drink the water or throw it back into the moving stream? (pause: If you drink the water, continue on with the meditation. If you throw it into the stream, skip to the last paragraph.)

The water feels cool and crisp on your lips and tongue. It is refreshing and energizing as well as calming and contemplative. You drink the water to the very last drop and, bringing the cup down, look directly into the eyes of Cessair. They sparkle merrily, and a suppressed grin curves the corners of her lips. She nods her head and receives the cup from you. "You have chosen to take the first step, my child," the goddess says as she easily places the cup back into her bag. "The water will bring you strength, but it may also carry sadness and despair. Risk taking embodies the very nature of life. It is unpredictable but … oh … so fulfilling." The goddess stands, as do you, and she gifts you with a warm hug. "Know that I am with you through this journey," Cessair continues, "and that you can come back to this crossroads at any time and I will be waiting for you."

Cessair backs up into the swirling mist. With a wave, she is gone, and you are left at the crossroads by yourself. As you begin to walk back across the meadow, following the twisting river, you notice sounds that were absent before. Chirping crickets. Whispering breezes. Singing birds. Jumping fish. And then the sun breaks out from behind the massive gray clouds, and you know that life's adventure awaits you and that you have taken the first step.

Now take a deep breath, in through your nose and out through your mouth. Take another deep breath, filling your stomach, your diaphragm, and finally your lungs. Hold this breath for five seconds … 1-2-3-4-5 … and exhale, allowing the breath to exit your lungs first, then your diaphragm, and finally your stomach. Breathe deeply once more, and as you breathe in, feel the energy and the wonder of the world around you in your fingers, your toes, your legs, and your shoulders, even the top of your head. As you exhale, wiggle your fingers and toes. Shake your legs and move your shoulders up and down. Take another deep breath and, as you exhale, move your head from side to side. Feel the ground under your body touching every nerve ending and muscle. Hear the rustlings of the people around you. Notice the movements outside. Continue breathing. Stretch your arms out above your head. You are returning to the present, to the here and now. Continue stretching. Continue breathing. When you are ready, open your eyes, blink and focus, and sit up.

INVOCATION TO CESSAIR

Whispering trees and riverbed breezes
Oh knowing one
Forgotten idols and voyages unknown
Oh powerful one
Adventure awaits
Across the ocean deep
Into the flowering blue
On a green land.

Secret invocations and wild waves
Oh trusting one
Strident voice and unexpected command
Oh caring one
Land Ho
Upon the rocky shore
Against unknown odds
At the rivers' crossroads.

Feminine strength and heartwise wisdom
Oh loving one
Waist-deep water and eternal bliss
Oh everlasting one
Water flows
Against the tide
Over the land
Welcoming you home.

The mother's embrace is your embrace.

Oh Cessair

Your sacrifice is our courage.

Hail Cessair!

We remember

In a land apart

With our heart's truth

Through time immemorial.

MAGICAL ACTIVITIES

Natural Magic: Feeling the Land

Items Needed: White T-shirt, beige pants, and foggy, rainy, or overcast day

Moon Phase: Any

Seasonal Period: Any, but especially spring and fall

It is necessary to find a day (preferably early morning or late afternoon) when fog has formed. If you live in an area where you rarely see fog, wait until a day when a light rain is falling. At the very least, the sky should be overcast and a chilly breeze should be blowing. Once you have found the perfect day, go outside in a simple white T-shirt and beige pants. If you have performed the pathworking to Cessair, wear clothing that resembles what the goddess wore when she presented herself to you. You will probably feel a little cold. This spell is meant to wake up your whole body, inside and out, so you may experience a little discomfort. But don't worry, as the spell lasts a relatively short time.

Step outside and deliberately walk to a quiet and secluded spot where you will be surrounded by nature. If you can access a place near a burbling brook, all the better. However, at least find a place that has a tree or some grass. After you have walked to your place, take three deep breaths. Listen to the world around you. Acknowledge the slamming car doors and giggling children. Hear the singing birds and the rustling animals or tree branches. Feel the powerful current of the streambed. Whatever setting you find yourself in, send out your inner senses and experience the land around you.

Now open up to the weather—to the mysterious fog, the dark sky, and the pattering raindrops. Feel these energies brushing against your skin and flowing through your hair. Breathe them in through your nose, and with each breath, open your skin to the essence of the fog, wind, rain, and clouds. Allow them to enter your body and become one with you. Breathe deeply, opening yourself more and more until you feel as if you will burst with all of the extra energy inside you. When you feel ready, bend down and place your hands on the ground. Exhale all of the excess energy into the ground, requesting its aid for the healing of Mother Earth. Although the natural energy is no longer inside you, your body remains awake and alert. You have released parts of yourself that previously had been closed and hidden. You are experiencing your full body, your full mind and heart, for the first time. Relish this feeling.

Having grounded the weather energy into the earth, take a few moments to honor the fog, clouds, wind, and rain in your own words, and then return to your house or car to warm up and dry off. You can repeat this spell as many times as you would like. It is especially useful during times of stress or at any time when you are feeling tight and constricted emotionally, mentally, or physically.

Incense Magic: Union

> Items Needed: Frankincense resin, myrrh resin, dried forget-me-nots, dried red clo-
> ver, a mortar and pestle, a plastic container with an airtight lid, charcoal incense
> discs, a charcoal disc incense holder or a fireproof bowl with sand, and a lighter
> Moon Phase: Full
> Seasonal Period: Spring

As Cessair traveled from the east to become the founding goddess of Ireland (in the west), this spell is designed to unify opposites. It can be used to bring together a deteriorating relationship or situation through understanding and kinship. It allows all involved to see things from a different point of view, expanding their perspective on life.

Take the frankincense and myrrh and hold them in your hands. These resins represent the east in Cessair's story and were probably the resins used to honor the idol that she crafted in order to find a solution to the Great Flood. Both frankincense and myrrh are extremely spiritual resins that help to protect. Frankincense also cleanses and can be used in divination and meditation, while myrrh is used for healing, especially in overcoming physical or emotional loss. Hold these resins and think about the situation you would like to heal, and then place them in the mortar. Grind the resins with the pestle while still thinking of the situation. When they are ground to your liking, empty the contents of the mortar into the plastic container.

Hold the forget-me-nots and red clover in your hands and think about the situation and how you would like it to be resolved. These herbs symbolize Ireland and the west in Cessair's story and were probably some of the local vegetation that she noticed when first alighting on Ireland's shores. Red clover is good for protection and cleansing, but it also revitalizes the spirit and brings mental clarity, money, and luck. Forget-me-nots, on the other hand, represent hope, true love, and remembrance. Once you feel the herbs are infused with the energy of the situation and your solution, place them in the mortar and grind them up. When they are at a consistency of your choosing, empty them into the plastic container. Now stir the resins and the herbs so that they mingle together.

When you are ready, place the charcoal disc on your incense burner or in a fireproof bowl filled with sand and light the disc. The disc will flare briefly before turning gray. As the gray seeps across the disc, sprinkle your resin and herb mixture onto the disc. Smoke will form, bringing your wishes up to Cessair. You can add incense until the disc collapses, or until the incense runs out, or until you feel as though your wish has been received by the goddess. Follow your intuition. After the spell, carefully dispose of the charcoal by running it under cold water to make sure it is completely out, and placing it outside or in a potted plant. Any leftover incense can be saved in your plastic container for a later time, in case you want to repeat the spell or connect to the goddess Cessair.

Symbolic Magic: Across the Waters

Items Needed: A bathtub, swimming pool, or large body of water; a large clam or scallop shell; earth-safe, waterproof markers or paints; your union incense (this time dedicated to Cessair only); a loaf of homemade wheat or spelt bread; and anointing oil

Moon Phase: New

Seasonal Period: Any

This spell has two parts, both of which are equally powerful and magical. The first section of the spell involves collecting all of the items. You will need to scour beaches, shops, or Internet sites for a large shell that resembles a boat. A bivalve mollusk works best, as you can separate the two halves and use one half for the spell and the other as an incense holder, jewelry container, or powerful reminder of your spell. After locating the shell, you will need to bake your bread. This is actually easier than it appears. Simply find a recipe that appeals to you and dive into the process. Remember, it doesn't have to be perfect! You will also need to create some more union incense, this time focusing on

Cessair and her trip from east to west rather than any disruptive situation in your life. If you have performed the union spell, do not use that particular batch of incense as you will have infused it with a particular situation and solution. Create new incense.

Gather all of your items near your body of water. Make sure it is large enough to represent the ocean and a voyage from old attitudes to new ones. In a pinch, however, you can use your largest kitchen bowl or garden pail. Take a deep breath and ground and center. Relax all of your muscles and open your heart, mind, and soul. Be accepting of the divine into your life. When you are ready, break the loaf of bread into three equal parts. Holding one of the sections of bread up, turn to the east and say:

> *By the Sky, high above,*
> *I honor thee.*

Place the bread in the east and, holding your second hunk of bread, turn to the west and say:

> *By the Sea, all around,*
> *I honor thee.*

Place the bread in the west. Pick up the last section of bread and, turning to the north, say:

> *By the Land, underneath,*
> *I honor thee.*

Place the bread in the north. Sit down and hold your shell in your hands. This shell represents your vessel, your ship, as you voyage from the complacency of your known life into the uncertainty of the future. It is this bark that will hold and comfort you as you take a risk and choose to look without and within to create wholeness in yourself. Using the markers or paints, decorate the shell with symbols and colors that will aid you and strengthen you on your journey. Take as much time as you need.

When you are finished, take a look at your vessel. While allowing the markers and paints to dry, meditate on what you are leaving behind and where you hope to venture forward. Allow the goddess Cessair to speak to you, touching you through the veils of mist and fog. Feel her comforting, calming presence. Once your shell is dry, anoint it with your oil. Start at the back of the ship, and using sweeping motions, rub the oil from back to front. This symbolizes your desire and dedication to move forward, leaving behind outmoded ideas and needs.

Put a pinch or two of incense in the shell and place it in the water, in the east if possible. Name the east with words that represent where you currently are in your life. These can be positive or negative experiences, adjectives, or nouns. Some of these you may wish to leave behind in the east. Others you may want to carry with you in your vessel. Even though you will be venturing into unknown areas, like Cessair, you will still be your own self. Parts of your current life will always remain with you.

After you have named the east, push the boat toward the west. Watch as it moves through the water. Pay attention to the movements of your ship. Is the path straight and true? Does your ship bob and weave or turn in spirals? Perhaps your vessel gets caught on something that jumps in its path. Whatever happens, make note of it and help your ship find its way across the water, to the west. When your ship arrives at the west, open your heart and express what you hope to gain from your risk taking. Do you wish to leave an unpleasant situation behind? Do you want to come into your own power? Talk confidently in front of groups? Realize your true self? Whatever you hope to achieve, state it now while holding your ship in the west.

After you have said your dreams out loud, pull the boat out of the water. Kiss it while facing the north, west, and east and thanking the land, sea, and sky, respectively. Take your bread and your boat (with the incense still cradled inside) and, in a secluded spot somewhere on your land or near your house, bury it with ceremony. If you wish to plant a flower or plant at the site, do so in order to honor this new phase in your life. Huzzah! Go home and try a food you've never had before in order to celebrate your new risk-taking self.

MEETING ERIU,
QUEEN OF IRISH SOVEREIGNTY
Connecting to the Land Around You

ERIU: IRELAND, HERSELF

It seems odd to equate a goddess with a piece of physical land on this green, wondrous earth. The Greek goddess Gaia, as the deity of our blue and green planet, is commonly invoked by Pagans, environmentalists, and concerned folks when the health of the earth is discussed. Yet her name is starting to become a euphemism for the earth and environmental causes, and her connection to deity overlooked and cloaked in shadow. Ireland, on the other hand, remains deeply entrenched in its reverence of the land, of the actual green plains and rolling hills of the fertile, mystical island of the Gaels and the Tuatha de Danann. There is power in the rocks and hills, in the very soil itself, and the Irish have never forgotten this truth. Eriu (pronounced AIR-oo) is the land of Ireland; her trees, her winds, her rivers and wells are all part of the goddess. Lie on her grass and feel her comfort. Step on her dirt and feel her support. She is alive and breathing every day, smiling on the children that make their way to her shores.

Eriu is yet another example of an Irish triple goddess. With her sisters, Banba and Fotla, she creates a triplicate reminiscent of Brigid and Morrighan. In fact, Eriu, Banba, and Fotla share the same mother as Morrighan, being the first goddess triplets born to Ernmas, the she-farmer and bountiful mother. In the *Lebor Gabala Erenn*, the eleventh century Book of Invasions or Conquests, Ernmas births two sets of girl children as well as five boys, displaying her prowess as a goddess of fertility and plenty. Undoubtedly, her fertile nature extends through her female children, especially her first three daughters, since they are the very land from which abundance spills to feed the people of Ireland.[1] The fertility of Eriu, Banba, and Fotla extends past sustenance to the granting of kingship upon their husbands and worthy warriors, giving them a larger role in the shaping of the land of Ireland and its future. Perhaps this universal point of view is derived from their father (and half brother), Fiachna. Ernmas, in true goddess fashion, does not discriminate in her choice of lovers and, according to the *Lebor Gabala Erenn*, beds her son Fiachna in order to conceive the three sovereign goddesses.

It is not uncommon to find older family members having sexual relations with younger family members in the *Lebor Gabala Erenn*. The goddess Danu births her sons Brian, Iucharba, and Iuchar after relations with her father, Delbaeth, and Morrighan brings Brigid into the world with help from her nephew, the Dagda. The fertility deities of the Tuatha de Danann do not seem to harbor the strict judgments and limitations

---

1. Macalister, *Lebor Gabala Erenn*, verses 62 and 64.

of our human ancestors and, indeed, even ourselves. The kin connection is important for the bloodlines and the familial energy and power that run therein. As deities, love is universal and they are not hampered by genetics or societal mores. This is the family that spawns the goddess Eriu—wild abandonment, fierce freedom, unlimited growth and prosperity. Anything is possible with these gods and goddesses.

Eriu exhibits her own innate ability to grant sovereignty when she is young in spirit and unknown to the touch of man. In *The Second Battle of Mag Tuired*, an Irish saga first written down in the ninth century, Eriu sits looking at a perfectly smooth sea when a shimmering silver boat appears. It sails directly for her and lands nearby. A beautiful man disembarks, with clothes of golden thread, jewel-studded swords, silver spears, and golden torcs. He requests an hour of lovemaking with Eriu, who initially rejects his suggestion, saying, "I certainly have not made a tryst with you."[2] (Perhaps she thought he mistook her for another woman.) But the man is very persuasive, and before long, Eriu and the mysterious stranger have "stretched themselves out together."[3]

After the hour of lovemaking, when the man stands up to leave, Eriu begins to cry. When the man asks the reason for the tears, Eriu gives two reasons. First, she is sad that he is leaving, and second, that she has given her virginity away. The man quiets her fears by gifting her with a golden ring that he entreats her never to give away unless to a person whose finger it fits. Then he tells Eriu that he is Elatha mac Delbaith, king of the Formorians, the race of beings that lived in Ireland before the Tuatha de Danann arrived on her shores. (It is the Formorians that the Tuatha de Danann fight in the Second Battle of Mag Tuired in order to secure Ireland for themselves alone. The Formorians and the Danann mingled quite a bit in mythology, intermarrying and birthing children.) "You will bear a son as a result of our meeting," Elatha states to Eriu as he is leaving, "and let no name be given to him but Eochu Bres (that is, Eochu the Beautiful)"[4]

As Elatha foretold, Eriu gives birth to a son who is indeed beautiful to look upon. Named Eochu Bres (or Bres, for short), the boy's divine nature reveals itself through his unnatural growth spurts. After one week, he is as big as a fourteen-day-old, and he doubles in growth until, in seven years, he is the age of fourteen. When King Nuada's hand is cut off in the First Battle of Mag Tuired, Bres is appointed the new leader of the

---

2. Gray, "Second Battle of Mag Tuired," verse 17.

3. Ibid., verse 18.

4. Ibid., verse 21.

Tuatha de Danann. He marries Brigid, and they have a son together named Ruadan. Unfortunately, Bres expresses parsimonious and stingy tendencies as king, eschewing the traditional rules of hospitality—of bread and board. This causes the Danann princes to oust him for their old leader, Nuada.

Despite the fact that Bres was king for only a short while, it is important to note that his mother is Eriu, the king-maker and sovereign goddess of Ireland. In her first sexual encounter, Eriu, the goddess from the fertile family, conceives a child that becomes a king. Her son is no mere love child; he is the king of Tara. As the land itself, Eriu grants sovereignty to her son, having remained stable and unchanging so that the current of the sea is able to carry Elatha's silver boat to her, to the land, which is the goddess herself.

As the years progress, Eriu marries another Irish king, Cethor. Son of Cermait, grandson of the Dagda, Cethor has two brothers named Sethor and Tethor who also serve as the kings of Ireland, marrying Banba and Fotla, respectively. These sons of Cermait also are known as "son of" the individual gods that they worship: "Mac Cuill—Sethor, the hazel his god; Mac Cecht—Tethor, the ploughshare his god; Mac Greine—Cethor, the sun his god."[5] As the land of Ireland, it is interesting to note Eriu's connection with the sun through Mac Greine. The land and the sun work together to sustain crops and vegetation for the people of the earth. Both are needed to create life. Since the sun and the earth are sometimes married in mythology, they are symbiotic entities that need each other in order to create bounty and abundance. Eriu's marriage to Mac Greine and her encounter with Elatha show a goddess who is flexible and has an ability to work with others. As a fertility deity, she is comfortable with the power that comes from losing oneself in the merging of another to create something that is greater than either.

The way in which the three kingly brothers and their sister queens rule exemplies the intrinsic nature of Eriu, Banba, and Fotla. The kings shared the rulership of Ireland, dividing their sovereignty into thirds. The land remained whole, but the time they ruled was divided up, so each brother ruled for only approximately ten years out of the twenty-nine they held power. Every year, the crown would shift to another brother and the name of the land changed to that of the queen. So, when Mac Greine held power, the land was called Eriu, but when Mac Cuill wore the crown, Banba was the name of the land.[6] Thus, all three goddesses hold the sovereignty of Ireland, yet Eriu makes the biggest impression in the ancient mythology. It is Eriu who not only makes a king

---

5. Macalister, *Lebor Gabala Erenn*, verse 64.

6. Keating, *History of Ireland*, 223.

through marriage but creates one from her womb. It is Eriu who is described as "generous"[7] when her sisters' personalities are not mentioned. And it is Eriu who changes the fortunes of the Tuatha de Danann when the Milesans arrive on the island of Ireland.

The Milesans are the last of the mythological invaders of Ireland. They arrive from Spain to avenge a fallen comrade, Ith, who was killed by the Danann nobles out of jealousy for the land of Ireland. After Ith praises Ireland for its plentiful harvest, fish, honey, wheat, and moderate climate, he seeks to return home and is ambushed by the Danann lords.[8] They react to Ith's compliments as though the land is a woman and Ith an unwelcome bridegroom coming to steal her away in the dead of night. Although the Danann race wields powerful magic, the threat of abduction is very real to the Danann men, perhaps even more so for Mac Greine, Mac Cuill, and Mac Cecht, whose wives are the very soil of the land. The Danann lords' hasty reaction and decisive strike against Ith intimates at the character of Eriu and her sisters. Like the land itself, it is possible that Eriu, Banba, and Fotla care little for the actual group that rules Ireland, as long as the caretaking of the land holds sway. After all, Eriu has already had sex and birthed a child with the Formorian race. Perhaps the land wishes to be honored for the power that she is, not for the power she can bring.

After hearing of Ith's unwelcome treatment in Ireland, the Sons of Mil gather their forces and sail to Ireland. The Danann princes use magic and Druidry to hide the island from the Milesans, but after circling the island three times, the invaders find purchase at the harbor of Inber Scene. They walk out to explore the land and enact their revenge. Three days after landing, they meet Banba with her retinue, who states that the land is named after her, and she asks that the invaders give the island her name. Her visit is followed by that of Fotla, who also claims the name right of the land, praying that the Milesans allow her name to remain on the island. Neither sister tries to stop the invaders through words or deeds. Indeed, the daughters of Ernmas appear to accept the appearance of the Sons of Mil as appropriate and expected. Instead of pushing the men back into the sea, they request boons and favors from the men.

The reasoning for this acceptance is explained when the Milesans finally meet Eriu in the very center of Ireland, at Usneche. Eriu welcomes the invaders with grandeur and nobility, stating, "Welcome, welcome to you. It is long since your coming is prophesied. Yours will be the island forever."[9] Obviously, Eriu, Banba, and Fotla have divined the

---

7. Ibid., 225.

8. Cross and Slover, *Ancient Irish Tales*.

9. Ibid.

fate of their land and have seen that the Dananns will not live on and rule the island forever. Gracefully, as branches swaying in the wind, the sovereign queens of the land accept the change of rulership and honor the line of new kings. Yet Eriu demands her own respect as well, exacting an equal, give-and-take relationship with the Milesans. When one of the men scoffs at Eriu's words, boasting about his own gods and demeaning her power, Eriu states that the power of his gods means nothing in the claiming of Ireland. She suggests that only through her will the land be taken. Then she insists that the land be named after her. The chief bard of the Milesans, Amergin, undoubtedly noting her power and sovereignty, agrees, stating, "It will be its chief name forever."[10]

Despite Eriu's divinatory skills and the might of the Milesans, the Danann men do not relinquish their hold on Ireland easily. They seek to destroy the Milesans with elemental magic, convincing the Milesans to return to their boats and travel nine waves away from the island. The two sides come to an agreement: if the Danann lords can block the Milesans from landing on Ireland using only magic, then the Sons of Mil will return to their homeland. Once the Milesans are out at sea, the Danann lords send a furious, Otherworldly wind that causes ships to spin and men to fall overboard. One ship is dashed upon the shores of Ireland, causing all aboard to perish. Donn, the Milesan who disrespected Eriu earlier, cries out that the Milesan bards and cunning men are not doing their duty by protecting the ships from the magic of the Dananns. Amergin, the chief bard, stands in the heaving ship and offers a remedy. He invokes the land to protect the Milesans. He invokes the aid and protection of the goddess Eriu and her sister sovereign queens. Amergin does not call on the power of his own gods; rather, he taps into the essence of the land of Ireland, the land they wish to invade and live upon.

Amergin sings the praises of Ireland's fertile sea, bountiful mountains, and teeming waterfalls and woods. He praises the land, yet he is clever, for he links this bounty to kingship and the right to rule:

> *I invoke the land of Ireland.*
> *Much-coursed be the fertile sea,*
> *Fertile be the fruit-strewn mountain,*
> *Fruit-strewn be the showery wood,*
> *Showery be the river of water-falls,*
> *Of water-falls be the lake of deep pools,*
> *Deep pooled be the hill-top well,*

---

10. Ibid.

A well of the tribes be the assembly,
An assembly of the kings be Tara,
Tara be the hill of the tribes,
The tribes of the sons of Mil,
Of Mil be the ships the barks,
Let the lofty bark be Ireland,
Lofty Ireland Darkly sung,
An incantation of great cunning;
The great cunning of the wives of Bres,
The wives of Bres of Buaigne;
The great lady Ireland,
Eremon hath conquered her,
Ir, Eber have invoked for her.
I invoke the land of Ireland.[11]

This poem of magic and cunning irrevocably links the power of the land to the kingship of Ireland, calling down the protection and blessing of Eriu and her sisters. Is it any wonder that Eriu, who has slept with and birthed a Formorian king, married a Danann prince, and negotiated with a Milesan bard, listens and heeds its call? She has seen the divinatory signs and knows that the lifespan of the Dananns on her island is at a close. Their respect for her power and might has diminished, and Amergin, the honey-tongued, woos her with his sweet words of honor and glory. Just as Amergin's song ends, the winds die down and the seas become tranquil yet again. The Milesans are able to sail to shore.

Adhering to the compact made between the Milesans and the Dananns, the Milesans troop onto the island and, amid much bloodshed, rout the Dananns. During the final battle, the queens Eriu, Banba, and Fotla and their kings Cethor, Sethor, and Tethor die. The essence of the land is returned to the soil, to the winds and waters from which it sprang. The power of sovereignty returns to the living land under the feet of the Milesans, to the green rolling hills of Tara, to the stark mountains and roiling seas. But it can never truly die, for as long as the land thrives, the goddess Eriu lives.

She arises once again to grant sovereignty in the eleventh-century manuscript *Baile in Scail*. In this, she is known as Flaith Erenn, the bearer of the cup of sovereignty and power. Many years after the struggle between the Dananns and the Milesans, a descendant of

---

11. Ibid.

the Sons of Mil, Conn, is greeted by the sovereign goddess. After stepping upon the Stone of Destiny, or Lia Fail, and hearing its screams, Conn's Druids tell him that he and his children will be kings of Ireland. After this proclamation, a mist forms around Conn and his advisers, and they are spirited away to an unearthly house. There, they meet a mysterious horseman, the god Lugh, and a young female cupbearer, Eriu. The men eat and drink of the bounty of Ireland and are made most welcome. At the end of the feast, Eriu asks Lugh, "To whom shall this cup be given?" and he tells her to give it to Conn.[12] She does, naming every ruler of Ireland until Judgment Day. Then she and Lugh melt into the shadows, the fog lifts, and the house disappears. However, the cup of sovereignty remains with Conn.

Like the cup, Eriu stays with each of us who has been touched by the beauty and majesty of the land of Ireland. The land is alive, a deep spirit that roots each of us into the very heart and soul of Ireland and the Irish goddess Eriu. Eriu is Ireland. She cannot be separated from its birds and beasts, from its air and rain, from its mist and shining sun. Through the invasions of seven peoples, through the use of ploughshares and the building of highways, she remains, living, breathing, and gifting us with her solid presence. She is the very essence of Ireland, and praises deserve to be sung in her name. Hail Eriu, mother of Bres! Hail Eriu, queen of Cethor! Hail Eriu, lover of Amergin! Hail Eriu, cupbearer of Lugh! Hail Eriu, essence of the land!

THE LAND: FEEL HER POWER

Not all of us are lucky enough to travel to Ireland and experience the joy and wonder of Eriu firsthand. Pictures are beautiful, but they do not invoke the essence and spirit of Eriu like actually feeling the wind, the waters, and the grasses with our bare hands. Despite this, Eriu teaches us a very powerful lesson: respect and honor of the land. Every land. All lands, no matter how they look or in which country they reside, are connected to Eriu through underground water tables and molten rivers of lava, through jets of air streams and oceanic currents. We are all connected on this planet. We just have to remember how to get in touch with one another.

With that, it is time to begin with your land, the land around your house or apartment building, the land that springs forth with flowers and offers sustenance to the trees and birds and bugs and humans who trod upon her every day. Think about the land as you walk around from appointment to mailbox to work to soccer practice. No-

---

12. Dillon, *Cycle of the Kings*.

tice her subtle changes. Relish in her beauty, no matter how she presents herself to you. In short, pay attention to the land around you and give her honor and praise. It is time to stop being oblivious to the living world around us. It is time to realize that outside of our safe houses and cozy cubicles, a rich and diverse world begs for exploration. For contemplation. For gifts. For song. For love.

THE PATHWORKING

The guided meditation to visit Eriu is perhaps one of the most challenging in this book. It is not very detailed, and it forces you to rely on your own inner sight and deep-seated experience to come to know the goddess. As the land of Ireland, Eriu knows all and is everywhere at once; therefore, her personality is less well-defined than that of other goddesses. She is the nurturer, the sustainer, the giver of life. Yet she is also the death-dealer, the rioter, the chaotic energy of Mother Nature. She is a primal force, not to be tampered with lightly. If you seek her out, be prepared to stand on your own two feet and work through the situations and confrontations presented to you.

Due to the nature of the goddess Eriu, the following meditation contains many instances in which you are asked to look into your own self to color the Otherworld around you. This can be disconcerting at first, as the guided meditation simply leaves you time to explore the Otherworld of Eriu on your own, without outside words or phrases. It is important to take your time and not rush through these pauses in the meditation. This is where you will gain your deepest insight, your most profound wisdom. Also, remember that your messages and knowledge may come to you in various forms: images, sounds, smells, feelings (both literally and emotionally), and intuitive flashes of insight. Accept anything and everything that comes to you. Do not discount any message, as they all have meaning for you.

Should you find that you are having trouble gaining messages while in meditation, don't feel discouraged. Eriu's meditation is a transition path to pure journeywork, which occurs without words at all. It takes time to master new skills, so accept where you are on your journey and honor your time there. Breathe deeply while in meditation and try to remove any expectations about receiving a message. Allow yourself to simply enjoy the relaxation of the meditation. And remember, you can always listen to the meditation again.

GUIDED MEDITATION: THE HILL OF TARA

Take a deep breath, in through your nose and out through your mouth. Take another deep breath, filling your stomach, your diaphragm, and finally your lungs. Hold this breath for five seconds … 1-2-3-4-5 … and exhale, allowing the breath to exit your lungs first, then your diaphragm, and finally, your stomach. Take one more deep breath and as you breathe in, feel the energy of the sturdy, warm ground around you supporting your fingers, your toes, your legs, and your shoulders, even the top of your head. Hold the breath for seven seconds … 1-2-3-4-5-6-7. As you exhale, feel all tension leave your fingers, your toes, your legs, and your shoulders, even the top of your head. Continue breathing deeply, in through your nose and out through your mouth. Feel the damp grass under the soles of your feet, soft and springy. The air is charged with power and the earth is swaddled in thick fog. It blankets you, calming you and removing any tension, any stress, any worry. Feel your anxieties becoming absorbed by the warmth of the fog, melting away any tightness in your muscles. (pause) You have never felt so relaxed, so secure, so calm.

You are sitting on the Hill of Tara, surrounded by fog. You cannot see more than one or two yards in any direction. The world is a cotton ball of white, reduced to you, the land, and the fog. You close your eyes and breathe in deeply. The fog cools your throat and your lungs and mingles with your vital essence, the warmth of your body. You can feel the fog seeping into your cells, deep within. It is strong. Powerful. It is the same fog that has enshrouded the island for thousands and thousands of years. It is eternal. It is the breath of the goddess Eriu.

And as her name enters your mind, you open your eyes and see the fog shifting, ever so slightly, ahead of you. It eddies and swirls very slowly, as if awakening from a deep slumber. You get the urge to yawn and stretch your hands above your head, but you settle for shifting your shoulders and sighing softly. The fog begins to shift around you, sparking blue and light green, but you don't move. You are rooted to the Hill of Tara, unable to stand up and walk away. Not that you'd want to. The lights are dazzling and sharp and electric. They burst with energy and then dissolve just as quickly. They remind you of tiny, pastel fireworks, mere inches from your nose and eyes. Enjoy them as long as you like. Perhaps a message is hidden within for you. (pause)

Suddenly you glance through the fireworks and see a dark shape taking form in the mist. It is tall, but you cannot make out its nature due to the thick, heavy fog. It begins to move toward you, and you wait, anchored by the ground, energized by the sparks, and calmed by your breathing. The movements of the fog become more erratic now, quicker and choppier. The dark shape is moving toward you, pushing away the fog. (pause) And then it emerges, tearing through the fog with sure strides and powerful movements. The shape stands before you, a mere arm's length away. The fog reforms behind the shape, knitting itself back together in a solid wall of white. Now it is just you, the land, the fog, and the shape: the goddess Eriu.

She stands before you in a simple, draped white gown. Her arms are bare, as are her feet. Her dark hair hangs loose, unadorned.

"The goddess Eriu," you say, bending forward at the waist and placing your forehead on the ground ahead of you.

She chuckles quietly and intones, "That is one of my forms, the land. But I am right before you. Look at me, child." And you do. And you see so much more than you did before. (pause)

The goddess steps forward toward you, arms outstretched, and motions you to stand. You scramble up, noticing how Eriu takes up every inch of space, every breath of air within your fog blanket. You breathe shallowly for a few minutes before she places her hand at your throat with a smile and breathes into your mouth. The tightness in your chest subsides, and you are able to smile back at the goddess.

"The land anchors you, my child, sustains and nourishes you. We mother you and love you," the goddess says, her voice echoing deep inside your head. Her voice is rich and teeming with life. It is deep and full and boundless. It is wildness, barely tamed. Eriu holds her hands out to you, and without thinking, you grasp them with your own.

Immediately, you are thrown backward and down with a powerful pulse of energy. Roots shoot out from your feet, diving, searching for water. You can feel brittle bark forming around your legs and belly. It is hard and unyielding, making you secure. Your skin begins to change color, turning into tree-colored brown; your fingers sprout tendrils and new green leaves. But you notice all of this from a long way off, as your consciousness, the very essence of yourself, follows the driving roots deep, deep, deeper into the earth. (pause) Down, down, down you go.

And then the roots stop, and you do too. Look around. See with root eyes, accustomed to the blackness deep within the land. Hear with root ears, used to the silent quiet. Smell with a root nose, familiar with the mustiness of enclosed spaces. You have reached the power center of Eriu. See what the goddess sees. Hear what the goddess hears. Smell what the goddess smells. Can you hear the laughter of children playing outside? Do you hear a snippet of song? A rattling bulldozer? A crying mother? (pause) Can you see the earthworms burrowing through the rich soil? A small chipmunk nestled in his winter nest? A leaf moldering slowly, turning into nutrients to sustain the land?

(pause) Can you smell the smoke from a barbecue? A forest fire? A beeswax candle? Do you smell the strength of the soil? The oil from a spill? The fumes from thousands and thousands of cars? (pause) Do you see, really see? And hear? And smell? (pause) Join now with the land and become one with the goddess Eriu. (long pause)

When you are ready, you feel a brief bit of pressure on your hands. Your spirit zooms up the roots and returns to your body, which, miraculously, has returned to its original form. No more bark or leaves or snaking tendrils of roots. "You have seen the truth," says Eriu. "My truth. Do with this knowledge what you will. But know that I am always a part of you, just as you are always a part of me." She squeezes your hands one last time before releasing them and walking backward the way she came, through the fog. The white veil swirls around her until she is once again a dark shape in the mass of eddying white. And then she is gone, and only a slight movement of the fog shows that she was ever standing with you at all. And then her voice echoes through the shrouded land, "Remember."

Now take a deep breath, in through your nose and out through your mouth. Take another deep breath, filling your stomach, your diaphragm, and finally your lungs. Hold this breath for five seconds … 1-2-3-4-5 … and exhale, allowing the breath to exit your lungs first, then your diaphragm, and finally your stomach. Breathe deeply once more, and as you breathe in, feel the energy and the wonder of the world around you in your fingers, your toes, your legs, and your shoulders, even the top of your head. As you exhale, wiggle your fingers and toes. Shake your legs and move your shoulders up and down. Take another deep breath and, as you exhale, move your head from side to side. Feel the ground under your body touching every nerve ending and muscle. Hear the rustlings of the people around you. Notice the movements outside. Continue breathing. Stretch your arms out above your head. You are returning to the present, to the here and now. Continue stretching. Continue breathing. When you are ready, open your eyes, blink and focus, and sit up.

INVOCATION TO ERIU

The fog shifts
And she stands, waiting,
Watching, smooth and silent.
"I have seen it all," she states.
Her voice molten.

Her eyes ice.
"And I have been waiting."

So you lift your voice
For the first time
Or the hundredth
And you sing
From your heart,
From your belly,
From your fire.

Hail Eriu, mother of Bres!
Hail Eriu, queen of Cethor!
Hail Eriu, lover of Amergin!
Hail Eriu, cupbearer of Lugh!
Hail Eriu, essence of the land!

Then you take a deep breath and you sing again
Louder.
And again, and again, until your throat is sore.
But you have touched the eternal,
The cup of queenship (kingship),
And you are quenched.

And now you whisper,
Hail Eriu, mother of Bres!
Hail Eriu, queen of Cethor!
Hail Eriu, lover of Amergin!
Hail Eriu, cupbearer of Lugh!
Hail Eriu, body, spirit, and soul of the land!

MAGICAL ACTIVITIES

Elemental Magic (Earth): Getting Your Hands Dirty

Items Needed: Dirt from your land, nearby land, or the garden store; a bucket; water;
a sunny day; and a blanket (optional)

Moon Phase: Waxing

Seasonal Cycle: Summer

Set up all of your items outside, in the light of the full sun. Close your eyes and take some time to attune to the natural world around you. Hear the insects and birds. Feel the wind in your hair and the earth under your body. Lie down on the ground and, while meditating, feel yourself sink into the earth, being welcomed by her soft, warm embrace. This elemental spell can be used to energize and activate any magical intent that you wish to pursue. However, it is best used with "drawing" spells that manifest specific goals in your life, rather than "banishing" spells that remove unwanted influences. While you are lying down in the sun and meditating, decide on the goal you most want to manifest in your life.

When you feel ready, sit up and place your hands above the soil that you have collected. Take seven deep breaths, reaching out with your intuition to the soil below you. If it is from a store or a different piece of land, notice any differences between the dirt under your hands and the dirt under your body. When you have acclimated your body to the vibrations of the new soil, allow your hands to drop gently onto the soil. Welcome the dirt's energy into your body, allowing it to seep up into your hands, through your arms, and down into your torso. At the same time, feel the energy of the earth moving up your legs and through your abdomen to join and mingle with the energy of the pile of soil under your hands. You are the conduit between these two similar, and yet dissimilar, items of earth energy and power. You and they are now united.

With deep reverence and utmost care, scoop seven handfuls of the collected and now-energized soil into your empty bucket. With each scoop, say a meaningful phrase or line that reinforces your magical intent. So, for instance, if you wish to bring prosperity into your life, you might say something like, "The earth provides for all her children." You can repeat the same phrase seven times or create different phrases for each handful of dirt.

After you have placed your seven handfuls in the bucket, plunge your hands into the dirt. Don't be afraid. Working with earth energy can be messy, so dive right in there. Pour your magical intent into the dirt through the tips of your fingers. Now pour the water into the bucket and mix it around with your bare hands. Swirl the mud in a clockwise direction, chanting your purpose for the spell. Call on the earth energies that you see around you to aid you in empowering the spell. So, for instance, you might see a pine tree, feel a soft breeze, or notice a puddle nearby. They can all help you in performing your magic if you ask (nicely) for their aid.

When you sense that the mud is completely charged with the power of your spell, lift your hands out of the bucket, hold them above your head, and shake them vigorously. This will cause a mud shower all over you and the earth around you, so it is best to wear old clothes for this spellwork. Scatter the mud all over your land, leaving mud droplets, mud puddles, and mud piles in random places. Have fun and play with this part of the spell. Run and skip and jump! Make mud pies and silly mud faces! In short, allow the little child inside to come out under the warm sun and play in the mud. When your bucket is empty, wipe your hands one last time on a fallen leaf or a patch of grass or clover. Lie down on your blanket and take seven deep breaths. Once again, feel the warm embrace of the Earth Mother. This time, thank her for allowing you to share in her exuberance, her creative power, and her long and luscious life. Know that you have begun a long relationship with the earth, having received some of her energy and given some of yours. You have placed your magical wish into her safekeeping; she will provide for you, the caring, sustaining mother of us all.

Incantation: Amergin's Praise Poem

> Items Needed: A copy of Amergin's poem (provided in the first section of this chapter), two pieces of parchment paper, a pen, several beeswax candles, and lavender and chamomile flowers (fresh or dried)
> Moon Phase: Full
> Seasonal Cycle: Any

About a week before the full moon, sit down and read Amergin's poem. Read it at least once, but you may need more readings to truly comprehend its meaning. It is not simply a poem, but a rather complex magical incantation that showcases the verbal abilities of our ancient Celtic ancestors, who honored and prized word knowledge. Even if you are not a poet or an accomplished writer, you can still utilize the format of Amergin's praise poem in an incantation to accomplish your magical desires. Your spell does not have to be as elaborate or long. Simply follow the general structure of the poem to verbally state your magical intent.

Now, for the whole week, gather information to aid you in crafting your incantation. First, take a look at the world around you. At this exact moment, what do you see, hear, and smell? What colors are predominant? What animals or birds are around? Are there trees nearby? Flowers? Herbs? Are they wild or cultivated? Write down on your first piece of paper everything that you notice about the natural world around you. This will constitute the first section of your poem.

Once you feel you have identified all of the natural elements presenting themselves to you, focus on your magical intent for this spell. Since this spell is meant to be performed at the full moon, you can request something to be brought to you (drawing magic) or you can request something to be lifted from you (banishing magic). Either one will work with the full moon energy, although some people feel that drawing magic is more closely aligned to the full moon, while banishing magic resonates with the dark moon. Consider your own feelings on this concept and choose a magical intent accordingly.

Continue to use your first piece of paper, write down everything that jumps into your mind concerning your magical intent for the spell. Don't limit yourself. Write down every single word, phrase, and sentence that comes to mind. These may seem inconsequential or out of sync with your original intent, but they are connected in some way, through your mind, spirit, and emotions. Everything holds meaning, so write it down! Do this for between fifteen minutes and a half-hour. At the half-hour mark, stop brainstorming and reread what you have written. Try to form connections and notice similarities between the various ideas and concepts. This will help you to create your second section of the poem.

Finally, write down your family lineage for at least two generations, starting with you. You can choose to include your children and/or significant other, but definitely write down the names of your parents, their parents, and any great aunts and uncles. Try to remember their full names, including maiden names and middle names, if you can. You'll probably have to talk to members of your family for some of this, so allow yourself a few days to collect the information. Also, find out the founding men and women of your town and the approximate date that it was created. If you own land, search for the names of the people who owned it before you. If you rent, write down the name of your landlord or the owner of the property company. This last bit of information will make up the third and last section of your poem.

On the night of the full moon, gather your magical items and place them in the light of the moon. Light your candles with words of praise to the goddess Eriu, to the earth, to the animals and plants, and to any inspirational and creative muses, including the bard Amergin. Hold one of the lit candles in front of your face, near your third eye, and say, "May the light of inspiration sweeten my words, allowing them to flow unhindered and unchecked." Blow a kiss to the candle and honor it with some lavender and chamomile flowers, either fresh or dried. Breathe deeply and ground and center as you normally do. Allow yourself to fall into a soft yet conscious meditative state. Pick up your pen and your blank sheet of paper, and begin to write with the natural world as inspiration.

Start with the sentence "I invoke the land of (*your town or your land holding*)" and continue until you have described the world around you to your satisfaction. If you want, try linking the lines of your praise poem together, as in Amergin's poem. For instance, if your first line is "The leaves shine gold and rust," your second line might be "Gold sunlight radiates from above," and your third line could be "Above the tree line, cardinals chirp." Whatever you do, don't overthink your incantation or get so stressed that you jump out of your meditative state. Allow the words to flow.

After you have described your natural world, move on to the reason for your spellwork: the goal you wish to accomplish with this spell. Utilize your brainstorming phrases and statements for this section of your incantation. If you can link your spell to the natural world through your poem, do so. You could write something like, "As the branches of the trees reach to the sky, so do I hunger for divine connection" or "Baby birds fill the nests above my head, reminding me of the power to procreate." This can be a little tricky, so simply write down the connection that first comes to mind. If no nature alignment comes to you, don't worry. Your magical intent is already attached to the earth around you through your poem. Describe your magical intent as fully and completely as possible in your incantation. Don't leave out anything.

Lastly, find your genealogical, town, and land information and compose the third and last section of the poem. This section tells the universe and the earth exactly who you are in relation to others around you. This is important, as it links you to other powerful people in your family and in your past. In essence, you are drawing on their power to help activate and charge the spell, so pick the ancestors and people to whom you are most closely connected. If you didn't like your great uncle Joel, don't include him in your spell. End the poem as you began it with the sentence "I invoke the land of (*your town or your land holding*)."

Now, taking the candle that you held up to your forehead and honored with flowers, go outside and proclaim your spell. In a loud voice, read your incantation. After you have stated it out loud, hold your poem to the candle flame and burn it. Scatter the ashes to the winds. When there is nothing left of your incantation, go inside and douse all of your candles except the one that you brought outside. Allow that candle to burn down to nothing, making sure that you keep it in a safe place, away from any curtains, paper, or other flammable objects. If you need to go to bed, douse the candle, but relight it at your next earliest convenience.

You have tapped into the ancient power of the bard Amergin. Your spell is heard for all generations. Be glad!

Natural Magic: Awakening the Land

Items Needed: A tiki torch and oil, a lighter, a drum, and cornmeal (or another agricultural item that represents your area of the world)

Moon Phase: Any

Seasonal Cycle: Any

As this ritual grants you the honor and responsibility of being the steward of the land, the elemental energies are invoked to bear witness to your rite. If you feel uncomfortable requesting their presence, do not ask them to join you. This rite is sacred in intent and should not be undertaken lightly or on a whim. Becoming a custodian of the land means that you have to consider every action in relationship to its connection to the world around you. This rite will change the way you view the world, especially the land on which you reside. If you feel unable to accept this responsibility, do not feel obligated to perform this rite. Honor the land in your own way until you wish to take on more responsibility. Anytime you work with the land, even if only once a year on Earth Day, you are bettering the world in which we all live. Take pride in all your earthly actions, no matter how small.

Gather your items outside in a central location on the land you wish to adopt or steward. Starting with the north and turning in a clockwise direction, honor each direction by looking at the land around you. After you have watched, heard, and smelled all that you can at each direction, say, "Spirits of the north (east, south, west), I honor you and ask you to bear witness to my rite."

Take the torch and light it, using your lighter. Say, "The flame of truth burns bright in my heart. I vow to honor this land with sacred fire. May its wisdom reside in me." Walk around the periphery of the land, holding the torch high. As you walk, feel the shape of the land under your feet and watch the smoke from the torch color the landscape. You are centering yourself in the scope of the land around you. After you have completed your circuit around the land, stick the torch in the ground in the center of your land. Take a few moments to take in the significance of what you have done.

When you are ready, hold up your cornmeal or other agricultural product. Say, "The bounty of the green earth grows strong in my heart. I vow to honor this land with sacred cornmeal (or other product). May its abundance reside in me." Walk around your land, stopping to sprinkle the cornmeal at places that call to you. You may choose to put some under a tree, on some moss, at the edge of the woods, or inside a rippling puddle. Wherever the landscape calls to you, leave a handful of cornmeal. Take note of these places, as they form part of your sacred trust with the land. These are your power centers, and it is here that you will honor the land with offerings, listen to the land in meditation, and connect with the land through words and deeds. When you have completed your exploration of the sacred centers of your land, return to the center and drop a handful of cornmeal at the base of the sacred fire torch. Breathe deeply for a minute or two to connect with your actions.

Finally, pick up your drum. Say, "The heartbeat of the living earth resonates deep in my heart. I honor this land with sacred drumming. May its love and power reside in me." Begin to drum while walking around your land. You will probably find that you start off slow, but as your connection to the land intensifies, you will begin to drum and walk quickly. You may find yourself running or dancing in celebration of the wonder of your natural surroundings. Surrender yourself to the moment, to the wind, the water, the earth under your feet. Move through the land, within it, not just on top of it. Feel it entering your very soul. You are forming a relationship with the land. Give thanks to Mother Earth. All praise!

As your drumming and dancing subsides, begin to wend your way back to the central spot on your land. Lay your drum next to your torch and cornmeal, and turn to each of the four directions. With arms outstretched, say at each direction, "I thank the forces of the north (east, south, west) for witnessing my rite. I am honored by your presence. Pray, return to the areas where you are most needed." If possible, allow your torch flame to burn for a few more hours, illuminating and energizing the land.

You have now committed yourself to being the steward of a small section of this green earth. Be sure to honor the sacred power spots with offerings at least twice a month. Spend time in your land and meditate, play, hold ritual, and relax outside as much as possible. Pick up any trash, and craft small sanctuaries for birds and faeries and elementals. Enjoy your land, and relish your intimate connection to the world around you.

MEETING MACHA, IRISH GODDESS OF POWER AND SPEED

Recognizing Your Inner Strength

MACHA: GODDESS OF INITIATION

The goddess Macha (pronounced MAH-ka) shifts characteristics and professions throughout Irish mythology. She is a deathly crow, a battle queen, and a winsome *sidhe*. She runs fast, acts decisively, and kills without compassion. Yet for all this power and energy, Macha displays mothering qualities and even gives birth, in a very public forum. Macha is an enigma: life and death, love and hate, wrapped together in a goddess whose energy opens up opportunities and new avenues for all. Clearer of fields, obstacles, enemies, land, and clutter, Macha creates space for life, for living, and for movement and change. She gives you a place to find your own strength and courage and to achieve your own goals and dreams.

According to the *Lebor Gabala Erenn*, Macha is one of the three illustrious daughters, often known collectively as the Morrighan, of Ernmas the she-farmer. Her sisters, Badb and Morrighan (who is also known as Anand or Anu), are generally considered to be goddesses of war and death.[1] Yet there is a fertile aspect to their nature, derived, no doubt, from their mother, who is a prolific and abundant goddess. Ernmas births eleven children: five boys and two sets of female triplets, including the goddesses of the land of Ireland, Eriu, Banba, and Fotla. It is no wonder, then, that the fruitfulness of Ernmas spills over onto her female children, however slightly. Macha's name is sometimes given the meaning of "plain," and as the wife of Nemed (the leader of the third group of invaders of Ireland), she is said to have cleared plains. Felling trees and moving rocks to create a plain or field indicates an interest and talent for agriculture. Macha, as the mythical wife of Nemed, works to provide sustenance for her people, making a space for them to cultivate crops. She is not the land itself, like her sisters; rather, she is the drive and energy to work hard and wrest a living from the soil. She is the power that gives us the space to create. Yet Macha, like Morrighan and Babd, is as intimately involved with destruction as she is with creation.

The reasoning for the innate warrior characteristics of some of Ernmas's children is never explained in the *Lebor Gabala Erenn*. Perhaps it stems from the warlike environment in which they were born. (The Tuatha de Danann are in constant struggle with either the Formorians, the Fir Blog, or the Milesans throughout the *Lebor Gabala Erenn*.) Or perhaps, as Miranda Green suggests in *Celtic Goddesses*, the goddesses bridge

---

1. While generally true, this assumption leaves out the important connection of the goddess Morrighan to the fertility and abundance of the land and all of the people upon it. See chapter 13 of the book *Goddess Alive!* for a more detailed explanation of this phenomenon and for additional bibliographic resources.

two halves of a cyclic whole—life and death, love and hate, war and fertility—signifying a connection to sovereignty.[2] In any event, Macha and Morrighan display tantalizing glimpses of fertility and abundance, whereas Badb is relegated to the central figure of the carrion-eating crow.

Macha is also known to assume crow form and is so described in the ninth-century text *Cormac's Glossary*. The crow is often seen as a harbinger of death, destruction, and war in Celtic mythology. As an eater of the dead, the crow was an inauspicious omen for men on their way to battle. Seeing a crow or, even worse, a murder of crows indicated death on a grand scale—and probably your own. Yet the crow (and its cousin, the raven) was a bird of augury, prophecy, and initiation as well. Its dark feathers reminded one of night, mystery, and death, while its ability to fly indicated a connection to the divine and inspiration and movement. The crow, like the goddess who could take its shape, teetered on the edge of light and dark, death and life, having an ability to venture into either and perhaps to pass through one to reach the other. *The Druid Animal Oracle* states that the raven (and its cousin the crow) "marks the death of one thing, which gives way to the birth of another."[3] As such, it is a fitting bird for a fertile and deadly initiatory goddess like Macha.

Further reading of *Cormac's Glossary* shows additional proof of Macha's dual nature by describing "the heads of men after their slaughter" as "Macha's mast."[4] *Mast* comes from the Old English word *mæst* and probably from the Old High German *mast*, which means "food." *Mast* in Middle English, as used in *Cormac's Glossary*, means "acorns" or "nuts on a forest floor often collected for food, especially for animals." Describing the heads of dead men as "Macha's mast" juxtaposes the image of food needed for life with the bloody scene of a battlefield. Once again, Macha straddles the doorway of death and life and, like her sister Morrighan, chooses which will hold sway. Unlike other "gateway" goddesses (such as Cymidei Cymeinfoll and Cerridwyn), Macha does not have a connection to rebirth or transformation of the soul. Rather, she is the pivotal point at which light dwindles into darkness and darkness bursts into light. She is the energy and essence that pushes one way or another, that selects the path opening before us. As the crow, Macha chooses birth or death but does not actively participate in the process.

---

2. Green, *Celtic Goddesses*, 71–72.

3. Carr-Gomm, *Druid Animal Oracle*, 66.

4. Green, *Celtic Goddesses*, 43.

Indeed, in Irish mythology it is difficult to find an instance of Macha's interference in a battle. The *Lebor Gabala Erenn* states that Macha, Badb, and Morrighan were "sources of bitter fighting,"[5] but there is little evidence of Macha's direct connection with war in her goddess form. During the First Battle of Mag Tuired, when the Tuatha de Danann fight the Fir Blog (an earlier race of beings that inhabited Ireland), Morrighan and her sisters Badb and Macha attack the Fir Blog at Tara with a very physical form of their magic. "Enchanted showers of sorcery and sustaining rainclouds of mist and mighty showers of fire, and a downpour of red blood poured down from the air upon the warriors' heads; and they did not allow the Fir Blog either to leave or to disperse for three days and nights."[6] Both Morrighan and Babd are mentioned in the Ulster Cycle, which includes the epic tale "The Cattle Raid of Cooley," a bitterly fought war between Maeve of Connaught and Conchobar of Ulster over a magical cow. The goddess Morrighan plays a significant role in another famous battle, the Second Battle of Mag Tuired, which highlights the struggle between the Formorians and the Tuatha de Danann. Both Macha and Babd make cursory appearances in this epic but do not display any of their amazing battle magic.

Macha does, however, showcase an amazing ability for warcraft in a small section of the tale "The Wooing (or Courting) of Emer." In this story, Macha is known as Macha, the Red-haired, daughter of Aed Ruad (or Aed the Red), who, with his peers Dithorba and Cimbaeth, rules Ireland on a cyclical basis. Every seven years the power of the high king of Ireland shifts, moving from one man to the next (an arrangement that is reminiscent of the husbands of another set of Ernmas triplets, Eriu, Banba, and Fotla). For sixty-six years, these men rule Ireland, each wielding power for seven years and then quietly stepping aside to allow the next man his chance to reign, until Aed Ruad drowns. When Macha, Aed's only child, demands the kingship in her due time, Dithorba and Cimbaeth refuse, stating that "they would not give kingship to a woman."[7] Naturally, their attitude does not sit well with Macha, who promptly goes to war against the two leaders and routs them, earning the kingship (or queenship) of Ireland for herself.

At the end of her seven years of rule, the five sons of Dithorba (who by now has joined Aed Ruad in the Otherworld) demand the kingship. Macha refuses, saying,

---

5. Macalister, *Lebor Gabala Erenn*, verse 64.

6. Epstein, *Morrígan*, 77.

7. Meyer, *Wooing of Emer*, 151.

"Not by favor did I obtain it but by force in the battlefield."[8] She fights and, once again, trounces her opponents, leaving a "slaughter of heads"[9] on the battlefield, an undeniable reference to the goddess Macha and the term "Macha's mast" coined in *Cormac's Glossary*. Not content to destroy the sons of Dithorba on the field of war, Macha pursues the brothers into the wilds of Connaught, where she catches up with them in the woods as they roast a boar. Although she is dressed as a leper, the sons of Dithorba invite her to sit and eat with them. Before long, the men begin to lust after Macha, and one of them guides her into the woods to lie with him. In no time, Macha emerges from the woods, but without her erstwhile suitor. When the men question her about their brother, she says, "He is too ashamed to come to you, after having lain with a leper."[10] The men laugh and exclaim that there is no shame, since they will all lie with her. Then they each go into the woods with her, but not one of them emerges. When the last brother traipses into the woods with Macha, we learn that Macha has subdued each of the sons of Dithorba with her strength, binding them so they cannot move or speak. She then chains the brothers together and leads them back to Ulster.

When her warriors see the sons of Dithorba, the traitors who tried to kill their queen, they clamor for their deaths, yearning to kill them. But Macha has other plans. Instead of publicly executing the sons of Dithorba, an action she feels will undermine her queenship, she makes them her slaves, and forces them to build her a rath, or fort. In essence, she forces her enemies to create a seat of power for her. Macha, harking back to her plain-clearing days as the wife of Nemed, marks out the spot for her fort with her brooch and so named her rath, according to the legends, Emain Macha (*eo imam muin Macha*, or "brooch on the neck of Macha").[11]

Another story, perhaps the most well-known about the goddess Macha, gives a different explanation for the meaning of the name Emain Macha, claiming that *emain* is the word for "twins." The story, often known as "The Curse of Macha" or "The Pangs of Ulster," is a prelude to "The Cattle Raid of Cooley" and explains Maeve of Connaught's reasoning and timing for attacking the king of Ulster, Conchobar mac Nessa, in order to heist the brown bull. "The Curse of Macha" begins with a very lonely, very rich landlord

---

8. Ibid., 152.

9. Ibid.

10. Ibid.

11. Ibid.

in Ulster named Crunniuc mac Agnomain. Crunniuc's wife has recently died, and he is all alone on his land in the mountains with his sons. One day, when Crunniuc is all alone at home (and undoubtedly feeling sorry for himself), he sees a beautiful young woman (Macha) walking toward him. She enters the house and, without a word, begins to set things in order. She cooks and cleans, creating a warm, welcoming environment. That evening, after the sons are in bed, Macha sleeps with Crunniuc, effectively becoming his companion.

This arrangement continues for quite some time, until Crunniuc decides to attend a fair at the high seat of Ulster. Macha counsels Crunniuc to keep quiet about her when at the fair. She says, "It would be as well not to grow boastful or careless in anything you say."[12] Crunniuc promises her that he'll stay quiet and goes off to the fair by himself. (Macha does not go with him, as she is nine months pregnant with his child.) Crunniuc has a grand time at the fair, watching chariot racing, buying goods, and drinking the wildly accessible alcoholic beverages. After King Conchobar's horse and chariot team wins the races, the people of Ulster proclaim that nothing is faster than the king's horses. Crunniuc, without thinking, blurts out, "My wife is faster."[13] Conchobar, never one to be slighted without recourse, drags Crunniuc before the high seat and holds him there under guard while messengers go in search of Macha.

When the messengers approach Macha in her lonely house in the mountains, she tells them that she cannot possibly go to the fair, as she is about to give birth to a child. They reply, "He [Crunniuc] will die unless you come,"[14] and so Macha goes to the fair. At the fair, labor pains grip Macha, and she calls out to the crowd, "A mother bore each of you! Help me! Wait until my child is born."[15] It is obvious to everyone that Macha is heavily pregnant yet no one cares to champion her cause (afraid, no doubt, of the ire of King Conchobar, who was known for his wrathful temper). And so Macha is forced to race King Conchobar's chariot team even as she is in the midst of giving birth to her children. She wins but falls down at the finish line in agony. There, on the field, in front of the whole fair attendance, she gives birth to twins, a boy and a girl, forever naming the high seat of Ulster as Emain Macha, or the Twins of Macha. As Macha gives birth, she screams a curse that all who hear her screams will suffer from the same pangs of birth for five days and four nights during times of Ulster's greatest difficulty. And then

---

12. Kinsella, *Tain*, 7.

13. Ibid.

14. Ibid.

15. Ibid.

she dies, but her curse lives on for nine generations, affecting all of the men of Ulster so that when they have most need to fight, they cannot move from their beds, as they are wracked with labor pains.

Macha appears in numerous guises in Irish mythology. As sister to Morrighan and Babd, she is the carrion crow, chooser of life or death, connection to the gods, omen, prophet, seer. As wife to Nemed, she is the plain-clearer, the provider of plenty for her people, the drive to accomplish and live. As Macha Ruad, she is the warrior queen, the powerful conqueror, the ruler of a queenship earned. As wife to Crunniuc, Macha is the faery lover, caretaker of the unfortunate, counselor of wisdom, curser, mother, champion of right. And so, the differing stories of Macha may seem to have little in common, but this is not correct. In each incarnation, Macha opens up a pathway for herself and for others. She scythes through the unnecessary in order to achieve a goal, creating a clear space for new ways of thinking and new chapters in our lives. She clears the land for the Nemedians. She clears away the old kings (and their sons) in order for her to assume the queenship of Ulster. She clears away the clutter and despair of the widower Crunniuc so he can live a fruitful life, evidenced by her subsequent pregnancy.

Macha's stories indicate that she is the initiator of new phases in life and also in death, which to the ancient Celts was just an extension of this mundane life. Macha is the clearing wind that sweeps a path for you to follow. Sometimes this wind is forceful and turbulent, as with the actions of Macha Ruad. Other times it is a gentle breeze, calmly showing us the way. Yet despite Macha's soothing ways, it is best to remember that she is a crow goddess and that, in most of her stories, death is apparent. Macha's pathways open to the Otherworld, the land of the dead, as well as this mundane world, so it is wise to pay attention to her messages and judge them for yourself. A goddess of far-reaching power, Macha should be honored with respect and deference, but not with fear. After all, she is a daughter of Ernmas, the she-farmer. The death of one thing gives birth to the beginning of another. Macha knows and lives this truth as an abundant, deadly, fertile, and strong goddess of initiation.

HIDDEN STRENGTH: LOOK WITHIN

Moving from one phase of life into another takes an amazing amount of strength. When we move from being a child to a teenager, from being a college student to an adult, from single life to married life to parenthood, we are altering our entire way of life. Our thought processes change, and we think and act and perceive from a different center. Everything is viewed within a different context. These self-chosen life stages are complicated, and thorny issues arise from our movement and growth. These need strength, but not necessarily courage, as we experience these changes by biologic necessity (growing up) or by choice.

Courage comes into play when we are unceremoniously thrust into a new way of life without our consent and without any warning: The company downsizes unexpectedly. Your lover of thirteen years decides to leave. Your healthy mother or father catches the flu and dies. You win an obscene amount of money through the lottery. A coveted position at work opens up and you're given a promotion. You find out you have a child you didn't know existed. In these situations, all of a sudden your life has completely changed and everything on which you have relied is gone; your foundation has crumbled. You realize you have nothing to support you, except yourself.

Your inner strength materializes in these instances because you have no choice. Whether growing up, selecting a new lifestyle, or changing by force, you are in uncharted waters. You will experience sensations, people, events, and encounters that you have never seen before. And you will have little guidance, other than an occasional friend and your own inner will, in order to overcome any obstacles, persevere, and triumph. Change brings growth, joy, and abundance, but it can also cause heartache and turmoil as we slough off old attitudes, opinions, and actions. We change because we are human. It is part of our experience on this planet. So when you are confronted with such experiences (which inevitably you will be), think back to all of the other times you've handled sudden change with success. These are testaments to your will and strength. Honor them. Cherish them. And learn from them. They are the buttresses that support the foundation of your very self.

THE PATHWORKING

The journey to visit Macha takes place at the current site of Emain Macha or Navan Fort in Armagh County, Ulster, in Ireland. The landscape plays a big role in the meditation, so I recommend finding some pictures of the site, either online or in Irish travel books or brochures. If you can go visit the site in Ireland, even better! (It's a great excuse for some much-needed rest and relaxation.)

I have decided to set the meditation in the current era (rather than during Emain Macha's illustrious past), because Macha is a goddess concerned with moving ahead. She recognizes that the past has occurred, and she even understands its value, but she does not dwell on it. She is a continually moving goddess who brings with her great change, a great clearing of space, and an understanding of our place in the design of our lives. To visit the past would be unimportant to Macha, because it would not bring with it the lessons that are so clearly before us. Death, birth, love, heartache—they are all Macha's domain, because they are doorways to the beyond, to the subconscious, and to the inner knowing of ourselves.

So don't be afraid or nervous during this quest to remember your inner strength. It's there, whether you recognize it or not. But it's always nice to be reminded of its presence. After this meditation, you will have a tangible, visual token of your strength. You can choose to craft a replica for this mundane world, but it is not necessary. As a goddess of the threshold and of initiation, Macha brings that which lives in the Otherworld into this world. So your token is alive whether you can hold it in your hand or simply close your eyes and think of it. It is your gift from the goddess Macha.

GUIDED MEDITATION: MACHA'S GIFT

Take a deep breath, in through your nose and out through your mouth. Take another deep breath, filling your stomach, your diaphragm, and finally your lungs. Hold this breath for five seconds... 1-2-3-4-5... and exhale, allowing the breath to exit your lungs first, then your diaphragm, and finally your stomach. One more deep breath and as you breathe in, feel the energy of the sturdy, warm ground around you supporting your fingers, your toes, your legs, and your shoulders, even the top of your head. Hold the breath for seven seconds... 1-2-3-4-5-6-7. As you exhale, feel all tension leave your fingers, your toes, your legs, and your shoulders, even the top of your head. Continue breathing deeply, in through your nose and out through your mouth. Feel the soft grass under the soles of your feet. The air moves fitfully in strong gusts of wind and in soothing, caressing breezes. Allow the wind to remove any excess tension and stress. Feel your anxieties being wafted away on the breath of the wind. Allow your muscles to relax. (pause) You have never felt so relaxed, so secure, so calm.

You are walking across a green field on a sunny, warm day. Trees and bushes litter the plain but do not hinder your movement forward. A bird sings sweetly, relaxing you and transporting you to a time without worries, troubles, or concerns. The sun warms your skin while the breezes keep you cool and comfortable. It is an absolutely gorgeous and perfect day. In the distance, you see a low hill rising from the flat plain. Although the footing is difficult, as there is no path or walkway, you veer toward the mound, pulled by some indescribable force.

Rocks jut out and roll under your feet. Sand slips, and grasses undulate. The breeze intensifies as you walk closer and closer to the hill. It grows so strong that you have trouble looking straight ahead and must duck your head to protect your eyes. You reach into a pocket for a pair of sunglasses and instead find an unusual object. Pay attention to this object, as it is the link between you and the pathway to the goddess Macha. (pause) You safely secure the object back in your pocket just before tumbling up a small incline. A mounded bank runs in either direction, forming a circular design. This is followed by a four-foot ditch, which keeps to the same path as the bank. You easily climb over the bank and into the ditch.

The wind has lessened some, and you are able to look around without worrying about dirt and debris. The mound that you have been seeking stands right in front of you, round and glorious in the sun. Several trees stand lonely sentinel in front of the mound, which is surrounded by a small embankment made of grass, hay, and straw. Here is the end to your quest. You clamber out of the ditch and run toward a space in the embankment between two fully flowering trees. Just as you are about to pass through the opening and onto the rounded hillock, a woman steps out from behind the shadow of a tree and you are brought up short.

She is of medium height and build, neither beautiful nor ugly but cute, with high cheekbones, a smattering of freckles, and a pert nose. Her hair is dark, so dark as to be black—crow black. You catch a hue of blue among the riotous curls when she moves her head in the sunlight. She wears a brown leather vest and pants, high boots, and a simple shirt. You would not look askance at her if you saw her at the supermarket, even though her whimsical clothes might be better suited to a Renaissance fair or traveling theater troop. Although she is smiling, this woman's eyes are hard and knowledgeable. She has seen much. You do not dare push past her to reach the crest of the mound.

"Why the rush?" the woman asks, and her voice is deep, smoke-tinged around the edges with just the hint of a rasp. Search your mind and heart and soul. Why do you need to reach the summit of the hill? (pause) When you have found the answer, tell the woman. (pause) She nods in understanding and asks you questions about your quest, which you answer as best you can. (pause) "The heart of the quest lies within," the woman says, tapping you firmly on the chest. "It is in here. Do you have the heart to proceed? Do you have the strength?" You think about this for a few moments. Consider all of the obstacles you have faced and surmounted in your life. Think of all of the changes you have undergone. (pause) Looking the woman directly in the eye, tell her of your findings. (pause) Then show her the unusual object you found in your pocket.

The woman takes your object and holds it in her hands. She smiles. "Ah, yes," she says, "the pathway to Macha." Her voice lowers to a whisper. "The pathway to me." She takes the object and squeezes it in her hands. At that instant, the crow form descends upon her body. You can see the giant wings folded against her back and the long beak on her face. You see both crow and woman at the same time. Feathers and skin. Light and dark. Death and life. But then the woman smiles and the crow form disappears, blown away by the steady winds. "I am Macha," the woman says, "the initiator, the bringer of power and truth and beauty. Do you accept my gift of change? Will you step forward out of the old and into the new? Will you forgo the safe past for the ever-volatile present and the unknown future?" Think on this for a moment or two. (pause) Knowing that growth comes from change and is the pathway of humanity, you nod your head.

Macha takes your unusual object and smashes it against the tree. The tree groans and shudders, as if absorbing something through its bark. "The tree is now linked to you," she says. "It is your guardian, your reminder of your strength and ability to move ahead and forge new pathways. Nurture this tree and you will thrive. Allow this tree to die and your power withers away." She lowers her hand and holds out your unusual object. It has completely changed. Sitting in the palm of her hand is a wooden pendant etched with the design of a tree—the exact tree, in fact, that stands next to you. As the wind shakes the branches of the tree, so do the branches on the pendant move. You are entranced, mystified, and not a little overwhelmed by this gift.

"This pendant represents the core power of your strength," Macha says. "It cannot diminish unless you allow it to. It will grow with every obstacle you overcome, with every situation in which you triumph. Pay attention to this pendant, and every time you feel your strength ebb, put it on. It will immediately connect you to this place, to this tree, to me. It will remind you of your power." You take the pendant and slip it around your neck. It feels warm and comfortable against your skin.

Macha glances up at the sun and smiles wryly. "My time is at a close. Learn, love, and grow. This is just the beginning of an exciting adventure. Live it! Grasp the experience with both hands, stay true to yourself, honor your inner strength, and live!" Macha reaches over and kisses you soundly before encircling you in her strong arms. A tingling sensation runs over your skin, and you see that Macha once again has turned into her crow form. This time, however, you are not afraid. You feel her warm, soft feathers tickling your arms, and you know that this is but one more change, one more incarnation of the many that are to come. You stroke the feathers along her back, and with a squawk, Macha rises into the sky and resumes the size of every other earthly crow. You shield your eyes from the hot sun to watch her flight. As she wheels over the rounded mound in salute to you, she is joined by two more crows who circle and dart around her. They fly once more around the mound before starting off toward the west, cawing a raucous goodbye to you.

Without Macha's body blocking the way, you race through the two gateway trees and up the rounded hill. Clouds scuttle across the sky, and the wind whips across the land. Your clothes blow behind you as you spread your arms wide and twirl. Before you get too dizzy, you stop and shout triumphantly up to the sky. With raised fists, you claim your strength, and then you run back down, full of the knowledge of your inner power, confident in your ability to face any challenge.

Now take a deep breath, in through your nose and out through your mouth. Take another deep breath, filling your stomach, your diaphragm, and finally your lungs. Hold this breath for five seconds … 1-2-3-4-5 … and exhale, allowing the breath to exit your lungs first, then your diaphragm, and finally your stomach. Breathe deeply once more, and as you breathe in, feel the energy and the wonder of the world around you in your fingers, your toes, your legs, and your shoulders, even the top of your head. As you exhale, wiggle your fingers and toes. Shake your legs and move your shoulders up and down. Take another deep breath and, as you exhale, move your head from side to side. Feel the ground under your body touching every nerve ending and muscle. Hear the rustlings of the people around you. Notice the movements outside. Continue breathing. Stretch your arms out above your head. You are returning to the present, to the here and now. Continue stretching. Continue breathing. When you are ready, open your eyes, blink and focus, and sit up.

INVOCATION TO MACHA

Glorious one,
Of wind and change,
Of beginnings and endings,
I honor you
For you are the thrust of life.

Steely-eyed, you face down foes.
Soft of limb, you embrace love.

Feather-down, you mark the gateway.
Rough of hand, you clear the space.

To live
To grow
To birth
To sustain
To transform
To convert
To move
To kill
To die

You are the ever-changing,
Glorious one,
Macha.
I honor you
For you are the thrust of life.

MAGICAL ACTIVITIES

Elemental Magic (Air): Sweeping Away the Clutter

Items Needed: A broom; a raven, crow, or simple black feather; sage; purified water in a navy blue spray bottle; cornmeal; a gray candle; a lighter or book of matches; and a dustpan

Moon Phase: Waning

Seasonal Cycle: Any (but especially powerful when conducting spring cleaning)

Go to the sacred space where you typically perform your magic and rituals. Keep all of your items outside the space, except for the broom. Holding the broom in the center of your ritual space, take a deep, cleansing breath and let it out slowly. You are here to clear away any old magical energies that may have lingered in your area, cleansing yourself in the process.

Standing in the north and keeping your magical purpose in mind, physically sweep the floor or ground of your northern space, from the outer edges of the area toward the center. Do this as many times as you need to, and then sweep your broom in a counterclockwise direction toward the west. Sweep the western energies into the center, and then turn to the south. After the south has been swept, move to the east, and then finally, go back to the north. After sweeping your entire sacred space, you should have a pile of debris in the center of your circle. Place your broom with the rest of your items and sweep the pile into the dustpan. Hold on to the magical residue until after the spell is complete. Bring the dustpan outside your magical area and bring in the feather, sage, purified water, cornmeal, and candle and lighter.

Take your feather and, once again beginning in the north, sweep the air of your ritual space in a counterclockwise direction. While doing this, you might wish to say the Invocation to Macha, chant her name over and over again, or create your own Macha poem. You are calling on her energy as space-clearer and remover of the unnecessary. When you are finished with your sacred space, be sure to sweep the feather down your body as well, getting rid of long-held beliefs or issues that are not conducive to your growth.

Next, take the cornmeal and go to the northern area of your sacred space. State out loud all of the qualities of the north that come to mind. Name animals, gods, goddesses, crystals, colors, faeries, and so forth. When you are finished, place a small handful of the cornmeal on the ground and sprinkle some on the top of your head. Continue naming each of the elemental energies while moving in a clockwise direction, using the sage for east, the candle for south, and the purified water for west. Be sure to take the time to connect with each direction and to finish each elemental offering by purifying yourself with the smoke, flame, and water. (Do not burn yourself with the flame of the south. Simply allow the flame's glow to caress your body, enveloping you in its heat and light.)

Your sacred space is now cleared of any leftover magic and you are purified of past negativities in your life. Rejoice and praise Macha, the space-clearer, the initiator, goddess of the gateway! When you leave your sacred space, take all of your implements with you, especially the dustpan full of debris. Save this dust and dirt in a plastic, air-tight container until a very windy day. Then go outside and release the debris, allowing the wind to carry it to the four corners of the earth, cleansing it as it travels.

Candle Magic: Your Power Candle

Items Needed: A large red pillar candle, a lighter or book of matches, a needle or inscribing tool, thyme essential oil, a wet facecloth (optional), and paper and pencil (optional)

Moon Phase: Full

Seasonal Cycle: Any, but especially powerful during the summer

On a clear, moonlit night, gather all of your items together in a place where you can easily view the full moon. Take a few moments to ground and center. When you feel relaxed, think of all of the symbols that represent people and events in your life and throughout history that remind you of strength and courage. If you wish, write down these symbols on your piece of paper so you will not forget any later on. Consider these symbols in your meditative state until you have sorted through them all and chosen the nine that resonate most strongly with you.

With the moonlight bathing your body and your magical implements, inscribe these nine symbols onto your red candle using your needle or inscribing tool. Take your time with each symbol, naming it out loud and running your fingers over the rough surface it creates. Feel the smooth softness of the candle and the hard edges where the symbols bite into the wax. Become intimately aware of the changes you are making on the surface of this candle.

When you have inscribed and named the last symbol, take the thyme essential oil and rub it thoroughly into the candle, sweeping from the bottom up to the top. Use your whole hand, and cup the candle as you massage the oil into the wax. Don't be afraid to get your hands oily. Make sure you have covered every inch of the candle with oil, even the bottom and top. While you are putting the oil onto your candle, continue to focus on your nine symbols of courage and strength. If your mind is wandering, name the symbols out loud as a way to increase your concentration.

Light the candle and place it in the moonlight. Allow the candle to burn until you go to bed. Keep the candle in the light of the moon while you sleep, soaking up the energy of the Goddess until the next morning. This candle is meant to be a holder of power for you. Anytime you need an extra boost of strength or courage, take out this candle and light it. The symbols will infuse you with their power, giving you easier access to your inner will and strength.

Faery Magic: Creating Macha's Gateway

Items Needed: A piece of 8 x 10 paper; colored markers, crayons, or pencils; a tree pendant; sparkles; dried honeysuckle; a clove of garlic; a small trowel; a flat rock; a blanket (optional); a flat board or lap desk (optional)

Moon Phase: Dark or new

Seasonal Cycle: Any

As a multilayered, dualistic, Otherworldly goddess, Macha has much in common with the fey. Her role as caretaker and fruitful provider in "The Pangs of Ulster" has many faery overtones, especially her warning to keep quiet about her skills, her silent demeanor when she first arrives, and her amazing speed and skill in outrunning a pair of horses. The fact that she is described as beautiful, that Crunniuc never calls her by name, and that she has the ability to shape-shift are also clues to her connection to the denizens of faery. It is important to note that while we in the modern era think of faeries as tiny, light, ethereal beings with wings, the ancient Celts possessed a broader view of the appearance of "the good folk." Faeries were both good and bad, beautiful and ugly, and kind and mean in the ancient past. Macha fits right in with all of the other "goodly neighbors" when viewed with this knowledge.

On a day when the sun is bright and the sky is blue, gather all of your magical items and head out into the great outdoors. Allow yourself to wander about, sensing the environment for the perfect place for your ritual. Ideally, there would be several trees about, preferably surrounding the sacred space, but as long as there is one tree nearby and the space feels right, you should trust your instincts.

Once you have found your sacred space, set up your items and, spread out your blanket if you have a blanket. Sit down and, holding your tree pendant, think back to your meditation with Macha. Consider all of the experiences in your life that have forced you to grow and increased your well of inner strength. Name at least three specific experiences while holding your pendant. When you feel like you are sufficiently connected to your own personal power, get up and hold your pendant at each of the nearby trees in your sacred area. At each tree, say, "This tree is the tree on my pendant. My pendant tree is the tree at Emain Macha. The tree at Emain Macha is me. Through the mysteries of the Otherworld and by the magic of Macha, this tree and I are one." Slam your pendant against the tree, mimicking the actions of Macha in your meditation. When you have connected to all of the trees in your sacred space, return to your magical items and sit down.

Take out your paper and colored markers and pencils. The time has come for you to create a visual reminder of the gateway of Macha, the space between day and night, life and death, and love and war that Macha straddles. When times get difficult, as they are wont to do, you can visit this gateway in the physical and astral planes in order to gain perspective, tapping into your inner wisdom and knowledge.

Sit with your paper in your lap and your colored markers, crayons, and pencils within easy reach. Close your eyes and relax, allowing your mind to drift. Think of all of the elements and symbols in Macha's stories. Consider Macha herself as well as your journey to visit with her. Allow a doorway or gateway to form in your mind. See it in all its splendor and glory. Where is it located—near a brook, a forest, or a field? What color is it? What materials is it made out of—stones, wood, bricks, bones? Now draw that image on your paper to the best of your ability. Take as much time as you need, and don't be afraid to take breaks during the creation process. Close your eyes and visualize the gate as often as you like. Stretch your legs and visit with the trees in your sacred circle. Listen to the birds and the small animals and bugs. But always keep in mind your goal of creating Macha's gateway to the Otherworld. After exploring your inner and outer worlds and drawing on them for your inspiration, complete your drawing by signing your name and sprinkling it with some sparkles. Take your rock and, using markers, draw a symbol on the stone that reminds you of your doorway and of the goddess Macha.

Stand up. Hold the paper and the rock to your heart, then up to the sun. Twirl around nine times, and (while dizzy) stagger around your sacred space until you fall down. Mark that spot and dig a small hole. Rip up your picture into lots of tiny pieces and fling them into your hole, repeating the phrase, "Macha's gateway is here for me, hidden away from all who'd see," until the entire picture is inside the hole. Next, add a handful of dried honeysuckle with the words, "Life, light, abundance, growth." Drop in the garlic with the phrase, "Death, darkness, resistance, decline." Cover the hole with the dirt, saying, "I honor Macha, goddess divine." Now place your rock on top of the newly covered hole, knowing that this is your physical connection to the gateway of Macha. Without looking back, gather all of your remaining magical items and leave your sacred space, touching each of the trees with your tree pendant to release your intimate connection with them. You have now created a sacred link to Macha, and you can visit your sacred space anytime you need to remember your own inner strength and power.

LESSONS FROM
THE NORSE

MEETING FRIGGA, NORSE GODDESS OF PROPHECY AND THE HEARTH
Increasing Your Psychic Power

FRIGGA: LADY OF CONTAINMENT

Frigga (pronounced FREE-gah) is the goddess of women, secrecy, fated knowledge, and the household. She is the queen of heaven, who looks out over all of the worlds from the high seat of Hlidskialf—the only other god besides Odin (her husband) to have such a privilege. Knowledge of ancient Norse women's ways is hidden in her mysteries, behind the folds of her voluminous skirts. As the seeress, she is connected to the Norns, mythic beings and energies reminiscent of the Greek Fates. Like them, she is forever entwined in the fabric of humanity through her spinning and her distaff. If you desire fertility and motherhood (or fatherhood), Frigga will hear your plea and intervene on your behalf. Wish for a loving companion and partner, and Frigga will assist you. She is a goddess who knows the power of a happy home life and is pleased to help you create your ideal in the world. Frigga knows that the power of the world resides not in its political centers, but in its homes.

In the Poetic Edda, one of several medieval Norse mythological manuscripts, Frigga is said to be "Fjorgynn's maid," a term usually translated as "daughter." Little is known of Fjorgynn, except his fatherly role to Frigga. However, the name "Fjorgyn" is connected to the birth of another Norse god, Thor. Fjorgyn is the mother of Thor, first wife of Odin, and it is also one of many names for an ancient earth goddess. It is tantalizing to speculate that Fjorgyn and Fjorgynn are related in some way, but there is no mention of a connection between the mother of Thor and the father of Frigga in the Norse Eddas.[1] However, brother-sister and husband-wife partnerships can be found in Norse literature in the pairings of Freyja-Frey and Nerthus-Njord; therefore, there is the possibility that Frigga is sister to Thor, as well as stepmother.

Odin, Frigga's husband and Thor's father, is well-known for his extramarital affairs. (See the chapter on Skadhi for an example.) As the wife to the All-Father of the Norse gods, Frigga accepts her husband's wandering and philandering ways. She tolerates his retinue of beautiful Valkyries, his varied pairings with giantesses, and even his marriage to Freyja in the guise of "Od." Indeed, while Odin goes off to travel amid the worlds, searching for information and wisdom, Frigga stays at home, safe and secure with her own inner knowledge. (Loki, Norse God of chaos and mischief, charges that she actually takes two husbands in Odin's absence: Odin's brothers, the gods Vili and Ve. This may be a case of the queen granting sovereignty and the right to rule to her husband,

---

1. Gundarsson, *Our Troth*, 326.

through the sharing of her bed and her body.[2]) When Odin returns from his adventures, he reclaims his place by Frigga's side, relishing her security and safety. It is possible that Frigga's stabilizing presence allows Odin to feel comfortable in journeying far and wide and undergoing fantastical and exceptional triumphs and trials. Her blanket of protection may give him the strength to venture forth and push the boundaries of accepted conventions and social mores.

When Loki crashes a dinner of the gods and begins to criticize and ridicule each god in turn, in the Poetic Edda's "Lokasenna," it is Frigga who stands up for Odin. When confronted by some of her husband's more salacious activities, Frigga simply reminds both Loki and Odin that such talk is inappropriate. Outlining proper behavior to the gods, she says:

> Of the deeds ye two of old have done
> Ye should make no speech among men;
> Whate'er ye have done in days gone by,
> Old tales should ne'er be told.[3]

Since Frigga does not refute the charge, she is probably embarrassed not by Odin's past activities, but the impropriety of speaking about them in a large gathering. Just as Odin needs Frigga for her stability, so Frigga needs Odin for his wildness and freedom. Throughout the Eddas, Odin is referred to as "Frigg's delight"[4] and "the joy of Frigg."[5] He is said to lie in "Frigg's embrace,"[6] and it is obvious she cares about him from an exchange they have in the "Vafthrudnismal" in the Poetic Edda.

Odin announces his intention to visit the giant Vafthrudnir to pit his wisdom against the all-wise giant. Immediately, Frigga voices her desire for Odin to stay at home, safe and secure in Asgard, the world of the gods, saying:

> Heerfather here at home would I keep,
> Where the gods together dwell;

---

2. Paxson, "Beloved."

3. Bellows, *Poetic Edda*, 160, verse 25.

4. Sturluson, *Edda*, 55.

5. Bellows, *Poetic Edda*, 22, verse 53.

6. Sturluson, *Edda*, 67.

Amid all the giants an equal in might
To Vafthruthnir know I none.[7]

Odin, ignores her wish, stating that he wants to know what kind of hospitality is offered at the giant's hall. (In truth, he wants to know the wisdom and knowledge that
Vafthrudnir keeps.) Frigga counters with a chant of protective wardings that sound
magical in tone and cadence. She states:

Safe mayst thou go, safe come again,
And safe be the way thou wendest![8]

Frigga's power to protect keeps Odin from harm on this occasion. However, she does
not reserve her protective embrace only for the All-Father. Utilizing her foreknowledge,
Frigga's faithful followers are also shielded from harm.

Strong, caring, and wise, Frigga dares to oppose her husband on several occasions
in order to care for her loyal devotees on earth. Yet her resistance to her husband's will
is not blatant. She gets her own way through careful planning, knowledge of the inner
depths of the soul and the future, and sly cunning. In *The History of the Langobard Folk*,
a Germanic text written by Deacon Paul of Warnfriet, Frigga and Odin are backing opposing sides in a war between the Vandals and the Vinnili. Odin promises the Vandals
that he will grant victory to whichever side he sees first upon awakening, and since the
Vandals are positioned on the side on which he wakes up, they are assured victory.

That evening, Gambara, the mother of the leader of the Vinnili, prays to Frigga, asking for success for her tribe. Frigga tells Gambara to have all of the women of the Vinnili
leave their tents before sunrise on the following day with their hair combed over their
faces. Some sources indicate that Frigga turned Odin's bed around so he would see the
Vinnili women upon arising, others that she directed the women where to stand. Either
way, Odin awoke to the sight of the Vinnili women and their long, hair-covered faces
and exclaimed, "Who are these long beards?" Thus renaming the tribe, Odin was forced
to grant them victory through the craftiness of his wife.[9]

Frigga's power, then, is not in her manipulation of the material world, as with spellwork or magic, but in knowing the truth of a person and situation and being able to

---

7. Bellows, *Poetic Edda*, 69, verse 2.

8. Ibid., 69, verse 4.

9. Deacon Paul, *History of the Langobard Folk*.

turn it to her will. As the keeper of great knowledge between the worlds, Frigga is a powerful seeress, yet she keeps her wisdom to herself. When speaking up for Frigga in the "Lokasenna," Freyja states, "The fate of all does Frigg know well, / Though herself she says it not."[10] This foreknowledge is not simply prophecy or the possible future outcome of various actions. Rather, Frigga is the possessor of *orlog* (Old Norse for "destiny"), universal forces, actions, and laws that are unalterable and that affect both humans and the gods.

Orlog contains those parts of yourself and your destiny that are unchangeable: your immediate family, your ancestors, your country of origin, your genetic makeup, your innate skills, and the past actions and events in your life. It also encapsulates the unalterable destinies of larger groups of people, and even the world. Orlog is beyond fate, because it cannot be changed. It makes up the backbone of fate, the very basis of ourselves and our world.[11] Think of orlog as the warp on a loom, the stabilizing threads between which the shuttle weaves. The thread in the shuttle, known as weft or woof, represents our current actions and choices, otherwise known as *wyrd* (Old English for "fate"). We can change the color of the weft, the pattern of the overall piece of cloth, and the speed at which the shuttle moves. However, we can never change the threads between which it moves. The orlog remains absolute, that which has happened yet still affects us on a daily basis. Both orlog and wyrd make up our lives and our fates (and both collectively can also be known as wyrd), and it is this beautiful weaving, the emerging tapestry, that Frigga is able to discern.

The weaving of life is managed by the Norns, Norse goddesses of fate and destiny. They sit at the roots of Yggdrasil, the World Tree, and gaze into the Well of Urd, monitoring the actions of humans and gods alike. The three most well-known Norns are the sisters Urd ("that which is"), Verdandi ("that which is becoming"), and Skuld ("that which shall be"). As a textile goddess, it is not surprising that Frigga shares the knowledge of the universal loom of life with the Norns. Frigga is often depicted spinning, and the distaff serves as one of her most powerful symbols. The constellation of Orion is

---

10. Bellows, *Poetic Edda*, 161, verse 29.

11. Orlog and wyrd are very complex concepts. Whole books have been written about them. This definition is, of necessity, in simplified form, and has been taken from the writings of Freya Aswynn, *Northern Mysteries and Magick: Runes, Gods and Feminine Mysteries* (St. Paul, MN: Llewellyn Publications, 1998), 241–242.

known in the northlands as Frigga's distaff,[12] and the magic of spinning gauzy wool into one stabilizing thread is a powerful symbol for orlog and wyrd. Through her spinning, she is often able to bend fate in order to protect her worshippers, lovers, and friends.

There are two occasions on which Frigga, despite her foreknowledge, is unable to change fate, bowing instead to the universal force of orlog. Both involve the two loves of her life: her son Baldr and her husband, Odin. The true fate of Odin has yet to play out, as he is destined to die by the jaws of the huge wolf monster Fenris, child of Loki, at the world-ending, god-killing battle of Ragnarok. The story of Baldr, however, has already occurred, unfolding in the "Gylfaginning" in the Prose Edda. Baldr, golden god of light who made everyone smile and made everything bright, was tormented with horrible, prophetic dreams of his death. The gods decided that they would ask everything in the known world to promise to spare Baldr, thus forestalling his death. Frigga journeyed throughout the worlds, asking all of the metals, plants, animals, and people to give their oaths not to harm her son. They all willingly pledged to save Baldr, and Frigga returned home to Asgard, secure in her son's safety.

The gods of Asgard now took to throwing random objects at Baldr as a game, watching him come to no harm no matter what was thrown. Ever the mischief-maker, Loki disguised himself as a woman and, traveling to Fensalir (Frigga's Hall), learned that Frigga did not extract an oath from the small, puny plant known as mistletoe. Loki gathered the plant and, taking it to Asgard, gave it to Baldr's blind brother, Hod, prodding him to "Follow other people's example and do Baldr honor like other people. I will direct you to where he is standing. Shoot at him with this stick."[13] Needless to say, Hod hit Baldr squarely with the mistletoe and Baldr fell to the ground, dead.

It is in her capacity as the weeping, wailing mother of Baldr that Frigga displays her connection to motherhood and the bond between mother and child. Her knowledge of orlog is said to come to her as she stands at the birth of every child born. And although she could not change her son's fate, she is known to intercede in the lives of couples who wish for children.[14] Frigga is the universal mother who understands the pains of life and does her best to guard her loved ones. She is the mother who tried to snatch her beloved

12. Gundarsson, *Our Troth*, 332.

13. Sturluson, *Edda*, 48.

14. Byock, *Saga of the Volsungs*.

son from the jaws of death, only to realize that her power does not extend to the laws of the universe.

Yet Frigga holds sway over the four elements of earth, air, fire, and water. As Baldr's mother, she is able to reach out to the plants and animals of the earth in order to extract promises from them. As the queen of heaven, she stands at the All-Father's side and is able to look into all nine worlds that compose Norse cosmology. As the goddess of the household, the hearth fire is her domain, warming all who enter her presence with the security of kinship and the safety of love. As the mistress of the Hall Fensalir, or Marsh Hall, she lives in the boggy ground of shifting patterns, which gives her future knowledge and the power to prophesy.

Strong and silent, Frigga stands among the Norse gods as an embodiment of human life on earth. She knows all but says nothing. She loves deeply, risking her heart despite the knowledge of impending doom. She is not misty-eyed with love or consumed with passion. She is neither a knowledge-seeking scholar nor a green-thumbed farmer. She is a mother and a housewife, and yet she is so much more. As the spinner of the life force of mankind, she is the connector, the link between earth, air, fire, and water. With her threads, Frigga creates the bond between the Gods and humanity, between women and men, between mother and child. Frigga consorts with the future but lives in the present and remembers the past. She is ancient and old beyond reckoning yet forever changing shape and focus and skill. She is as transient as a cloud of smoke and as stable as your mother's arms. And throughout it all, she loves with an open heart, forever pure and selfless, forever willing to hear our voices and our cries for help. (Just don't expect her to say very much!)

PSYCHIC POWER: THE INNER REALMS

The power to see into the future is glamorized by our modern society. We see telephone psychics on infomercials getting rich by giving advice on everything from business to love to money. Psychics help police find missing children, seek answers for grieving mothers and fathers, and even talk to the dead. They have access to a world that is hidden from most of humanity. Psychics see, hear, and feel things that others do not comprehend. Their power is tangible. We can see the results, but we do not know the inner pathways by which they realized those results. We see the point of origin and the destination on the map, but not the roads that connect them.

Everyone is born with varying degrees of psychic ability. Not everyone can talk to the dead, just as not everyone can bake a soufflé or dance in a ballet or paint a masterpiece. Psychic ability is as much an art as dancing, writing, or painting, and as such, there are no clear-cut ways to learn, experience, and express your psychic skills. You may be able to tell when your mother is going to call. You may have dreams that come true and materialize as déjà vu. You may be able to get images and meanings from a deck of tarot cards or from passages in the Bible. You may hear a ringing in your ears when you enter a cemetery or a tingling in your hands and feet when you walk into the woods. All of these experiences are examples of innate psychic ability, and they all have worth and merit.

Using your own inner self as guidance, begin to work with the psychic skills that you have. If you know when the phone rings that it's your mom on the line, try sending a psychic message to her to call you, and then see if she does. If your dreams come true, begin keeping a dream journal and try lucid dreaming, a technique of ordering the outcome of your dreams. If you feel sensations at different locations, go visit them and meditate there. Write down any information that comes to you spontaneously, either while you're walking around or while you're in a trance. Practice reading tarot for friends and see if your predictions come true. In short, work with yourself. Honor your own psychic gifts and make them your own.

THE PATHWORKING

When we meditate, we are outside of the boundaries of time and space. We are one with the flowers and trees, one with our breathing and our blood, one with past ancestors and generations to come. Yet it is easy to become obsessed with moving forward quickly. Instead of enjoying the moment we are experiencing in the meditation, our brains try to skip ahead, wondering what could come next and guessing our next move.

Your upcoming visit with Frigga is very slow, with little action. You must be able to sit and simply be in the moment. This meditation is an exercise in taking your time in order to notice everything around you, to acknowledge your feelings, and to connect to the land of the queen of the Asynjur. Every step, every fiber of cloth, and every fireside spark should be noted and experienced fully. Oftentimes, the most insignificant detail adds meaning and insight to a journey into the Otherworld.

Should you find that you are having difficulty taking your time, focus on one small detail in the meditation. It could be the pattern of the tiles on the floor, the shape and texture of your hands, or the sound of a scurrying mouse or squirrel. Centering your attention will help you to sink into that exact moment in the meditation and will remind you that you do not need to rush to get to the end. Remember, the journey itself is the path you seek.

GUIDED MEDITATION: INCREASING YOUR PSYCHIC POWER

Take a deep breath, in through your nose and out through your mouth. Take another deep breath, filling your stomach, your diaphragm, and finally your lungs. Hold this breath for five seconds … 1-2-3-4-5 … and exhale, allowing the breath to exit your lungs first, then your diaphragm, and finally your stomach. Take one more deep breath, and as you breathe in, feel the energy of warm hearth fires enter you, supporting your fingers, your toes, your legs, and your shoulders, even the top of your head. Hold the breath for seven seconds … 1-2-3-4-5-6-7. As you exhale, feel all tension leave your fingers, your toes, your legs, and your shoulders, even the top of your head. Continue breathing deeply, in through your nose and out through your mouth. Feel the close, comforting warmth of a communal fire. Pine scent wafts toward you as bits of sap snap and pop, exploding into bursts of light. You are encircled by a glowing circle of gold, warm and secure, safe from the harsh outside world. Allow the warm, protected heat to melt away any remaining fear and anxiety. You have never felt so relaxed, so secure, so calm.

You are walking in a gray world of marsh and fog. You can see nothing but the swirling mist and the soft, boggy green ground directly under your body. After each step, the world behind you disappears, swallowed up by the dank mist. A bullfrog croaks off to your right and you hear the splash and hiss of a water snake entering the marshes. From behind, you feel the wind from many fluttering wings as a pack of geese rises from the branches of a waterlogged tree. Their voices soar and squawk behind you and far above, becoming fainter and fainter until eventually they disappear altogether. You are alone and not alone in this world of fog as you tentatively place one foot in front of the other, careful to test your footing before placing your full weight upon the boggy ground. Alert, tense, without the sense of sight, you follow the path before you, one step at a time.

After what seems a very long time, the path opens up to a large section of land. The mist thins slightly, and you can see that the land forms a large island in the middle of the marshlands. The trees fall behind you, giving rise to narrow strips of pastureland where fleecy sheep graze contentedly. A large, gray, two-storied wooden dwelling materializes out of the mist. It appears strong and sturdy, with heavy beams serving as posts and crossbeams. Symbols are carved into the wood, and a single sculpture of a mask hangs over the doorway. Marsh mist from behind you tickles the nape of your neck, causing an uncomfortable shiver and compelling you to knock on the door.

A shining lady in deep garnet red answers the door. She smiles at you and beckons for you to enter the holding. You step over the threshold, and the door swiftly closes behind you. The click of the latch reverberates inside your head. The lady swiftly and gracefully sweeps through the second door of the lodging, holding it open for you to pass through. You catch a glimpse of a multitude of keys hanging from her golden belt, and a modest white chemise peeks out above the bodice and below the sleeves of her gown. Her ginger hair is upswept, forming a loose knot at the back of her head and showing off a long neck and regal face. Her cheeks are plump, her bosom full, and no lines or wrinkles form around her warm, serious, knowing eyes. The second door clicks softly into place, and the lady gestures you to the right, toward a huge hearth.

Your feet tap gently on the gray flagstone floor as you silently walk behind the lady toward the fire. The hearth is enormous, taking up the whole wall of the large room. At the edges it recedes into a formless darkness that seems to drift endlessly. The hearth towers above you by six or eight feet, the fire larger than anything you can imagine or comprehend. Yet the heat is calming and soothing, relaxing, making you want to curl up on the hearthside rug and take a nap. The lady motions you to a wooden seat, high-backed and shaped in the form of flames of fire or fronds of leaves. The lady sits beside you in a similar chair, but a spinning wheel, a basket of carded wool, and a length of yarn rest next to her. With deft hands, she picks up a handful of wool and begins to spin it into thread.

"I am Frigga," she says as she works, her eyes downcast and focused on her moving hands. "I am lady of this holding. Who, may I ask, are you?" You tell Frigga your name. (pause) She nods knowingly, her mouth upturned in a slight grin. "Why do you visit me here at Fensalir, braving the marshy depths and boggy bottoms?" the goddess asks. "What do you seek?" She turns her eyes toward you, and you see the swirling cosmos in them. You see the knowledge of all that is to be hidden in their unreachable depths.

Tell Frigga your reasoning for venturing beyond your own self to her hall of wisdom. Tell her of your wish to access your own psychic powers and see into the heart of the universe. (pause)

Frigga sighs. "The power of foresight is not to be granted lightly. With my wisdom comes pain and suffering, knowledge of that which cannot be changed. You must have the fortitude to see the future for its truth, the courage to accept what cannot be altered, the wisdom to know when impending actions may indeed shape the course of destinies, of lives, of fates. Do you accept this responsibility? Think on it now. Do not rush into an answer." You think of your current psychic skills and the abilities you hope to attain. Ask yourself why you wish your powers to increase. Be aware of your motives and the reasoning for your quest. (pause) When you are satisfied with your answers, give Frigga an answer to her question. (pause: If you choose not to enhance your psychic skills at this time, skip to the last paragraph of the meditation. If you choose to accept the responsibility of her power, tell Frigga now.)

"Very well," Frigga says, her hands ever busy at the spindle of her spinning wheel. "I would ask you to give your oath to me that the power of prophecy will not be misused by you for illicit profit or gain. I ask for your word that you will use your psychic skills for the benefit of those around you." In your own words, state your unbreakable, binding oath to Frigga. (pause) As you utter your last word, Frigga stands and moves to the side of her chair.

"Come, my child," she says warmly. "Come and sit in my seat of power." The fire roars before you, and darkness encompasses the edges of your vision. You sit in Frigga's seat. Firelight bounces off the thread in the spinning wheel, landing on the skein of wool that materializes in your hand. Golden and amber light flickers at your feet, forming a circle around your body. Blackness envelops the rest of the room; you sense a vast space without time and distance, an immenseness that is frightening and thrilling at the same time. (pause) You no longer see Frigga but feel her hands upon yours as you begin to deftly spin the wool into yarn, as you begin to view the creation as one of a multitude of yarns in the warp of the world. The spinning wheel whirls faster and faster as your hands gently tug and pull the life of the thread into existence. Images begin to form in the blinding, merging union of the turning wheel. View the visions and remember them for later. (long pause)

As the spinning wheel slows its frantic pace, you begin to leave your trancelike state. You see your hands working the wool quite expertly now, and without the weight of

Frigga's guidance. You feel the hands of the goddess on your head, soothing, imparting assistance and help, should you ever need it. (pause) Her touch is firm, strong, and sure, linked to the bounty of earth, the wisdom of air, the passion of fire, and the emotion of water. She is one with your ancestors, and with your children, and with your children's children for generations to come. She is the All-Mother, peaceful and secure, first among the Norse goddesses, Beloved.

The spinning wheel stops, and you rest your hands in your lap, still clutching the remnants of the thread you created. You feel a soft kiss brush the top of your head, and then you are lifted effortlessly from the seat and placed on the hearth rug in front of the fire. Suddenly, you feel very tired, and you melt into the warming embrace of the heat from the fire. Soft hands smooth the hair from your face and settle blankets along your body.

"You have done well, little one," Frigga's voice floats to you from afar, soft and melodic. "Sleep now, knowing that I will watch over you." You take a deep, contented breath and drift into dreamtime.

Now take a deep breath, in through your nose and out through your mouth. Take another deep breath, filling your stomach, your diaphragm, and finally your lungs. Hold this breath for five seconds … 1-2-3-4-5 … and exhale, allowing the breath to exit your lungs first, then your diaphragm, and finally your stomach. Breathe deeply once more, and as you breathe in, feel the energy and the wonder of the world around you in your fingers, your toes, your legs, and your shoulders, even the top of your head. As you exhale, wiggle your fingers and toes. Shake your legs and move your shoulders up and down. Take another deep breath and, as you exhale, move your head from side to side. Feel the ground under your body touching every nerve ending and muscle. Hear the rustlings of the people around you. Notice the movements outside. Continue breathing. Stretch your arms out above your head. You are returning to the present, to the here and now. Continue stretching. Continue breathing. When you are ready, open your eyes, blink and focus, and sit up.

INVOCATION TO FRIGGA

Frigga, beautiful one
Blessed among goddesses and women.
I care for thee and speak to thee from the heart.
Do me honor and listen.

Sovereign Mother of kingship, I welcome thee.
All-powerful Queen of Heaven, I honor thee.
Subtle Spinner of life's thread, I respect thee.
Wise knower of orlog, I revere thee.

I wish you happiness always—
Kindling love of Odin,
Warmth of hearth and home,
Peace of heart and mind,
Knowledge of future events,
Changing power of old.

May your bright wisdom shine on me,
Illuminating my love,
Brightening my future,
Heating my heart and my soul.
Bring to me your wisdom of all.
Cradle me in your arms of strength.

Frigga, beautiful one
Blessed among goddesses and women.
I care for thee and ask you to speak to me from the heart.
I do thee honor and listen.

MAGICAL ACTIVITIES

Incense Magic: Up in Smoke

Items Needed: Incense in your choice of scent and an incense holder
Moon Phase: Any
Seasonal Cycle: Any

Incense is magical in its own right. It is a physical object that, when burned, emits a pleasing aroma and disappears into a pile of soft ash. It can uplift the mood, dissipate depression, and spread peace and harmony. Not only does incense evoke a magical essence by itself, but it is often paired with ritual behavior. It is common in Eastern religions for incense to be used as an offering to the gods or ancestors. The smoke drifts up to the deities and ancestors and lets them know that they are remembered and honored. Since Frigga is connected to all four elements, incense magic works with her air-aligned, regal nature as the queen of heaven, wife to the powerful All-Father of Asgard, the highest of the nine worlds in Norse cosmology. In this aspect, Frigga can grant powerful wishes, especially those concerned with family life, fertility, protection, security, and prophecy. Frigga understands all human needs, and by honoring her, you enrich your life in many, varied ways.

Decide on a general purpose for your magic spell. You might simply choose to pay respect to Frigga and invite her into your life, allowing her to bring her many gifts and skills. However, if you have a magical goal, you can certainly ask Frigga for her help in that specific area of your life as you light your incense in her honor. The choice of incense scent and style should be based on your individual needs. Some people prefer loose incense that is burned over charcoal discs, as it often has a stronger scent and is not mixed with other unknown substances. Others like stick and cone incense, since they are simple to use, easy to find, and last for a long time. The choice is yours. All three types of incense produce smoke, which is what you are after.

The scent of the incense is completely up to you. You might want to use an herb that is related to your goal, or you might wish to burn incense specific to the goddess Frigga. Scott Cunningham lists mistletoe as Frigga's herb.[15] Although this herb is associated with Frigga in Norse mythology, I personally would not burn it in her honor, as it would be a reminder of the death of her son and her inability to protect him. Raven Kaldera, a well-known Pagan author, has compiled a Norse herbal that connects several herbs with each Norse deity. For Frigga, he lists the herbs birch, lady's mantle, shepherd's purse, thyme, weld, and flax.[16] You can try any of these scents or follow your own intuition and go with one of your own choosing. While the scent is important, your intent is equally powerful.

Once you have chosen your incense, it is time to light it and send your respects and wishes up to the queen of Asgard. Think for a few moments on Frigga, your goal, and your life and how it will be enriched by the granting of your desire and by a deeper connection with her. When you feel ready, light your incense, and know that your thoughts are being brought up to Frigga by the smoke. Watch the smoke. See if it forms any inter-

---

15. Cunningham, *Encyclopedia of Magical Herbs*, 154.
16. Kaldera, "Northern-Tradition Shamanism Herbal."

esting patterns. Can you see the future in it? Allow the incense to continue to burn, and after a few moments, go about your everyday life. The smell of the incense will probably linger in your house, in your hair, and on your clothes, reminding you of your connection to the goddess Frigga and her power to help you manifest your goals in your life.

Elemental Magic (Fire): Bringing Peace into the Home

> Items Needed: A fairly large fire, your family, candles (one candle for each room in your house), candle holders for each candle, marshmallows and sticks (optional), a book of Norse myths (optional), and blankets and pillows (optional)
>
> Moon Phase: Waxing or full
>
> Seasonal Cycle: Winter

As the tender of the hearth fire while Odin wanders on his adventures, Frigga understands the importance of a well-kept, ordered, peaceful, and happy home. The energy of our home life seeps into all aspects of our lives, affecting us in ways we can only briefly understand. Our homes are our sanctuaries, the one place where we can rest our heads, remove our shields (both psychic and physical), and truly relax.

For this spell, you will need a working fireplace. If you don't have one in your home, use a large- to medium-size cauldron or a fire pit outside. This spell would be best performed in the evening hours with all electric lights turned off so that the light and warmth from the fire can create a soothing, comforting feeling. It should be rather like wrapping yourself in a warm, snuggly blanket. Any time of the year will work, but the spell will be especially powerful during the shorter, colder winter months, which are evocative of the northlands in which Frigga makes her home.

Light a fire in your fireplace, cauldron, or fire pit. Gather together your family, and roast marshmallows over the fire. Gaze into the fire and try to discern the future from its flames. (Remember, Frigga is a seeress who sees all.) Read aloud a myth about Frigga and discuss this powerful goddess with all of your family members. (Children are more receptive than you might think!) Perform any number of fun activities with your family, pouring your family's positive energy into the leaping flames.

I realize that keeping a family focused and positive is difficult, especially if you have children that are often at odds. Explain to them that you are seeking to lighten the energy in the house, creating a happier, more peaceful environment for everyone. If they slip into negative behavior, don't worry that your spell may be ruined. Simply ask the fire to burn away the negative energy and transform it into positive. You can even make a game out of it with your children, hopefully lightening any tense moments. However your family reacts, it is up to you to focus on the positive energy created by their togetherness. This is the energy you want to keep in your house: the happy, peaceful, loving energy of a family in harmony.

After you have enjoyed the light and heat from the fire, light candles from the central hearth fire, making sure you have one candle for each room in your house. Have your family members distribute the candles around the house in the dark, using only the light from the candle to guide them. (Make sure they have a pocket flashlight to use on their way back to the fireplace.) You are now spreading the harmony, peace, contentment, and protection of the hearth fire throughout your house. Keep the candles lit until the first member of the family goes to bed, and then snuff them out so that the energy of the candles is not dissipated but remains focused inside the candle. Light the candles anytime you feel negativity inside your home.

Sympathetic Magic: Rewriting Your Wyrd

Items Needed: A small toy loom, yarn or "loops" in specific colors, a bowl of water, four white candles and candle holders, and a lighter or matches

Moon Phase: Full or new

Seasonal Cycle: Yule or early spring

Rewriting your wyrd celebrates your ability to shape your own life according to your desires and secret wishes. It is a time for you to focus your intent on one or two important goals that can be accomplished in a fairly short period of time (no more than one year). You might wish to meet your one true love, for example. However, wishing for a marriage partner, children, a house in the country, picket fence, and a dog would entail many, many years of work and thus would be unsuitable for the ceremony. Also, be sure to wish for goals that are yours and yours alone. It is unwise to manipulate the wyrd of anyone else that you know, whether with positive or negative intentions. Focus on goals for yourself, keeping things open-ended if one of your goals involves true love or a better work situation. Before you begin, fully conceptualize your ideals. Choose only two or three, and take some time to think about them and all the details that would go into achieving them. Identify each goal with a color that reminds you of the true essence or spirit of the goal.

Once you have chosen your colors, go to your local toy shop and purchase a pot-holder loom, a lap loom, or even a table loom. These range in price from $10 to $100 and can be difficult to find in large, generic toy stores. You may have to hunt out smaller, local stores, craft shops, or far-flung Internet toy companies that specialize in unusual toys. Once you've purchased your loom, buy yarn (or "loops" if using the potholder loom) in the colors of your goals. Most specialty toy stores will stock the correct type of yarn next to the looms. These goal colors will be the weft of your finished weaving. The warp or stable lines (your orlog) can be any color that appeals to you and that comple-ments the colors of your weft.

Once you've outlined your two or three goals, assigned them colors, and purchased your loom and yarn, you're ready to change your life.

The best time to perform this ceremony would be during a waxing moon, a full moon, or a new moon. It is best done inside, in a fairly private place where you can be comfortable. Before you begin, set up the candles at each of the four directions and place the bowl of water, your loom, and the yarn or "loops" in the middle of the circle. You do not have to weave on the floor; just place a small table and chair in the center of your circle and work there. You can even set up your candles at the four corners of your dining room table and use that as your ceremony space.

Wherever you choose to hold your ceremony, after you have laid out the candles and your objects, sit in front of your loom and take several deep breaths. Ground and center, and begin to focus your mind on your two or three goals. When you start to feel relaxed, turn to the north, light the candle, and say:

Baldr's Mother, earth communicator, I honor you and the Spirit of Earth.

Think of all of the aspects of earth that you hold dear. When you feel ready, turn to the east, light the candle, and say:

Queen of Heaven, wife of the All-Father, I honor you and the Spirit of Air.

Think of all of the facets of air that make you smile. When you have experienced as many as possible, turn to the south, light the candle, and say:

Goddess of the household, builder of the hearth fire, I honor you and the Spirit of Fire.

Focus on all of the characteristics of fire that warm and excite you. After several min-utes, turn to the west, light the candle, and say:

Mistress of Fensalir, prophetic seeress, I honor you and the Spirit of Water.

Reflect on all of the features of water that calm and soothe you. When you are feeling very relaxed, turn back to your loom. Pick up the warp threads and hold them over each of the white directional candles in turn. As you do this, state:

This is my orlog, the unchangeable, the fixed. I accept this pattern as my destiny and vow to work within its guidelines.

Thread the loom with the warp thread, pondering all the while your ancestors, your culture and country, your genetic makeup, and your past actions and experiences. When you are finished, pick up one of the bunches of colored weft threads. Focus on the goal symbolized by the color. See it in your mind, smell it, feel it, and taste it. Make your goal come alive inside your mind and your heart. When you are ready, hold the thread over each of the white candles, saying:

This (state the color) *thread represents* (your goal). *As I weave it with my orlog, I manifest it in my life, creating and shaping my fate.*

Do this for each of the bundles of colored thread.

Now that you have purified and energized the weft and warp yarn, create a design of your own choosing on the loom. It doesn't have to be fancy or perfect. Remember, the finished product is as much an object of the universe as it is a creation of your hands and the material world. Through your weaving, you are merging with the spirits of the Norns and Frigga, altering your mindset and your life pattern. This is very serious work, so don't rush! Take your time. After all, time is relative, and the universe has no schedule to keep.

Once your weaving is complete, finish it off according to the instructions and hold it over the bowl of water. Sprinkle some water on the weaving as you state:

My fate has changed. My wyrd is my own. May my goals be manifest according to my desires and dreams.

Place the weaving down and, turning to the west, say:

Mistress of Fensalir, prophetic seeress, I thank you and the Spirit of Water.

Blow out the candle; turn to the south and say:

Goddess of the household, builder of the hearth fire, I thank you and the Spirit of Fire."

Blow out the candle, and then turn to the east, saying:

Queen of Heaven, wife of the All-Father, I thank you and the Spirit of Air.

Blow out the candle; turn to the north and say:

Baldr's Mother, earth communicator, I thank you and the Spirit of Earth.

Your wyrd ceremony is finished. Place your weaving in a prominent place in your household or use it on an everyday basis (such as a potholder or a scarf), and watch your goals materialize before your eyes!

MEETING SIF, NORSE GODDESS OF FAMILY AND HARVEST
Manifesting Abundance

SIF: MOTHER OF THE CLAN

Sif (pronounced SIF), beauteous one of the golden hair, is a goddess of many person-alities and many sides. However, they all condense down to her ability to work within a community. Sif is a goddess of the people—all people—and she is able to care for a great number of others at the same time. Like the image of the gentle, compassionate mother, Sif gives of herself until there is nothing left to give, and still she gets up to dry our tears and tuck us in at night. She cares for us all as individuals yet still has the ability to look at the big picture and direct the course of events. She is the ultimate vision of self-sacrifice for the good of all. And we love her for it.

In Norse mythology, Sif is known mostly through the actions of others. She is the consummate wife and mother who stands in the background and supports the deeds and actions of her family. And her family extends beyond her own marriage and her own children. As the wife of Thor, she nurtures his sons, Modi and Magni, by his mis-tress, the giantess Jarnsaxa, as well as her own daughter by Thor, Thrud, and her son, Ull, by an unnamed man. Her name, according to the Icelandic dictionary, is the singu-lar form of the plural word sifjar, which means "sib, affinity, connection by marriage."[1] So, through Sif's name and her actions toward her stepchildren, we can discern that Sif has the ability to welcome and accept all at her hearth. Despite her own personal feel-ings, she welcomes the sons of her rival to her table and her home. This takes an incred-ible amount of resolve and a willingness to place others' needs before one's own wishes. While we in the modern era might wish to see Sif's link to marriage bonds as evidence of the value of romantic love, it is important to note that our notion of love stems from the chivalric romances of the medieval era. Sif, as a goddess from an earlier time period, would have little knowledge of such romantic ideals. To the Norsemen, mar-riage was a business transaction that secured wealth and stabilized ties between families. Understanding, affinity, and affection certainly had their part in many marriages, but they were not the reasons for joining two people together.[2] The continuity and strength of the clan came first, before personal desires or dislikes. Sif, as seen in this context, personifies the ability to place the good of the clan (or family) above the desires of the individual.

The one myth that survives in full about Sif underlies her clan-centric behavior. In the "*Skaldskaparmal*," written by Snorri Sturluson in the Prose Edda, the trickster

---

1. Paxson, "Sif," 28.
2. Ward, "Courtship, Love and Marriage."

god Loki sneaks into Sif's room in the middle of the night, presumably when her warrior husband Thor is not at home, and cuts off all her hair. Sif's hair is much more to her than simply a distinguishing feature. It is, perhaps, the part of herself that best defines her character. She is described as "the most beautiful of all women, her hair ... like gold."[3] When her character is mentioned in the Norse texts, she is identified by her relationships to her family or by her hair, as evidenced in the "*Skaldskaparmal*": "How shall Sif be referred to? By calling her wife of Thor, mother of Ull, the fair-haired deity, rival of Jarnsaxa, mother of Thrud."[4] In fact, beautiful women are often solely described in the Norse sagas through the length and golden color of their hair. Their faces and bodies are rarely commented on, beyond their clothing. Keeping this is mind, Sif, as a goddess primarily associated with hair, would then be considered the most beautiful of the goddesses. Yet hair meant much more to the Norse people than beauty. It was a potent symbol of divinity and powerful life force.[5] To cut off Sif's hair shows a lack of respect for her, as well as for her entire god clan, known as the Aesir. It diminishes her sense of self and robs her of the sacred nature of her goddesshood.

Yet it is possible that Sif knew the mind of the chaotic god Loki and allowed the taking of her divine power and goddess might for the good of her entire clan.[6] In the prologue of the Edda, Sif's name is likened to the Greek notion of the "sibyl" or prophetess. In no other place in the Eddas or sagas is Sif described as possessing oracular powers. This brief mention of her abilities might be linked to the medieval practice of connecting any two similar words. Yet several Norse goddesses are known for their powers of future sight, and the Norse believed that women were especially attuned to psychic activity.[7] Therefore, it is not improbable that Sif is a seeress. If she allowed Loki's devious theft to occur, we must look beyond the relationship of her hair to herself and view her hair instead as an extension of her role as caregiver of the clan and thus of all humanity.

After Loki cuts off Sif's hair, Thor threatens to break every bone in his body. Loki, ever cunning, promises Thor that he will get a head of hair—better hair, hair of gold, hair of gold that would grow like any other hair—for Sif from the expert dwarven craftsmen in the land of Svartalheim, one of the nine worlds of Norse cosmology. Thor reluctantly

---

3. Sturluson, *Edda*, 3.

4. Ibid., 86.

5. Gundarsson, *Our Troth*, 380.

6. This concept is explored in the modern retelling of Sif's myth "How Sif Got Her Golden Hair," by Thorskegga Thorn, http://www.thorshof.org/howsif.htm (accessed January 2008).

7. Paxson, "Sif," 27.

agrees, and Loki goes forth to trick the dwarves into making the hair for him. He calls on the dwarves known only as Ivaldi's sons, and they agree to the job. Not only do they craft Sif's new hair but also Odin's spear Gungnir, which never misses its mark, and Frey's boat Skidbladnir, which can be folded up and put in a pocket. Never one to miss an opportunity, Loki takes these items and bets another dwarf, Brokk, that he and his brother, Eitri, cannot create three more objects of such magic and beauty. The two brothers agree to the challenge and craft Gullinbursti, Frey's golden boar that can run on water and air; Draupnir, Odin's ring that produces eight rings of equal weight every nine days; and Mjollnir, Thor's hammer that strikes hard, never misses, and always returns to its owner. These items define the powers of the Norse gods, heightening their magic and might. Sif's hair buys five magical tools and weapons that enhance the power of Odin, Thor, and Frey. Without the loss of Sif's hair, the Norse gods would have been a fraction of their powerful selves.

Whether or not Sif knew of the reward to the Aesir at the cost of losing her hair,[8] the fact remains that her hair brings abundance to her family members. If her hair had not been stolen, her husband, her father-in-law, and her close family friend would have never come into their full power. She grants them the tools to become greater than themselves, to fully grasp their innate skills, and to attain their highest potential. This is the gift that Sif, as guardian of the family, brings to us all. Her hair is the cornucopia, the horn of plenty, the cauldron of prosperity that spills across the land and opens each of us to the possibilities of ourselves.

It is not surprising, then, that Sif is often connected to cauldrons and cups—containers that hold the sustenance of the gods. In "Hymir's Poem," the giant Aegir is ordered by the Aesir to create the drink of the gods, but he says he cannot until Thor fetches him the huge cauldron of Hymir. In his capacity as cauldron bearer, Thor is labeled simply as Sif's husband. Thor's quest for the cauldron of Hymir is reminiscent of "Odin's winning of the mead of poetry, likely to be a Germanic survival of the original Indo-European tale of how the holy drink which sustains the god/desses was claimed from the Otherworld."[9] In fact, the Finnish god Ukko, who shares many characteristics

---

8. In an interesting sidenote, the Eddas and sagas do not state what happened to Sif's original hair. It is implied that she cannot grow hair and that her original hair cannot be reapplied to her scalp, thus the reason why Loki must resort to magical methods. But after stating that Loki took the hair, the medieval texts immediately launch into the creation of the six magical objects, forgetting about the original head of hair. It is up to you, dear readers, to determine for yourselves what happened to Sif's hair.

9. Gundarsson, *Our Troth*, 224.

with Thor (including an affinity for rowan trees, thunder and lightning, and a hammer weapon), associates fertility of the land and the people with the amount of beer that can be consumed. The more beer drunk, the more abundance graces the land. The beer, then, is the essence of the fertility of the god Thor, and the cauldron is the vessel in which it is created and kept.

Figure 6: The chalice of Sif serves to sustain the clan by granting
prosperity and abundance through service and sacrifice.
(Symbols on the above drawing were taken from the Gotland Picture Stone from Havor in Hablingbo.)

When another giant, Hrungnir, boasts in the Edda that he will bury Asgard (the home of the Norse gods), destroy Valhalla (one of Odin's halls in Asgard), kill all of the gods, and steal Freyja and Sif back to his home, he is drunk on mead served from Thor's goblets. Indeed, this scene in particular depicts the goblets as extensions of the power of Sif and Freyja. The goddesses are the vessels that house the spirit might of the Aesir, which is why the giant wishes to possess them, gaining for himself the might of the gods.[10] The cups, in this instance, symbolize the power of these goddesses to store the life force of the Norse gods. They house the holy drink of the gods that brings fertility to our world, known as Midgard in Norse cosmology. After sampling this power by drinking from the cups, the giant Hrungnir wishes to possess it forever by kidnapping the goddesses. Sif, then, becomes the sacred chalice in which the divine, fertile drink of Thor is kept.

The most well-known story of Sif as a cup bearer takes place in the "Lokasenna" in the Poetic Edda. In this story, Loki arrives at a party uninvited and proceeds to insult the gods and goddesses one after another. In an effort to calm Loki's raging heart and restore peace to the hall, Sif steps forward and pours mead for Loki into a crystal cup, saying:

> Hail to thee, Loki, and take thou here
> The crystal cup of old mead;
> For me at least, alone of the gods,
> Blameless thou knowest to be.[11]

In this capacity as cup bearer, Sif acts as the representative of her lord and husband, Thor. She is an extension of his might and power, and her claim that she is "blameless" reflects on her husband as well as on her entire household. She works to create peace and promote unity and cooperation among the guests in the hall. Once again, we see Sif (the cup) working to benefit the group (by promoting peace) by working with the powerful force of her husband (the drink within the cup) in order to bring about change.[12]

Loki goes on to claim that Sif is not blameless but rather has made a cuckold of Thor by sleeping with Loki himself. In the process of proclaiming Sif's adultery, Loki says that

---

10. Gundarsson, *Our Troth*, 380.

11. Bellows, *Poetic Edda*, 168, verse 53.

12. Enright, *Lady with a Mead Cup*, chapters 1 and 2.

she is both "shy and fierce towards men,"[13] an opposing combination of attributes that enhances our understanding of Sif. She must appear quiet around men other than her husband, yet with a discernible barrier or wall of reserve that cannot be breached by flattery or cajolery. She is the ripe flower hidden away behind the locked fence, waiting for the gardener with the right key to enter. She is inaccessible to most, but Loki says that he has tasted of her delights. (But then he also claims to have had sex with most of the goddesses at the gathering.) However, Odin, disguised as a ferryman in "Harbard's Song," corroborates Loki's claim by telling Thor that "Sif has a lover at home."[14] (Of course, Odin is a trickster as well and is trying to win a battle of wits against his son. He might say anything to disorient Thor and win the battle.) It could be that as the cup of the mighty, as the cornucopia of plenty, Sif has the ability to fertilize the dreams and desires of all men, but she chooses among her devotees wisely, being discriminate in who she gifts her bounty.

Sif's abundance has often been connected to the grain harvest, due to the color and texture of her hair. When a breeze blows through a field of ripe wheat, it looks like the brushing or stroking of long, fair hair. Snorri Sturluson in the Prose Edda claims that *Sif* is another word for "earth," and in England, old folktales tell of the power of lightning to fertilize and ripen a field. It would be easy to categorize the relationship of Sif and Thor as the fertile marriage of an earth goddess with a sky god, but that would diminish their considerable powers and divergent characteristics. Sif's bounty is not merely of the earth. Her hair is another term for gold in old Norse writings and is a symbol for the divinity and spirit spark of the gods. She is the cup that holds the mead of life, bringing abundance to the land. She is the land as well, and yet her magnificence spreads to all aspects of life that flourish and grow, making life better and fuller.

Sif's profusion begins with the earth but extends to the depths of our souls, where she fosters our ability to become our best and brightest selves. Just as she sacrificed her hair for the benefit of the gods, she gives of herself to foster and encourage our inner strength and powers. As the mother of the clan, she wishes for all of her children to achieve their highest potential and clasp their innate skills and powers. Sif is the cauldron keeper, the cup bearer, the bringer of bounty, the giver of plenty. It is Sif who tips

---

13. Larrington, *Poetic Edda*, 93, verse 54.

14. Bellows, 134, verse 48.

the cup and brings fertility to the land, to the people, to the very gods themselves. And we praise her for it!

ACCEPTING ABUNDANCE: WHO, ME?

One of the hardest things about abundance work is accepting that we deserve material goods and that we deserve to live free from worry and anxiety. For most of us, abundance translates into money, into gold, into cash, which again translates into material possessions such as cars and houses and designer handbags and season tickets. We want abundance so we don't have to worry about that sly orthodontist bill, the surprise car repair, or the here-before-you-know-it college tuition. We want to be able to cruise the Caribbean once in a while and take the grandkids to Disney World. We want to enjoy life. Is that so bad?

Traditional, monotheistic religions have told us for years that abundance is bad. Poverty, want, humility—these are the attributes that buy you a ticket to heaven. We have been taught that abundance corrupts. More money will make you a bad person, take you further from your spiritual center, and turn you into a cash-craving monster. And if we are honest, in the deepest part of our soul, we believe this rhetoric, even if just for the smallest of instants. But could this idea be merely a consolation prize for the less well-off, so people can say, "I'm not wealthy, but I'm going to heaven"? Possibly. Probably. After all, the Catholic Church was notoriously corrupt in its early years. The bishops often lived in luxury while their followers starved. But wealth and abundance do not have to bring callousness and depravity in their wake. You can choose your own course of action.

How are you going to use your abundance? Make a plan ahead of time. Will you pay off your mortgage and those of your best friend and sister? Will you support AIDS research, worldwide female education, or a cure for cancer? Make a list to show yourself exactly where your money would go. Cut out pictures from old magazines and create a collage. Research worthwhile nonprofit organizations and vacation destinations. Allow yourself the freedom to dream—to dream big, in Technicolor, with all the multitude rainbow hues of the world. Give yourself the permission to use your money to make your life better while helping others. Abundance will not change your core truth. It will simply heighten it and give you the means to explore different sides of your personality. Prove it to yourself by planning for your abundance. And then believe!

THE PATHWORKING

The following meditation is unlike any other in this book, as it compels you to meet not one divinity but two. While Sif will be the primary personage of power in the meditation and the divine energy that you will converse with the most, you will also meet her husband, Thor. Thor is not a god to be feared, as he has a wonderful paternal instinct and is sworn to protect Asgard and Midgard from forces that would do them harm. Unlike modern portrayals in comic books, Thor is not a warrior who uses any excuse to fight. Rather, he fights when he feels it is necessary to defend his clan.

It is essential to include Thor in the following meditation because Sif, as the cup, needs Thor to be the liquid, the essence of fertility, inside the cup. As the cup bearer, Sif has the power to dispense the abundance, but her family (especially Thor) is the sustenance within the cup, the actual agent of growth. They are connected on a very intimate, esoteric level. You cannot have one without the other; otherwise, you'd have an empty cup or a handful of liquid spilled on the ground.

Sif holds the divine spark, the might of the gods, and cherishes it and keeps it safe. This energy was kept in her hair, which she bartered for the magical objects of power for Odin, Frey, and Thor. This energy is within her still but has been transmuted to be shared by all. Her golden strands link the gods together, heightening their collective powers and strength and giving them the instruments to achieve their greatest deeds. For Sif, the power is always shared by all, made greater by the community. As such, it is only right that the meditation reflect this aspect of her character and her energy.

GUIDED MEDITATION: THE CUP BEARER

Take a deep breath, in through your nose and out through your mouth. Take another deep breath, filling your stomach, your diaphragm, and finally your lungs. Hold this breath for five seconds … 1-2-3-4-5 … and exhale, allowing the breath to exit your lungs first, then your diaphragm, and finally your stomach. Take one more deep breath, and as you breathe in, feel the energy of a warm, comforting fire around you, supporting your fingers, your toes, your legs, and your shoulders, even the top of your head. Hold the breath for seven seconds … 1-2-3-4-5-6-7. As you exhale, feel all tension leave your fingers, your toes, your legs, and your shoulders, even the top of your head. Continue breathing deeply, in through your nose and out through your mouth. Feel the soft rushes of a well-kept hall under the soles of your feet. Boisterous voices echo off the walls, beckoning you closer. Fur tickles your shoulders, causing a single bead of perspiration to trickle down your back. The fire is warm in the hearth. Allow the warmth to remove any excess tension and stress. Feel your anxieties being melted away by the heat of the fire. Allow your muscles to relax. (pause) You have never felt so relaxed, so secure, so calm.

You are walking inside a good-size medieval Viking hall. Rushes and hay crinkle under your feet, softening the hard-packed dirt and keeping the earth's chill at bay. Large wooden beams crisscross the ceiling, holding firm the sturdy, shingled roof. A central aisle as wide as two men abreast runs the length of the hall, punctuated by heavy posts that support the massive roof. Tiers of wooden benches spread out on either side of the central aisle. Currently they are filled to capacity with men and women garbed in linen clothes and woolen cloaks, with an occasional fur trim. Jewels and gold glimmer among the assemblage on neck brooches, rings, torcs, simple bracelets, and elaborate pins. Before them, big rectangular tables line up, piled high with tankards and mugs, trenchers and plates, knives and an occasional spoon. They are waiting for the feast to arrive. In the center of the homestead, a fire blazes bright, warming the chilly air. Dogs and children, too energetic to sit and chat, ramble and play. All is movement, warmth, camaraderie, and merriment. You smile to be in the midst of such cheer.

"You there!" The voice comes from beside you, gruff and commanding. "Are you going to serve the food or just stand there gawking?" Laughter bounces around the room, and a sharp elbow pushes into your back.

"Go, go," a small female voice whispers behind you, and you notice that you are carrying a platter of food and that you are standing in the doorway of the holding with a long line of servers behind you. You move farther into the hall and allow several servants to pass you by. You notice how they place their plates of food on the tables and then take up stations against the walls to see to the needs of the noblemen. You quickly move to the nearest table and make to place your platter down. Before you do, look and see what you are offering to the nobles. What are you bringing to the feast? (pause) Make a mental note to remember this item, as it is a clue to your present state of abundance and a personal link to the goddess Sif.

Before you can back away from this table, a hard hand grasps your arm. "Servant," the man growls, tearing into a hunk of bread, "we already have what you're serving at this table. See to the others." You stammer a quick apology and hastily grab the platter of food. Being careful not to spill any, you move from one table to another. But each table has already received its due portion. Explore these tables now and see what knowledge awaits you. (pause) Before too long, your arms begin to tire from the heavy platter and you begin to wonder if you will have to lug around this food for the entire night.

Suddenly, a movement catches your eye. There, at the back of the room and near the fire, rests the high seat. The owners of this holding sit there, amid the cacophony of their company. A delicate hand rises from the crush of bodies and the cover of smoke and beckons to you. You advance toward it, careful to avoid the dogs scurrying for bones and the other servants hastening to appease the guests. (pause) You arrive at the hall's high seat and bow your head respectfully, hoisting up the platter of food as you do. Your arms shake slightly, but you grit your teeth in an effort to control your muscles.

"Ah, good servant," a deep, mirthful voice rumbles, "place your platter here, between my wife and I, for we have not sampled of your wares as yet." Still not raising your eyes, you clumsily move forward to the table and place your platter upon it. You instantly give a sigh of relief as your aching muscles relax. As you back away from the table, a soft voice stops you.

"My lord," the gentle voice says, "is this not the guest we have been searching for?" You glance up inadvertently and are instantly dazzled by the bright light surrounding the lord and lady of the hall. It is sparkly and brilliant and reminiscent of the brightest noonday sun during the summer months. Heat, warmth, and light radiate from the high seat.

"I think you are right, my lady," the deep voice agrees, and suddenly the light dissipates on the edges of the smoke from the fire and the steam from the meats and you are looking into the greenest pair of eyes you have ever seen. They belong to Sif, lady of this hall, goddess of plenty, mother of the clan. Her golden hair glows around her, falling in soft waves down to the floor. Her gown is a light spring green, and she wears a cream kirtle hand-stitched with golden embroidery. The design forms flowers and leaves and vines and, if you look closely, is always changing ever so slightly. (pause) Her smile is bright, for you alone, and her face is open and welcoming. Next to her, on a seat carved with serpents, hammers, and lightning bolts, sits her husband, Thor, the lord of Bilskirnir, god of thunder and lightning, protector of the clan. His strawberry-gold hair hangs to his chin, waving slightly at the ends, decorated with two miniscule braids near his left ear. His facial hair is darker and outlines a hard, angular jaw and a mouth made for smiling. He wears a dark blue shirt, overlaid with a simple brown leather jerkin. Tan pants disappear into warm suede boots topped with white fur. And if you look carefully, you can just see a tiny bit of his red socks peeking out from the well-worn boots. His smile is welcoming, but his eyes, steel blue, are measuring you and considering your worth.

"What have you brought us?" Thor questions, looking down at the serving platter you have been carrying. Before your eyes, the platter of food morphs into items that symbolize your past hurts, issues, and concerns. (pause) They represent all that is holding you back from achieving your true abundance in life. Thor snorts and whistles lightly through his teeth. Swiftly he picks up his hammer, Mjollnir, and makes to smash the table. Sif jumps to her feet.

"Thor," she says, laying a hand on his arm, "why don't you go see to our honored guests? I will deal with the concerns of this one." Notably disappointed, Thor puts down his hammer.

"Very well, wife, I leave you to your women's work," he says. Then, with a kiss and a saucy pat on her rump, the god of thunder strolls away from the high seat to join the throng below. Sif sits down with an audible sigh and motions you closer.

"My child," she says, "you have come far with a large burden. It has made you tired and weak, but you have laid it before me and my lord. Do you wish to be rid of your burden? For I have the power to make it so." You walk to the platter on the table and look at the items that represent past hurts and pain in your life. Pick up each one individually and relive the painful memories. Remember that Sif sits right next to you, giving you her strength and guidance. She has lived through pain and knows what you are feeling. Allow her compassion to wash over you. When you have recalled and learned from each memory, place the object back on the platter and wipe your hands clean, saying goodbye to it. Take as much time as you need, as Sif has amazing patience and love. (pause)

When you have said goodbye to all of the unpleasant memories, walk away from the table, but stay within easy reach of Sif. She smiles at you and places her hands on either side of your face in a gesture of understanding and love.

"You are ready to transmute these painful memories into growth and abundance?" Sif asks you. You tell her that you are ready. Once she has received your assent, Sif waves her hands over the platter of objects. The golden threads of her dress reach out tentative tendrils that weave and undulate over and through the objects. (pause) They move slowly but deliberately, eventually covering the platter in a thick skein of golden thread.

With a wink and a smile, Sif removes the golden threads, calling them back into the elaborate pattern on her dress. As they unwind, the threads reveal a glorious crystal cup. (pause) Sif picks up the cup and hands it to you. It is full with the energy of the Goddess and vibrates slightly in your hand. It radiates with a silver glow. You look inside and see the amber color of mead. It reminds you of the color of Thor's beard.

"You hold the cup of abundance in your hands," Sif says, her hands clasped gently in her lap. "The essence of the fertility of the gods, the truth of your spiritual center rests inside there. Drink and you will be given your true power. Your life will flourish, and your might will be great." You look at Sif, glance at the amber liquid in the cup, and drink it down—every ... last ... drop. The mead burns its way down your throat, warming your belly. It blossoms inside you like spring rain and summer rainbows. Your potential is great, your possibilities absolute. You smile at Sif, drop the cup into her lap, and slide onto the floor. The potent drink has undone your mortal sensibilities. You hear her tinkling laugh and feel a light touch on the top of your head. You hear Sif's voice before you drift off to sleep: "Rest my child, for you have done well this day, and many adventures await you."

Now take a deep breath, in through your nose and out through your mouth. Take another deep breath, filling your stomach, your diaphragm, and finally your lungs. Hold this breath for five seconds ... 1-2-3-4-5 ... and exhale, allowing the breath to exit your lungs first, then your diaphragm, and finally your stomach. Breathe deeply once more, and as you breathe in, feel the energy and the wonder of the world around you in your fingers, your toes, your legs, and your shoulders, even the top of your head. As you exhale, wiggle your fingers and toes. Shake your legs and move your shoulders up and down. Take another deep breath and, as you exhale, move your head from side to side. Feel the ground under your body touching every nerve ending and muscle. Hear the rustlings of the people around you. Notice the movements outside. Continue breathing. Stretch your arms out above your head. You are returning to the present, to the here and now. Continue stretching. Continue breathing. When you are ready, open your eyes, blink and focus, and sit up.

INVOCATION TO SIF

Abundant blessings on your house,
Wife of Thor,

Mother of Thrud and Ull,
Stepmother of Modi and Magni,
Lady of Bilskirnir,
Mother of the Clan,
Horn of Plenty.

As goddess of the Earth,
You feed your people,
Bringing abundance
To the hearthstead.

As goddess of the Chalice,
You relieve our pain,
Showing the pathway
To our inner divinity.

Abundant blessings on your house,
Sweet Sif of the golden hair.
May the rafters echo
With boasts and cheer
To your generous self
And your magnificent family.

Hail Sif!

MAGICAL ACTIVITIES

Herbal Magic: Corn of Prosperity

Items Needed: A fresh ear of corn with the husk and silk attached; a lock of your
    hair, at least four inches long; scissors; a dollar bill; embroidery floss; a yellow
    candle; and a lighter
Moon Phase: Waxing
Seasonal Cycle: Summer

Set up your items in a sunny, warm place. You can do this spell during any time of the
day, but mid to late afternoon is best. Ground and center as you normally do, and when

you are relaxed, shuck the ear of corn, making sure the husk and silk remain intact. Set aside the ear of corn to eat for dinner.

Next, using the scissors cut off a four-inch or longer lock of your hair. While you are cutting, think about how your energy and sense of self is imbued in that length of hair. If you do not have long enough hair, purchase some embroidery floss that matches your hair color. Cut a five- or six-inch length of embroidery floss and some wisps of your hair. Lay the cut floss out straight and sprinkle the hair over the floss, saying something like, "As the hair touches the floss, so does the floss become the hair. The two are one, a part of me." (This is a form of sympathetic magic, in which you are creating a link between two seemingly dissimilar objects and unifying them. The floss is now your hair and will work in that capacity for this spell.)

Take the length of hair and weave it into the silk of the corn husk. You can braid your hair into the silk or simply tie it using knots and twists. Corn silk is often likened to Sif's hair, which she sacrificed (whether consciously or unconsciously) for an abundance of magical tools to aid the gods. In this spell, you are recreating that sacrifice by offering a part of yourself (your hair) for the abundance of greater prosperity. Keep your magical intent in mind while you are attaching your hair to the silk.

Once the hair and silk are entwined, tuck a dollar bill into the corn husk. Make sure it is touching your hair and the silk. While you are placing the dollar bill, say, "Sif, I have sacrificed a part of myself to welcome an abundance of prosperity. May my sacrifice yield positive results to (*state the address of your home*) while harming none." Light the yellow candle and pass the opened corn husk over the heat and light of the candle. This candle represents the warmth and power of the goddess Sif, as she nurtures your prosperity spell. Tie the husk closed by wrapping embroidery floss three times around the corn and tying it in a triple knot. The embroidery floss can be green or the color of your hair.

Set the corn spell over the main door of your house, resting it (if possible) on the ledge. If the ledge is too small, secure the corn in place using your embroidery floss. Keep the yellow candle burning until it extinguishes on its own. If you need to go to bed, extinguish the candle yourself, but relight it the following day. Allow the corn to stay in place as long as the harvest lasts. If it falls down before the end of the harvest, the spell is complete. You can ritually burn the corn spell as you see fit. If the corn does not fall down, remove the corn on the autumn equinox and ritually burn it. Be open to prosperity in all its many forms. You never know what will arrive at your doorstep!

Meditation/Creative Visualization: Winnowing the Chaff

Items Needed: Soft, calm, meditative music; sunflower incense; a lighter or matches; a soft pillow (optional); and a soft and warm blanket (optional)

Moon Phase: Waning

Seasonal Cycle: Any

Find a time in your busy life when you will have a complete hour of free time. This is actually harder to accomplish than you might think. It might take you two or three months to create the space in your life for this spell—no matter. When your free time materializes (as it certainly will if you look for it), you will know that the time is right to perform this magic. Once you have found your window of opportunity, place your "Shh…meditation in progress" sign on your door, turn off the phones, place any pets in a safe, out-of-the-way area, and set up your meditation space.

You can meditate anyplace in your house or apartment, but it should be relatively quiet and contained. If people walk through your meditation space, it will disrupt your creative visualization and your spell will not be as strong or effective. Try to find an out-of-the-way section of your house or apartment where you will not be disturbed.

Once you have found the perfect place and time, set up your area so that it feels calm and relaxing. You can use a soft pillow to sit on for comfort, or you can sit on the floor or on a rug. The choice is yours. I find that the more comfortable you are when meditating, the more you get out of the experience, because strange aches and pains are kept to a minimum. Wrapping yourself in a blanket helps to keep from getting cold, which often occurs when clearing unnecessary ideas and thought processes during meditation or creative visualization. It is not necessary to have a blanket, but as with the pillow, the fewer distractions you have, the deeper and more powerful your meditative experience.

After you have created your optimal meditation space, sit down and light the sunflower incense. Start your music and begin to relax. If you wish, invoke the goddess Sif by using the invocation provided in this chapter or by writing your own. Breathe in the smoke of the incense, and then ground and center, feeling yourself sinking into the lush, verdant, fertile earth. The soil is soft and warm, reminding you of a mother's embrace. It is all-encompassing, all around you, flourishing into the deep greens, sunny yellows, and blushing pinks of abundance. The smells overwhelm you, and you surrender to the earth's bounty, feeling tickling vines and nodding tree branches. Take some time to become acclimated to this lush Otherworld.

Before you know it, you find yourself at the edge of a farm, where forest and field meet. Spread out before you, in a never-ending tapestry of green and yellow, is row after row of corn, wheat, and rye. Sunflowers bloom straight and tall along the edges of the crop. Their heads droop slightly, waving in the gentle breeze. You begin down the nearest row of corn. Your steps are sure, but after only a few feet, you begin to feel a tugging on your clothes. You are striving to move forward, but you keep getting pulled backward. It is a constant battle to place one foot in front of the other. Unsure why you cannot get ahead, you hear a warm and smoky female voice say, "Why don't you look and see what is holding you back?" So you do. Two tiny imps caper across the row and amid the ears of corn. One is pink and the other is blue. They climb on your body and muss your hair, all the while grinning from ear to ear.

You sit down in the middle of the row, knowing that these are the forces holding you back. The goddess Sif towers above you, the colors of the rich harvest swirling around her in dress and shawl, scarf and hair. She wears no shoes. See her now as she presents herself to you. (pause) She indicates to you that you need to hold each of the imps and ask what they represent in order to find out what is holding you back from accomplishing your goals and reaching your true potential. This is easier said than done, as the imps cavort around you and the corn stalks. They are quick and agile and tricky, but eventually you corner the pink imp. Holding it, you ask, "What are you?" And the imp responds. (pause) Take this knowledge given by the imp and, placing it on the ground, cup your hands over its head. Transform the imp's answer into something positive, thereby renaming the imp. So, for instance, if the imp said that it was "Fear," you might rename the imp "Joy," or "Happiness," or "Courage." Feel Sif's powerful presence as you rename the imp. You might feel her hands on your hands or a subtle pressure on the top of your head or a tingling throughout your body. Whatever you feel, allow this power to build and grow, as it is Sif's energy melding and blending with yours. Once the pink imp is renamed, it hops out from under your hands, smiles disarmingly, and pops back into your body. Follow the same procedure to rename the blue imp.

When both imps have been renamed and have returned to your body, stand up. Feel the protective, strengthening embrace of Sif. She steps out into the corn row with you and, waving her arm, shows you an image of the open pathway ahead of you. "Now you are ready," she says. Ask her for an indication of your next step and wait and watch for a sign. (pause) Pay attention inside the meditation but also throughout the following weeks. Signs and omens may present themselves to you. Weird coincidences may occur.

These are all Sif's answers to your question. Put them all together and you will know the direction you need to walk.

After you have reveled in Sif's presence, receiving any guidance she has to offer, leave the corn rows and return to your meditative space and time. Take three deep breaths, wiggling your toes and fingers. Shake your arms and legs and move your head from side to side. Bring yourself back into this reality. Take some time to write down your experience with Sif, knowing that your spellwork has already started working. You are moving away from past negativities and striving forward into a bright and abundant future.

Rune Magic: Love Stone

Items Needed: A polished rose quartz stone, an ultra-fine-point gold permanent marker, and a rune book, preferably *Futhark: A Handbook of Rune Magic* by Edred Thorsson or *Northern Mysteries and Magick: Runes and Feminine Powers* by Freya Aswynn

Moon Phase: Full

Seasonal Cycle: Any

As with all things esoteric, such as tarot cards, rune stones, ogham sticks, and I Ching coins, the power of the item comes from combining the knowledge and will of the individual with the wisdom and infinite power of the universe. A magical practitioner should not attempt to access this power without doing a good amount of research. This is especially true of the runes, as there are instances recorded in the Norse sagas of well-meaning but unlearned people doing harm to those they wished to heal. Rune magic links the magician to a long line of ancestral rune workers, or *vitki*. The power and magic of the runes come from past uses of them, along with medieval and modern interpretations of their meanings. No two rune masters will totally agree on the uses of a rune. Yet the runes do have standardized general meanings with which most rune workers would agree. This leaves the novice rune magician in a bit of a bind, because different rune masters will choose varying runes to accomplish the same magical purpose.

With love magic, the choice of rune is especially problematic, as no one rune is directly associated with the modern concept of love. Our romantic ideal has been shaped by the chivalric romances of the Middle Ages and the Renaissance era. We want emotive, gushing, romantic love with all the flowers, candlelight, and, yes, sex possible. We want to relive the roles of the gallant knight and winsome maiden overwhelmed with a wellspring of emotion. Yet these ideas were not especially prevalent in Norse society. One married for position, power, wealth, security, and stability. You hoped for a comely mate who would serve as your steadfast companion through life, helping you create and sustain a family. "Listening to the heart" was not as important as "listening to the head." So it is no wonder that no rune in the Elder Futhark (the oldest of the three rune sets) corresponds directly to the concept of romantic love.

Despite this drawback, the runes connect to the core of the self at a very deep and intimate level. They are powerful tools for creating and manifesting your reality and, with the help of Sif, can help you achieve love in your life. You just have to be specific about the love you want to attain. Below is a list of possible runes that you could use in a love spell. These are my personal interpretations, so please do not take them as the end-all and be-all of runic knowledge. They are meant to give you some direction in your own individual quest for rune wisdom. Do some research on your own, using either of the books listed at the beginning of this spell. Remember, any good spell begins with the maxim "To Know," and this is especially true of rune magic. Don't skimp on the gathering of information, or you may be unhappy with the results of your magic.

Figure 7: Kenaz

Kenaz: A rune often connected to inspiration and the fire within, Kenaz is great for drawing passionate sexual partners or for reigniting the flame of a current relationship.

Figure 8: Gebo

Gebo: This rune is often stated to be the "rune of love" in commercially created runic talismans and pendants. It is a rune of "give and take," of equality and charity, so it might be better applied to an existing relationship than a future one.

Figure 9: Wunjo

Wunjo: This rune links and bonds people together, creating connection and harmony. As such, Wunjo is excellent at attracting long-term love, the kind that leads to extended partnership and the sharing of assets and lives.

Figure 10: Ehwaz

Ehwaz: A rune used to describe working together (like a matched pair of horses), Ehwaz is wonderful for promoting accord in any relationship. It can be used for drawing a mate of similar mind or for stabilizing a rocky situation at work or in your extended family.

Once you have chosen the rune that best describes your desired type of love, sit down with your rose quartz, gold pen, and rune of choice. Holding the rose quartz between both of your hands, chant the name of the rune. Take your time, and allow the power and vibrations of the rune chant to enter your body, mind, and spirit. (If you are unsure about rune chanting, you can always listen to Freya Aswynn's CD *Songs of Yggdrasil* for some ideas.) When you feel like the power of the rune has entered your body, channel the energy into the rose quartz in your hands. When the crystal is filled up with the power of the rune, release any excess energy by placing your hands on the ground and allowing the earth to soak up the remainder. Now write your rune on the rose quartz, using your gold pen. The written symbol is a reminder to you of the runic power held in the rune. The power is there whether you write on the stone or not, but the writing helps to seal in the runic energy.

While you allow the gold ink to dry (five minutes or so), continue to softly chant the rune, focusing on your magical objective. Once the ink has dried, hold the rose quartz between your palms again and say out loud, "*Sif, help me achieve the love that I please.*" Then kiss the crystal and place it in your pocket. Carry the stone around for the rest of the day so that your energy intermingles with that of the stone. You can choose to continue to carry the stone around, or you can place it in your purse or briefcase, in your car, or on your magical altar. Now keep vigilant and alert, for your love will be arriving soon!

MEETING SKADI,
NORSE WARRIOR GODDESS
Activating the Warrior Within

SKADI: GODDESS OF SELF

Fierce winter winds, snowcapped mountains, and the howling of wolves all welcome you to the realm of the snow goddess Skadi (pronounced SKAH-dee). Called "shining bride of the gods," "snowshoe goddess," and "ski goddess," Skadi is actually a giantess who became a goddess through marriage. She rules over the cold winter months and the areas of the world covered by snow and ice. Skadi can be found traveling about on skis and hunting with her bow and arrow. (She's quite a good shot!) She is the protector of all women who choose an independent lifestyle, single moms and dads, and any individual who chooses a military career, but especially women warriors. Strong and forceful, yet beautiful and emotional, Skadi believes in the bond of family and in the integrity of the self. She makes no excuses for her actions, but simply chooses her path and follows it, navigating with her own inner truth.

Skadi bursts onto the scene of the Norse gods bristling with fury and aching for vengeance. Her beloved father, the giant Thiassi, has been killed by the Aesir (one branch of gods in the Norse pantheon), and she vows to extract payment for his death. According to the *Skaldskaparmal* in the Prose Edda, one of several medieval books of Norse mythology to survive to the present day, Skadi, armed with "helmet and mail-coat and all weapons of war,"[1] descends upon Asgard, the home of the gods. Obviously, Skadi has belief in her own strength of arms as well as in the justice of her cause. Her father is dead due to the manipulations of the Aesir. Her family (of which only her father is known) has been destroyed, and she demands the payment that is due her by Norse law. Impetuous, Skadi acts on instinct, without thinking her actions through. Yet her character is such that, as a giant, she does not fear the gods, and she could conceivably cause them much harm with her weapons.

Knowing her power, the gods choose not to fight her, offering her compensation for her father's death instead. This wergild consists of marriage and laughter rather than blood and death. Just and fair, Skadi agrees to the terms of agreement, which state that she will choose her own husband from among the gods and must be entertained enough by the antics of the gods to laugh out loud. Odin, All-Father of the Gods, true to his word, allows Skadi to pick her husband; however, with typical cunning, he limits her ability to see them, allowing her to choose based on their feet alone.

---

1. Sturluson, *Edda*, 61.

Skadi views all of the feet and in a relatively short time selects the most beautiful pair, rationalizing that "there can be little that is ugly about Baldr."[2] Baldr, the young, beautiful, golden son of Odin and Frigga, is Skadi's choice for a husband. True to her impatient, hasty nature, Skadi selects quickly. Much to her disappointment, the feet she chooses are not those of the lovely Baldr but belong to the old, crusty, patient, kind, and very wealthy god of the sea, Njord. Njord forgives Skadi her initial regret, and the couple marries immediately.

After such dissatisfaction in her marriage, it would seem unlikely the Aesir could fulfill the second half of their wergild: that of making Skadi laugh. Enter the trickster god of the Aesir, a giant himself and blood brother to Odin, Loki. With serious aplomb and ease, Loki calmly ties one end of a string to his testicles and the other end to the beard of a goat. Hindered by Loki's great size from grazing to her delight, the goat begins to tug at the cord, much to the discomfort of Loki. Loki, in pain and wishing to retaliate, pulls back, and a hilarious tug of war ensues, with much screaming and cussing and shouting from both parties. When Loki is hauled off his feet by the goat, he lands clumsily in Skadi's lap. Skadi cannot contain herself any longer. She laughs out loud, and the wergild is satisfied.[3]

When Skadi leaves with her new husband, Njord, the first test of their marriage is to decide where to live. Skadi loves the wilderness of her father's mountainous hall, Thrymheim, but Njord feels more comfortable in his seaside home of Noatun. They decide to stay nine nights together at Thrymheim and then nine nights at Noatun in order to make the decision as to where they should live. After the eighteen nights together, Njord declares:

> I hate mountains—not long was I there, just nine nights:
> wolves' howling I thought ugly compared with the swans'
> song.[4]

Skadi makes no apology for her beloved home but counters with her own disparaging opinions of Noatun, saying:

> I could not sleep on the sea's beds for the birds' screaming;
> he wakes me who comes from out at sea every morning, that
> gull.[5]

---

2. Ibid.

3. Ibid.

4. Ibid., 23.

5. Ibid., 24.

Not able to reconcile their opposite natures, Skadi and Njord separate and live independently in their own halls.

This is not to say that Skadi divorces Njord. The Eddas are not clear on the exact nature of their relationship. It seems that in times of crisis, Skadi and Njord come together to form a united front. In the prose introduction of the "Skirnismal" ("Skirnir's Journey") in the Poetic Edda, both Skadi and Njord request the help of their son's friend and servant Skirnir in dissuading their son from romancing a giantess. Their son, Freyr, is Njord's son by blood; Skadi is only his stepmother. Yet this story indicates that she takes his welfare and her role as guardian seriously.

Indeed, it is not inconceivable to think that Njord agreed to having an "open marriage" with Skadi, where each is bound by responsibility but not necessarily by the bedchamber. In the "Lokasenna" in the Poetic Edda, when Loki is claiming that several of the goddesses are wanton hussies, Njord counters with this argument: "That's harmless, if, besides a husband, a woman has/a lover or someone else."[6] Njord's statement would seem to indicate that he has no problem with a wife having extramarital affairs and thus that, if they did remain married, Skadi was free to pursue alternative lovers.

Later in the "Lokasenna," Loki even claims to have been invited into Skadi's bed. After sneering over the way he engineered her father's death, Loki taunts Skadi by saying:

> More lightly thou spakest with Laufey's son,
> When thou badst me come to thy bed;
> Such things must be known if now we two
> Shall seek our sins to tell.[7]

Skadi does not refute his charges. To be fair, though, she does not have the chance, as Thor's wife, Sif, comes forward to pour mead, offering hospitality to Loki. If true, it would seem that Loki was only one of several gods to share Skadi's bed. According to the *Ynglings Saga*, Skadi also has sexual relations with Odin and bears him many sons.[8] One of their sons, according to the poem *Haleygjatal*, is Saeminger, the first in the line of the Jarls of Hladhir, fierce protectors of the ancient religion in Norway during the Christian conversion.[9] An assignation with Odin rings true to Skadi's character, as both

6. Larrington, *Poetic Edda*, 90, verse 33.

7. Bellows, *Poetic Edda*, 168, verse 52.

8. Sturluson, *Heimskringla*, chapter 8.

9. Gundarsson, *Our Troth*, 399.

gods have an affinity for wolves and battle. Also, neither of them is squeamish in administering punishments and retaliations, although Skadi usually acts out of a sense of fairness while Odin strikes for reasons only he can know.

Skadi's propensity for justice is exemplified in the vengeance she claims for the death of her father and in the punishment she inflicts on Loki for his part in the death of Baldr. After Baldr dies (due to a mistletoe dart thrown by the blind god Hod but guided by Loki), Loki is captured by Thor and imprisoned in a cave. Loki is forced to watch as one of his sons, Vali, is turned into a wolf. Beyond reasoning in his new animal form, Vali disembowels and kills his brother Narfi as Loki looks on, unable to stop the carnage. As if that was not enough punishment, the "Gylfaginning" in the Prose Edda and the "Lokasenna" in the Poetic Edda describe the gods tying Loki to a rock with his own son's intestines. In a final coup de grâce, Skadi places a venomous snake over Loki's face so that the poison may sting and burn him as it drips from the snake's mouth. Skadi places herself in the position of judge, jury, and executioner, taking on the power and ultimately the responsibility of disciplining Loki. Loki has caused the death of two people that Skadi cares about: her father, Thiassi, and the beautiful god Baldr. Using the strength of her emotions, yet accepting the consequences of her actions, Skadi enacts retribution from a giant-god who has caused her much pain and suffering.

Skadi is a brave, beautiful, forthright goddess who acts on her instincts and emotions, accepting her choices and trusting in her own inner truth. Lover of at least three gods, she allows her own needs to dictate her bedroom behavior. Unafraid of her power, Skadi acts in the name of what is right and just, reacting to her emotions and her own inner sense of fairness. Sexy and strong, Skadi makes a decision and does not veer from her chosen path. She is sure of herself and confident in her abilities. She is a woman in control.

An explorer and adventurer, Skadi will not coddle your insecurities and fears. Rather, she challenges you to confront your anxieties and conquer them. Skadi dares you to uncover the power hidden deep within yourself and, once found, actually use it. Direct, complex, powerful, and graceful, Skadi calls us to be the individuals we are destined to be—without excuses, without blame, without apology. "Be yourself," she screams over the screeching winds and howling wolves of her hall in the north. And with her help, we just might be able to accomplish that task.

THE WARRIOR WITHIN: UNLEASHING THE POWER

It is very rare nowadays to wield a sword or axe in battle, to learn naval tactics, or to destroy an enemy stronghold. In fact, except for members of the military, very few modern people have a chance to connect with their inner warrior. The job of the warrior is to protect. She protects the homestead, the children and spouse and friends, the morality of societal leaders, and the right decisions and actions. The warrior believes in herself and stands up for what she thinks is right. She doesn't allow anyone to step on her or talk down to her. The warrior knows her own heart and her own true worth. No one can take her sense of self away from her.

Although the days of rampaging dragons and marauding raiders are long past, the warrior still serves as a valuable part of our inner psyches. It is the "sixth sense" of the warrior that alerts us to potentially damaging and dangerous situations. It is the strength of the warrior that carries us through difficult physical tasks and emotional experiences. It is the morality of the warrior that urges us to speak out against unlawful and secretive activities. It is the will of the warrior that compels us to stand up for ourselves and our beliefs and ideas.

The power of the warrior is without bounds and can bring value into our lives. Although it is necessary in our society to behave diplomatically, it is also important to accept our inner warrior, which is a fundamental part of being human. To ignore the inner warrior causes blockages and pockets of negativity in our bodies and our lives. Sometimes you just can't swallow another of your boss's stupid lies. Sometimes you need to tell your friend that you don't want to go dancing (again) and that you'd rather see a movie instead. Our warrior energy balances out our mediating, accepting energy, giving us fuller, healthier lives. So allow your inner warrior to come out and roar! And don't be surprised if you suddenly want to decorate your apartment with replica broadswords, flails, and axes.

THE PATHWORKING

When traveling in the Otherworld, it is not uncommon to find yourself in difficult, unsettling circumstances. Trees may come to life and talk. Animals may dance and alter their shapes. Formless blobs or mythological monsters may suddenly appear, popping up next to you from (apparently) nowhere. The environs may be dark and spooky or simply zany and kooky. The rules and laws of our mundane world do not apply to the Otherworld, so there is no limit to what you may encounter.

Most of your visits in the Otherworld will be harmless, strange, exotic experiences in which you will gain insight and knowledge from the spirits, the Gods and Goddesses, and your ancestors. However, other visits may involve your whole psyche and soul, creating changes on the spiritual level, as well as the cellular. One such visit is the shamanic initiation, and the following Skadi meditation mirrors a traditional initiation experience.

An initiation involves a welcoming or blessing and an altering of your perception of the world and of yourself. Most shamans undergo an initiatory experience before their training is finished. In fact, many cultures consider the initiation essential to the creation of a shaman. They believe that without an initiation, the spirits have not fully accepted the spirit of the shaman and thus will not respect him or her when journeying to find information and to heal.[10]

Shamanic spirit initiations happen spontaneously and are as individual as the shamans themselves. However, there are a few occurrences that generally (although not always) take place. First, the shaman encounters a much stronger power than him or herself. This power could obviously destroy him or her if it so wished. After some time, this power eventually dismantles the shaman in the Otherworld. This can take the form of a beheading, of a ripping off of arms and legs, or of various body parts suddenly falling off the shaman's body. The destruction of the shaman's body symbolizes his or her release from the mundane world. Afterward, the shaman is put back together, either with or without the help of the power. Sometimes power animals or spirit guides will facilitate this restructuring. The shaman has now become as much a member of the spirit world as the mundane world. After the shaman's body has regained its original shape and form, the power may gift the shaman with an item. This could be a crane bag, medicine bundle, mask or helm of invisibility, or anything else that has meaning to the shaman and the shaman's culture. This gift is to be used by the shaman in future visits to the Otherworld and will signal his or her connection to the spirits. He or she may create a physical representative of this gift once the journey is complete. And, with this, the shamanic initiation is over.

---

10. This concept was first explained to me by Trish Casimira, a wonderful healer and shaman of Cherokee ancestry. Contact her at her Wendell, Woburn, or Sandwich, Massachusetts, offices by telephone at (978) 544-1155 or (508) 833-6300 or online at http://www.souljourneying.com/home.html. (This shamanic idea is also stated in numerous scholarly and spiritual books.)

Your visit to Skadi will not be as explicit as a traditional shamanic initiation. There will be no disfigurement or destruction of the body. However, in accessing your inner warrior, you will be asked to endure extreme cold, heat, and light. Skadi is not a small or gentle goddess. There will be times when her arms will weigh you down or she will inflict some pain. Remember, you are trying to birth the warrior who is hidden within yourself. Every birth has trials and tribulations, pain and blood. However, every birth also gifts you with strength, desire, and endurance. Every birth is a transition, a change—and it is not easy. However, all transitions, by their very definition, come to an end, allowing you to reach a whole new level of understanding and knowledge. Enjoy the Skadi meditation. Experience it. Live it at the very basic level. And when you are done, know that your inner warrior is alive and well and ready to fight for you.

GUIDED MEDITATION: ACTIVATING THE WARRIOR WITHIN

Take a deep breath, in through your nose and out through your mouth. Take another deep breath, filling your stomach, your diaphragm, and finally your lungs. Hold this breath for five seconds … 1-2-3-4-5 … and exhale, allowing the breath to exit your lungs first, then your diaphragm, and finally your stomach. Take one more deep breath, and as you breathe in, feel the energy of the crisp winter air around you supporting your fingers, your toes, your legs, and your shoulders, even the top of your head. Hold the breath for seven seconds … 1-2-3-4-5-6-7. As you exhale, feel all tension leave your fingers, your toes, your legs, and your shoulders, even the top of your head. Continue breathing deeply, in through your nose and out through your mouth. Feel the bracing, frigid breeze over your body, tracing around every inch of exposed skin. Goosebumps form on your arms and legs, along the back of your neck, and on the top of your scalp. With their forming, stress and worry are released from your body, floating out through your pores to be whisked away by the breeze. You rest on the earth, on a pelt of fur, warm in your cocoon, completely free of care and anxiety, loose and unresisting. The fir trees sigh high above you, and white clouds scuttle quickly over a piercing blue sky. You have never felt so relaxed, so secure, so calm.

You are in a mountainous terrain at the very heights of the world, where the snows gather for most of the year. The sun shines brightly, warming your body and energizing you, galvanizing you to roll out of your fur-lined bedding and strap on a pair of snowshoes. Leaving your gear under the protective boughs of a large pine tree, you walk northward, toward a nearby granite mountain. The trees guide your way, forming a walkway, a path of living green to the base of the mountain. (pause) Your snowshoes hiss and shush on the snow, the only sound in this harsh world of white and gray and green.

At the base of the mountain, a ragged path zigzags upward, disappearing behind fallen boulders and jagged rock faces. Although steep, it does not look to be particularly difficult or dangerous to climb. Unfastening your snowshoes and placing them in your pack, you step on the path and begin walking. The trees are sparse on the mountainside as the breeze becomes wilder and the air becomes thinner. For some reason, perhaps due to an enchantment or the steepness of the ascent, there is no snow on the path or on the craggy peaks you are walking past. However, sheets of transparent, iridescent ice form shining waterfalls on the slick, rocky mountainside. They sparkle in the sun, throwing tiny rainbows over the dirt path. They are beautiful, and the sight of them lifts your spirits, even as your lungs ache from trying to draw in enough oxygen.

As you follow the path around a large rocky outcrop, burrowing ever deeper into the heart of the mountain, you are blinded by a burst of sunlight reflecting off a sheet of ice. Instinctively, you close your eyes, groping forward until you sense some shade. When you open your eyes, orange, blue, yellow, and black spots float and dance in front of you, obscuring your vision. You blink rapidly as the sound of wolves rises all around you. The howling is endless. Blinking your eyes continuously to adjust them to the relative dark, you hope the wolves are not hungry enough to take you as their next meal.

The spots in front of your eyes dim and fade away, leaving the breathtaking view of a giant granite hall directly before you. It seems to rise directly from the rock face, gray and solid and commanding. If you looked quickly, you might think it was just a strange grouping of rocks or a unique phenomenon of nature. A commanding peak juts forward over a heavy iron door. Along the roofline, wolves too numerous to count sit staring over the frozen, barren wasteland. You think they are statues, part of the architectural design, until you see an ear twitch and a fang exposed. The ghostly howling begins again, announcing your arrival.

You raise and drop the knocker on the iron door once, and the sound reverberates throughout your body and through the stone of the great hall. The door opens immediately, as if waiting for the signal, and a large, thick warrior roughly ushers you inside. He towers above you, clad in leather and furs. His face is set in a perpetual scowl, with thick, heavy eyebrows and angry eyes. He clutches a large axe in his hand. His fingers flex anxiously, as if itching to put the axe to use. You smile nervously, hoping not to offend him and thus give him an excuse to lop off your head or cleave your arm from its shoulder.

The warrior stomps through a narrow guard booth lit only by the wavering light of two torches. It is cold in the depths of this stone castle, and you shiver uncontrollably. Pulling open a second door, the warrior motions for you to walk through. Then he steps out behind you and closes the door, effectively blocking any escape. You stand in a courtyard, open to the elements but surrounded on four sides by high, gray stone walls. Small buildings in varying stages of disrepair line the sides of the courtyard. Warriors, both men and women, spar with each other, using sword and shield. Several chickens and a few goats chew and peck at the straw littered on the ground, scrambling away noisily should any warriors come too close. In the far back of the courtyard, steam rises from washing tubs and cooking kitchens. Out of the doorway of the large, dominating hall sprints a young woman. It is Skadi, shining giant bride of the gods.

She wears fawn-colored pants tucked into worn brown knee-high boots. A dark blue cloak swirls around her shoulders, and you catch only a glimpse of a white shirt and heavy armor underneath. Skadi moves so fast toward you that her long light blond hair flies behind her like a banner, and she appears before you more quickly than you anticipated.

"I am Skadi, mistress of Thrymheim," she announces, putting her hands on her hips and spreading her legs wide. "Who are you, and what do you want here?" You tell Skadi your name and that you are looking to activate your own inner warrior. (pause) Skadi's icy blue eyes narrow as she gazes into the depths of your soul. Her stare is piercing, but you do not look away. (pause) Skadi nods, lowers her arms from her hips, and punches you on the shoulder. You feel her punch in the very marrow of your bone, with a dull throb and ache.

"So tell me," Skadi says, crossing her arms in front of her chest and leaning back gracefully, "what have you done to make me welcome you into my ranks?" You think of all the times you stood up for yourself, all the times when you chose to follow your own beliefs even if they were unpopular, all the times you protected someone less able. Consider every instance, from childhood to the present, and tell them to Skadi. (long pause)

"You indeed have the heart of a warrior." Skadi smiles, flashing brilliant white teeth. "But why do you need my help?" Explain to Skadi the reasons why you are seeking to activate your inner warrior. These reasons could be as varied as wanting to stand up to a bully, gaining confidence in going out alone at night, finding inner power during a difficult time in your life, or something completely different. Once you have decided why you wish to activate the warrior within, tell Skadi your answer. (pause)

Skadi nods and drapes one long, muscled arm across your shoulders. She guides you to a well-kept building, the closest one to the entrance of the great hall. The door is large and heavy, but Skadi kicks it open with the heel of her boot. Inside it is dark, as the only light trickles in from the newly opened door. The cold is numbing, chilling you through and through. You can no longer feel the tips of your fingers and so you shove them under the folds of your woolen cloak. As the darkness ebbs, and your eyes adjust, you see row after row after row of helms and breastplates.

"Armor," Skadi says, mirroring your own thoughts. "Every warrior needs armor." She gestures with her hand at the armor before you. "My storehouse is open to you. Choose a breastplate of your own." Stunned by her generosity, you move slowly into the cavernous room. "Choose wisely," Skadi calls from the doorway, "for the armor you choose cannot be returned. It is yours for life." Skadi turns and strides from the armory, giving you your privacy.

Overwhelmed with the task before you, you gaze at the hundreds and hundreds of pieces of armor in front of you. The breastplates are made of metal and leather. Some look to be brass or copper, some even gold. Others are shiny silver or heavy iron. Many have engravings and etchings. Meaningful scenes and phrases litter the armor in a colorful kaleidoscope. The leather cuirasses are worn in places, yet polished and malleable. Some sport fringe or fur, while others boast patterns and swirls made of studs or grommets. The array and assortment is breathtaking, and you take your time wandering amid the pieces of armor. (long pause) When you feel drawn to a particular piece of armor, pick it up, hold it in your hands, and study it. Look at the designs. Feel its energy. Compare and contrast two or three or four breastplates to which you are drawn. (long pause) Finally, when you find a piece of armor that you simply can't put down, that you absolutely must have, that you can't live without, put it on and step out the door of the small building. (pause)

"You have chosen well, my warrior," Skadi whispers into your ear as she ties the laces and adjusts the fit. The cuirass conforms to your body and fits as though it was made for you. Turning you around roughly, Skadi stares into your eyes. Lightning bolts flash in the depths of hers, and a blizzard blows beneath her lashes. A cloud covers her face, altering it, changing it into the terrible face of vengeance, the powerful face of battle, the quickening face of death. You try to step back, away from this dark vision, but Skadi's hands have gripped your shoulders with the strength of eagle talons. You can feel her fingernails piercing the flesh. You have no choice but to endure and wait for the final outcome.

Skadi's fingers clench harder, raking the bone. You grit your teeth, bearing the pain as best you can but refusing to look away from Skadi's stormy eyes. Just as you open your mouth to scream, trying to diffuse some of the pain, Skadi releases your shoulders and slams one hand into your chest and the other into your back, supporting you. She draws you upward, on tiptoe, just as the storm in her eyes bolts outward into your own in a crackling wave of icy blue light. The blue light blinds you, warming you with a strange, white-hot intensity. It is ferocious, so cold that it burns. You feel nothing but the radiating frozen heat of Skadi's power. You see nothing but the penetrating, piercing blue light mixed with Skadi's snow-white smile and the illuminating rainbows from the ice waterfalls on the mountain rocks. (pause)

"Rest, my warrior," Skadi's voice calls through the twinkling dark, over a large distance. "You have withstood my gaze and you have survived. The power you seek is within you, just as it always has been. Your breastplate is a symbol of this power. Don it whenever you have need and know that I am with you, guiding your actions, lending my power, giving you victory. You are a warrior!" And then her voice and the howling of wolves melts away into the sigh and shudder of the wind through the pine trees. You open your eyes just a little and see that you are once again in your furry cocoon of warmth, protected by the overhang of several large pine trees. You smile, thank Skadi, and close your eyes to rest after your ordeal.

Now take a deep breath, in through your nose and out through your mouth. Take another deep breath, filling your stomach, your diaphragm, and finally your lungs. Hold this breath for five seconds … 1-2-3-4-5 … and exhale, allowing the breath to exit your lungs first, then your diaphragm, and finally your stomach. Breathe deeply once more, and as you breathe in, feel the energy and the wonder of the world around you in your fingers, your toes, your legs, and your shoulders, even the top of your head. As you exhale, wiggle your fingers and toes. Shake your legs and move your shoulders up and down. Take another deep breath and, as you exhale, move your head from side to side. Feel the ground under your body touching every nerve ending and muscle. Hear the rustlings of the people around you. Notice the movements outside. Continue breathing. Stretch your arms out above your head. You are returning to the present, to the here and now. Continue stretching. Continue breathing. When you are ready, open your eyes, blink and focus, and sit up.

INVOCATION TO SKADI

Blue and gold lights play on freshly fallen snow
—Ah Skadi—
Wolves howl in the distance as we go
—Oh Skadi—
Warrior maiden, skiing free
—La Skadi—
Come, lend your strength to me.
—Hail Skadi—

Mistress, temptress, lover of the Gods
—Ah Skadi—
Only yours as your head nods
—Oh Skadi—
In assent and pleasure, yours to gift
—La Skadi—
Until your interest does sway and shift.
—Hail Skadi—

Vision of vengeance, tough and fierce
—Ah Skadi—
Sword-arm strong enough to pierce
—Oh Skadi—
Teach me well, of truth and right
—La Skadi—
That I may travel through the night.
—Hail Skadi—

Hail Skadi—Goddess of independence
Hail Skadi—Goddess of impatience
Hail Skadi—Goddess of intensity
Hail Skadi—Goddess of impulse

Be with me now.

MAGICAL ACTIVITIES

Physical Magic: Create a Power Bundle

Items needed: An eighth of a yard of cloth or leather; thread; a needle or sewing machine; several small sacred items; ribbon, rope, yarn, or twine; and thin black cording (optional)

Moon Phase: Full

Seasonal Phase: The extremes of the year—summer or winter

This power bundle will be a contained collection of trinkets that reminds you of your warrior nature. During difficult situations, it will help you maintain your strength of mind and body. In times of stress or anxiety, it will help you acknowledge the wisdom of your inner truth. When confronted by deception and falsehood, it will guide you onto the valiant path of justice. You can choose to wear your power bundle, keep it in a sacred place in your home, or store it in a hidden location until such time as you need it. This craft is fairly simple and, once you have gathered all of your items, takes very little time to accomplish. Children often enjoy making power bundles, especially if they are having difficulty with bullies or complicated tests at school.

Your first step in crafting a power bundle is gathering the items to put inside. These items should be fairly small, especially if you are planning on wearing your bundle. Since this bundle revolves around the goddess Skadi and your own inner warrior, you should gather items related to these concepts. As the number nine is sacred to the Norse culture, I recommend gathering nine items, in groups of three: collect three items that remind you of Skadi, three items that remind you of warriors, and three items that remind you of your inner warrior. You might choose to find small charms that recall the armor you received in the meditation or things that recollect Skadi's clothing or hall. Some suggestions might be dried herbs, colorful buttons, pieces of ribbon, a lock of your hair, semiprecious stones, coins, acorns or leaves, homemade paper snowflakes, glitter, or anything and everything else that calls to you.

After you have gathered your items together, visit your local fabric store and choose your cloth. I like transparent cloth, because then you can see the items in your power bundle and draw energy from them without having to untie the bag. However, if you are drawn to a dark wool or a vibrant snowy cotton, go with your instinct and purchase what feels right. Buy only an eighth of a yard of the fabric, and then choose some ribbon, yarn, rope, or twine to close the bundle.

Once at home, cut the fabric into an eight-inch rectangle and fold it in half, with the wrong side facing outward. Using a sewing machine or hand-stitching with needle and thread, sew the two long sides of the rectangle. If hand-stitching, make sure your stitches are fairly small and close together so your smaller items (like herbs) won't fall out. When you are finished, you will have an inside-out "pocket," with two sides sewn up, one side closed along the fold, and the fourth side open. Turn your pocket so that the right side of the material is facing outward.

Take each item that you gathered and name it before dropping it into your cloth pocket. For instance, you might say, "This is a piece of onyx, stone of protection and defense. I place its power in my power bundle in remembrance of the warrior." Once all nine items are placed in the bundle, gather the open end of your bundle together and tie your ribbon, twine, or rope around the end. If you want to wear the bundle, sew thin black cording (found in most craft stores in the jewelry aisle) on either side of the gathered edge, making sure the cording is long enough to fit over your head.

Runic Magic: Gathering Skadi Water

Items Needed: A fairly large bowl, a fine mesh strainer or cheesecloth, glass bottle(s) or container(s), a funnel, a rune book, and a rainy or snowy day

Moon Phase: Any

Seasonal Cycle: Winter

Water is a sacred substance, one of the four natural elements on this earth. It can be used to heal, to honor, to cleanse, to recharge, and to rejuvenate. You can drink it, bathe in it, splash it, sprinkle it, and pour it over objects. It is eminently versatile and flexible, persistent, patient, and strong but with a strength that is mutable and changeable. Is it any wonder that Skadi, ski goddess, father-avenger, Etin-Bride, claims water, in the form of snow, as her own?

For this spell, you must wait for a cold day when it is raining or snowing outside. Ideally, the rain and snow would be gathered during the winter months. Pay attention to power days, such as the first or last snowfall of the season, the winter solstice, Christmas, New Year's, or Imbolc, as snow or rain gathered on these days will be even more potent.

Once a cold and snowy or rainy day has arrived, place your bowl outside where it will collect the snow or rain. Be sure to place the bowl off the ground so as to avoid animal contamination. You are trying to gather the purest sample of winter water possible. If you live in an area where acid rain is prevalent, please do not collect any naturally occurring rainfall. Instead, purchase distilled water and pour some into a bowl. Place the bowl outside during a winter rain or snowstorm for five or ten minutes, allowing only a small portion of snow and rain to collect in it. This way, you will receive the essence of the winter water while still protecting yourself from harmful chemicals.

Once your bowl is full, bring it back inside and allow it to warm up (and melt, if you have snow). You will probably notice small bits of dirt, soot, and vegetation in your water. Strain these out of your water with the cheesecloth so that you can have a pure sample. Pour the clean, strained water into your glass bottle or container using the funnel, and then cap it. If you wish, gather more rain or snow until the bottle is full.

After you have gathered as much winter water as you wish, bring your water to a place in your home that is comfortable and relaxing while still affording a view of the snow or rain outside. Glance through your rune book and see what runes resonate with you. Read the sections on those runes. If you are already familiar with runes, you might find the reading to be redundant, but do it anyway, as it may give you additional insights into the runes. If you are not drawn to any particular rune, start with the runes Isa and Uruz, as I have found these runes work well with the goddess Skadi.

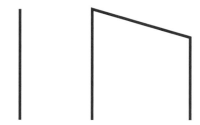

Figure 11: Isa, and Figure 12: Uruz

Meditate for a while on the runes that call to you. Feel their presence. Explore their hidden meanings for you, and for humanity. While still meditating, find a rune that represents the goddess Skadi. Focus on that rune. Hear it singing inside your head. Feel its power and strength. When you feel as though you have explored the rune entirely (at least for the moment), pull the winter water to you and chant the name of the rune into the water. Using your fingertips, sign the symbol of the rune over the water, feeling the energy of the rune entering the water and blessing it. Cap the bottle and shake the water three times, saying, "Skadi, goddess of winter power and might, I bless this water in your name and in the name of (*name of the rune*). May its strength purify, cleanse, and heal me and others around me. Blessed Be!"

You have now created sacred water that can be used during rituals, healing sessions, or everyday life. You have tapped into the wildness of winter, the fierceness of Skadi, and the power of the runes. You hold a bit of the Otherworld in your hands.

Symbolic Magic: Consecrate Your Power Bundle

Items Needed: Your Skadi water, wolf fur or a picture of a wolf, a knife or sword, the rune Isa drawn on a piece of paper or carved into a piece of wood, your power bundle, a sage wand, and a lighter or matches

Moon Phase: New or full

Seasonal Cycle: Winter

Consecration is the act of making an object (or person) holy. It is usually performed after the item has been cleansed of any negativity, and it is done through the use of sage, salt water, moonlight, or Florida water. Through consecration, the object is linked to the divine and actually houses some of the energy of the Goddess. Since your power bundle is a physical representative of your warrior energy, it is important to honor Skadi by asking for her blessing on your bundle by honoring it as a sacred link to her.

Place all of the items in the center of your sacred space and, holding your power bundle in your hands, sit down in front of your items. Ground and center, forcing your breath to be steady and even. You should feel extremely calm and connected to everything in the world and in the universe before you begin. Acknowledge the truth about yourself, and feel the peace and serenity that come from knowing your inner self.

Once you are relaxed, put down your power bundle, pick up the wolf fur or picture, and walk to the direction of the north. Hold the fur or picture up to Skadi and say:

Howling clan, protectors of Thrymheim, Skadi's constant companions. Aid me now in warding and protecting this sacred space. By the strength of Skadi's arm, I call you to me.

Sprinkle the bits of fur as you walk to the east. If you have a wolf picture, hold it facing outward as you walk to the east. Once there, hold up the fur or picture and say:

Den-lovers, protectors of Thrymheim, Skadi's constant companions. Aid me now in warding and protecting this sacred space. By the power of Skadi's voice, I call you to me.

Continue sprinkling the fur or holding the picture aloft as you walk to the south. Once there, hold up the fur or picture and say:

Fire-leapers, protectors of Thrymheim, Skadi's constant companions. Aid me now in warding and protecting this sacred space. By the lightning in Skadi's eyes, I call you to me.

Walk to the west, still sprinkling the fur or holding up the picture. Keeping your arms raised, say:

Wolf family, protectors of Thrymheim, Skadi's constant companions. Aid me now in warding and protecting this sacred space. By the quickening of Skadi's blood, I call you to me.

Return to the center of your sacred space, and if there is any more wolf fur, add it to your power bundle. Grasp the Isa rune and envision the beautiful, terrible, powerful giant goddess Skadi. Once her image is fixed in your mind, say:

Glorious Skadi of snow-blinded sun and frosty cold.
You are the strong one,
—impatient, impervious, intuitive, intense—
Your warrior skills gain respect from the gods.
I ask for your guiding hand and skill
in achieving and knowing my inner warrior.
This power bundle is a first step along the lifetime road
toward that goal.
I consecrate it, with your tools of power, in your name.

Hail Skadi, lady-wolf, bow-string Var, ski goddess, Njord's ill-suited wife, Thiassi's vengeful daughter! I honor thee!

Light the sage wand and allow the smoke to float over every inch of the sword or knife and the power bundle. Take your time as you are cleansing these objects of any and all negativity, getting them ready to be consecrated to the goddess. When you feel the objects are cleansed, put down the smudge wand. Place the Isa rune in front of you and then place your power bundle on top of it. Put the knife or sword on top of the bundle so that the power bundle is sandwiched between the rune and the knife. Take the Skadi water and sprinkle it on top of the knife, the bundle, and the Isa rune. Don't worry about getting every piece of the bundle wet. The Isa rune and the knife (sword) sanctify the bundle just as much as the water. Relax for a few minutes, relishing the energy and enthusiasm of Skadi. Feel the warrior inside you. If you wish to meditate and ask for a message from Skadi, do so now.

When you are finished consecrating your power bundle and meditating, thank Skadi for her help, saying:

Most strong-limbed Skadi,
Sword-wielder, wolf-tamer,
True Warrior,
I thank you for lending your energy to my power bundle.
May I walk your ways with honor!
Hail and Farewell.

Walk to the west and say:

Wolf family, protectors of Thrymheim, Skadi's constant companions. I thank you for warding and protecting this sacred space. By the quickening of Skadi's blood, I bid you Hail and Farewell.

Moving to the south, say:

Fire-leapers, protectors of Thrymheim, Skadi's constant companions. I thank you for warding and protecting this sacred space. By the lightning in Skadi's eyes, I bid you Hail and Farewell.

After walking to the east, say:

Den-lovers, protectors of Thrymheim, Skadi's constant companions. I thank you for warding and protecting this sacred space. By the power of Skadi's voice, I bid you Hail and Farewell.

And, lastly, at the north, say:

Howling clan, protectors of Thrymheim, Skadi's constant companions. I thank you for warding and protecting this sacred space. By the strength of Skadi's arm, I bid you Hail and Farewell.

Return to the center of your sacred space and place your knife, bundle, and Isa rune in a safe place where no children or animals will bother it. Allow the knife and rune to consecrate the bundle for the length of one night. The next day, remove the knife and the rune. Wash the knife reverently and, if the rune is made of paper, burn it safely and sprinkle the ashes to the wind. Put your power bundle in a safe place so that you can utilize its energy whenever you have need.

MEETING SUNNA, NORSE GODDESS OF THE SUN
Allowing Yourself to Shine

SUNNA: GODDESS OF ALL-TIME

Our sun is approximately 4.5 billion years old and will probably live for another 4 to 5 billion years.[1] Since humans have been on planet earth, she has hung in the sky, brightening our days, giving life to our plants, regulating our weather, and warming our lives. Think about that for a moment. There has never been a time in the vast scope of human life on earth that the sun has not existed. In fact, we exist because of her—and a lucky fluke of nature that placed us in the exact right spot to benefit from her powerful presence. She is the constant in our lives that sustains our planet and assures our survival.

The sun that we bask under on our beaches and in our backyards is the exact same sun that the Norse people worshipped hundreds of years ago. In the timeline of our sun, the Vikings trod the earth only a second or so ago. They did not see the earth's birth or her tentative early years of youthful growth. By the time the warriors of the north stepped into their longboats, the sun was in her maturity, just as she is now. Their sun is our sun. Our sun was their sun. In a supreme act of mind-bending time travel, the sun reduces the space between us and the Vikings. We are brothers and sisters, sharing the same stage of the sun.

In Norse mythology, the sun is a woman, differing greatly from traditional Greco-Roman, Egyptian, and Middle Eastern myths that give the sun a male persona. Traditional Wiccan mythology also deems the sun to be under the influence of the God, the male aspect of divinity. These are the myths with which we are most comfortable. After all, if the moon, with her fluctuations and watery emphasis, is female, then the sun, with his assertiveness and fiery ways, must be male. Or must he? To the northern peoples, the Norse of Scandinavia and the Celts of Britain and Ireland, the sun did not hold the same intense strength and power as the sun of the southern lands. In Greece and Egypt and in the deserts of the Middle East, the sun baked the land, destroying crops and drying up lakes and riverbeds. The sun gave life and destroyed life, depending on the time of the year. In the north, the sun loses some of its intensity. While it still helps the plants to grow and flourish, it does not burn them during the hot months. Instead, the sun melts away the cold and ice of winter, revealing a burgeoning earth underneath the snow. The sun, then, loses its negative qualities, becoming a nurturing, nourishing entity, not unlike a mother feeding her children. Is it any wonder that the Celts and the Norse related the orb of the sun with the Goddess?

---

1. University Corporation for Atmospheric Research, "About the Sun."

The Norse sun goddess is Sunna (pronounced SOO-nah), daughter of Mundilfaeri, sister of Mani, wife of Glen. She is a human who rose to the rank of Goddess with the help of the Norse gods. Sunna's father, Mundilfaeri (whose name means "Axis Mover"[2]), thought his children so beautiful that he named them Sun and Moon, respectively. The gods were unhappy with this proud father's choice of names and, seeking to punish him, took hold of Sun and Moon and threw them up into the sky, where they became one with their namesakes. Therefore, Sunna drives the chariot of the sun, and Mani, her brother, is the driver of the chariot of the moon. Both children of Mundilfaeri are hastened in their flight across the sky by two wolves, named Skoll and Hati, who run at the heels of their horses, trying to devour the sun and the moon.[3] During an eclipse, it is said that Skoll and Hati take bites out of the sun and moon, heralding the death of these celestial orbs during the Norse end of the world, known as Ragnarok.

During Ragnarok, most of the Norse gods die in battle while fighting the legions of fire giants and dead men led by the god Loki and his offspring, Hel (the Norse goddess of the Underworld), Jormungand (the world serpent), and Fenrir (the iron-jawed wolf). Ragnarok destroys the current incarnation of the world, allowing the rebirth of a new and brighter earth, with the sons and daughters of the gods taking the place of their fallen parents. For Sunna, the wolf finally catches up with her, dousing her light by swallowing her. Skoll is descended from a giantess named Jarnvidiur who births giants in wolf form in the Ironwood Forest. Born from this family, a wolf known as Moongarm "will swallow heavenly bodies and spatter heaven and all the skies with blood. As a result the sun will lose its shine."[4] He is known as "sun's snatcher in troll's guise" and the sun is described as "dark … for summers after."[5] Yet all is not lost. Like the other gods, at the end of Ragnarok, light still shines on the planet. Before her death, Sunna gives birth to a daughter as beautiful as her mother, and "she shall ride, when the powers die, the maiden, her mother's road."[6]

---

2. Schmitt, "Sunna and Mani."

3. Sturluson, *Edda*, 14–15.

4. Ibid., 15.

5. Ibid. Further evidence of the sun's demise can be found on pages 52 and 53. It is interesting to note that Sturluson, in his list of acceptable alternative phrases or names for the word *wolf*, does not list Sunna's chaser, Skoll. He also does not record Moongarm, although Mani's pursuer, Hati, makes the list, page 164.

6. Ibid., 57.

One contemporary scholar of Norse myth has concluded that Sunna holds the powers and attributes of a mother goddess, as compared to a warrior goddess, maiden goddess, or crone goddess. Lynda C. Welch, in *Goddess of the North*, postulates that since the Norse viewed the sun as a mature woman capable of giving birth, the sun radiates with classic mother-goddess attributes, such as the "Mother's ability to provide nourishment to sustain her children."[7] While this is true from a modern goddess-spirituality viewpoint, there is little evidence to support that the medieval Norse categorized their goddesses into a maiden-mother-crone continuum. This chronological triple-aspected goddess can be traced back to the modern Wicca movement of Gerald Gardiner, which first came to light in the late 1930s.[8] In fact, the only triplicate god form in Norse mythology is a male divinity, Odin, whose brothers, Vili and Ve, are often considered to be other aspects of himself. The fact that we cannot link her to a maiden-mother-crone triple goddess structure does not lessen Sunna's impact as a mature, mothering goddess. She is a mother not only to her surviving girl child, but also to all of the medieval Scandinavians who relied on her warming rays for food, as well as to all of us in the present day who need her to survive.

Despite Sunna's importance to the lifestyle of the medieval Scandinavians, there is little concrete mythological evidence of her worship, other than the myths pertaining to her family and her demise at Ragnarok. The fact that Snorri Sturluson includes her in his list of Norse goddesses (or Asyniur) in the "*Skaldskaparmal*" in the Prose Edda indicates that she was known to the medieval Norse chroniclers. Yet other medieval Norse sources indicate that Sunna, as the sun goddess, was not merely a character in the larger body of Norse mythology. She does appear to have had a sacred ritualized persona as indicated in the Old Norwegian Rune Poem, which dates from the late twelfth century. This poem gives a two-line description of each of sixteen Norse runestaves. The poem describes the rune Sowilo (the rune connected to the sun) this way: "The Sun is the light of the land; I bow to holy doom."[9] Although vague, there is a general feeling of worship in this stanza, especially since the writer "bows" to the sun. However, the extent and form of Sunna's worship is unknown.

---

7. Welch, *Goddess of the North*, 151.

8. While triple goddesses can be found in many cultures (Celtic, Roman, Greek, Hindu, and Mesopotamian, for example), the classification of the triplicity into a maiden-mother-crone format is distinctly modern.

9. Bray, "Old Norwegian Rune Poem."

Modern Icelandic folklorist Jon Hnefill Aalsteinsson suggests a possible example of sun worship in the *Laxdaela Saga*, an Icelandic tale written by an anonymous author around 1245 AD. In the story, a woman named Gudrun goads her husband into pursuing and killing his foster brother, her former suitor, and the one man who holds her heart, Kjartan. (In classic love-triangle fashion, Gudrun is tricked into marrying her husband, Bolli, while her true love, Kjartan, is being held hostage by the king of Norway. When Kjartan returns, both he and Gudrun are incensed at the situation and take their frustration out on each other.) On the morning of Kjartan's death, Gudrun awakes early, as Aalsteinsson translates, "when the sun was lifted or offered to."[10] This would be an allusion to the classic sacrificial offering to the gods in order to receive a boon. Gudrun wants Kjartan dead, so she gives an offering to Sunna so that her plans are accomplished successfully. Coupled with the fact that the dawn was often seen as a symbol of victory in medieval Norse literature,[11] it is possible that Sunna was a goddess who helped achieve goals and manifest wishes, bringing success and victory.

Yet Sunna's sacred attributes are more diversified than success in battle and growth of crops. In the Icelandic *Landnamabok Saga*, or the Book of Settlements, written during the thirteenth or fourteenth century, a dying man, Thorkell Thorsteinsson, requests that he be placed in the sunlight due to his sickness, indicating a correlation between the sun and death or the sun and sickness. Both theories can be backed up with other instances in Norse medieval literature.

In the "Solarljod" ("The Song of the Sun"), a poem written about the same time as the Poetic Edda and sometimes included within that series of myths, the journey of a man through death and the afterlife is described. From the title of the poem, it is obvious that the sun plays an important part in the man's journey, especially as he lies dying. In his death throes, the man crafts several stanzas beginning with the phrase "The sun I saw," juxtaposing her radiance with the dark, creaking gates of Hel (the Norse Underworld) and with his own failing body. Yet despite the dissonance, the man is linked to the sun through the experience of death. As the sun sets in the twilight sky, so too does the man die, indicating a connection between his death and the daily death of the sun. And through this connection, the sun appears mightier "than she was before" to the man. He sees "a glorious god" to whom he bows "for the last time, in the world of men,"

---

10. Gundarsson, *Our Troth*, 391.
11. Ibid.

harking back to the Old Norwegian Rune Poem, which indicated bowing as a form of honoring the sun and the Goddess Sunna. In the "Solarljod," the sun, although nameless, is given the feminine pronoun *she* while taking on human characteristics. The feminine sun beams "forth with quivering eyes, appalled and shrinking" and, to the dying man's way of thinking, seemed "seldom sadder."[12]

The appearance of the sun at two specific deaths indicates a correlation between the sun and the role of the shamanic psychopomp or guide into the Otherworldly realms of the dead. Since the deaths are not battle-related, the traditional psychopomps of warriors, the Valkyries, would not appear to the dying. Instead, Sunna emerges for one last comforting glimpse, one last warming embrace, before the dying slip into the great unknown. She materializes as the sacred caring mother wishing to ease the transition of her child from one level of existence to another. Her role in Ragnarok, as the birthing mother and the dying sun, also shows her affinity to be present at times of transition and to ease the burden of new experiences for humankind. Despite being eaten by a ravaging wolf, Sunna is still able to birth her daughter, who will continue in her mother's footsteps and shine the healing, growing, fertile rays of the sun on the world. While dying, Sunna gives birth not only to her own daughter, but also to humanity's only hope of continuing life on planet earth. The last activity of her existence puts her on the threshold of this world and the Otherworld twice—during death and during birth. The presence of Sunna at two separate deaths, her own demise at Ragnarok, and her neither fully human nor fully goddess lineage demonstrate a goddess familiar with transitory periods and one with an ability to aid those undergoing such changes and alterations.

One such transitional stage is illness. Being neither fully alive nor dead, sickness falls into a nebulous nether region of wounds, and boils, and phlegm, and general malaise. The second Merseburg charm, an incantation recorded in a tenth-century manuscript but believed to be much older, illustrates Sunna's ability not only to shepherd the sick to the Otherworld but also to heal the routine ills of everyday medieval life:

Phol and Wuodan rode to the wood;
then Balder's horse sprained its leg.
Then Sinthgunt sang over it and Sunna her sister,
then Frija sang over it and Volla her sister,
then Wuodan sang over it, as he well knew how,

---

12. Thorpe, *Edda Sæmund the Learned*, verses 39–44.

over this bone-sprain, this blood-sprain, this limb-sprain:
bone to bone,
blood to blood,
limb to limb,
such as they belong together.[13]

In this incantation, we are confronted with three major deities in Norse mythology: Odin (Wuodan); his wife, Frigga (Frija); and their son, Baldr (Balder). Many myths abound about Odin, Frigga, and Baldr, but one of the most common is the story of Baldr's death by mistletoe at the hand of Loki. (See the chapter on Frigga for more information.) Baldr dies, goes down to Hel's Underworld kingdom, and is then resurrected at Ragnarok to replace his father among the gods.

This mythic story follows the pattern of death presented in "Solarljod" and the *Landnamabok Saga*. Like the heroes of those tales, Baldr dies of sickness—poison from the mistletoe dart—and not in battle. There is no mention of Baldr's journey to Helheim in the Edda, so it is unknown if any goddess served as a psychopomp for him. However, the disposal of his body is fraught with descriptions of fire. Baldr's funeral is to take place on a ship, but none of the gods can move it off the pier. They call a giantess to help them, who "pushed it out with the first touch so that flame flew from the rollers."[14] Thereafter, Baldr's body is carried onto the boat and he, his still-alive but inconsolable wife, Nanna, and his horse are placed on a pyre and set ablaze. As Thor blesses the pyre with his hammer, a dwarf runs out from between his feet. His name is Lit, and a frustrated Thor kicks him into the pyre as well, where he burns freely. In the "Skaldskaparmal," Sturluson reports that the sun was often referred to as "fire of sky and air" and that fire was known as "sun of the houses."[15] Although not named, the many descriptions of fire at Baldr's funeral may have been alluding to the goddess Sunna in her psychopomp role, as evidenced in other medieval manuscripts.

The inclusion of Sunna in the second Merseburg charm undoubtedly comes by design rather than by happenstance. Sunna seems an odd choice of Goddess to include in a charm to heal a horse's leg, until one looks at the tale of Baldr's funeral and the fact

13. Storms, *Anglo-Saxon Magic*, 109. "Wuodan" is another name for Odin and "Frija" is his wife Frigga. "Phol" is generally considered to be another name for "Balder" (Baldr).

14. Sturluson, *Edda*, 49.

15. Sturluson, *Edda*, 93.

that he replaces his father among the gods after Ragnarok. Baldr, like Sunna's daughter, survives to aid and guide humanity after the destruction of the world as we know it. Both of them heal the world, knitting together the fragmented pieces of life after the chaos of Ragnarok. By birthing her daughter, Sunna performs the ultimate healing. She gives the earth the light necessary to survive utter destruction. The sun survives, gifting the world with her life-giving rays.

Healing, mothering, guiding, the sun shines on all of us from on high. Sunna, sun goddess of the northern lands, is much more than the growing, warming sun's rays. She is an active goddess who takes an interest in our everyday lives. She hangs in the sky high above and, when honored, helps us reach our goals. She heals our broken bones and our fragmented psyches with the gentle touch of a mother. And in the final action of our lives, our transition from this world into the Otherworld, Sunna shines bright, lighting our way and welcoming us home. For humans, Sunna has always hung in the sky, nurturing our planet. May we always feel her distant love, embraced by her warming light.

SHINING BRIGHT: BEING NOTICED

It's hard to envision the shining sun in the sky as a powerful, caring goddess. After all, we know the sun is a star. We know it is 93 million miles away from the earth and that its core reaches an average temperature of 15.6 million Kelvin, or 27 million degrees Fahrenheit. We know that it is not a solid planetary body and that its solar flares and solar wind cause the beautiful light storm known as the aurora borealis. It is a being of science, not mythology—but there you are wrong.

The wisdom of the sun bridges the worlds of science and mythology. Like Sunna herself, the sun straddles the fine line between fact and fiction, legend and lore, astronomy and astrology. For how many of us have ever set foot on the sun? How many of us have even seen it up close, in space? None. Man has set foot on the moon (about 250,000 miles away from the earth) but has not ventured farther out in space. The moon is still very, very far away from the sun, approximately 92,750,000 miles. So why, then, should we limit our knowledge of the sun to science? Why label her at all?

We label her because it's easy. We don't need to expand beyond the comfort zone of our society. We all agree: the sun is easily explained through the discipline of science. This pervasive philosophy limits the sun's existence. Her power is diminished. Her light grows dimmer. We push her into our conception of reality, boxing her into our truth, which may or may not be hers.

Society's need to box and label and compartmentalize is not limited to celestial bodies. Like the sun, many of us have accepted our prescribed "role." We are mother or teacher, lover or reader, worker, warrior, or friend. We don our supporting-cast costume and move out into the world, knowing our lines, knowing our blocking, and never venturing from the written script. We have allowed ourselves to be creatively thwarted, to be boxed into a corner. We have agreed to be only what others think we can be. We live in the shadow of their reality. Are we science or are we myth?

If we only forgot the limitations and expectations placed on us by society, we would realize that our existence is so much more than either science or myth. It is both. It is neither. It is something magical and mystical *and* scientific, and only you can create it! You have the power, the light, to shine in our world. Forget the restrictions of society, and be yourself—fully, totally, unbelievably yourself. Allow yourself to shine; it's time.

THE PATHWORKING

The passage of the sun is beyond our ability to comprehend. It is vast and unchanging, yet mercurial and transforming. The sun is larger and more powerful than we can even understand. Therefore, when meeting with a sun goddess, it is normal to feel slightly lightheaded and woozy. I have written these physical symptoms into the following meditation, because it is important to understand the differences between us and the realm of space on a tangible, visceral level. Our minds comprehend the numbers, but our hearts and bodies need a little explanation.

In fact, the entire meditation to visit with Sunna is slightly larger than life. Snarling wolves spray blood. Flaming horses snort and whinny. Shadows skulk in mysterious forests. Nothing is done halfway. This is the point. Sunna is a Goddess of the sun—the big, glorious gas giant that sustains our planet and our very way of life. The sun does not hide its brilliance or its light. The sun does not do things halfway in order to appease the constraints of others. The sun is wondrous and massive and full of life and death. It is experience at its most grandiose.

So, when entering into this meditation, expect exciting and nerve-racking episodes. Know that you will feel the warmth of the sun and the heat of violence. Be aware that this meditation gives you life at its most intense and extreme. And don't shy away from it. Embrace it, knowing that you are within a safe environment. Sunna is there to protect you, and your protective talisman is always by your side. Still ... if you don't like heights or feel nauseated by the smell of blood, you might consider performing this meditation on an empty stomach.

GUIDED MEDITATION: THE PATH OF THE SUN

Take a deep breath, in through your nose and out through your mouth. Take another deep breath, filling your stomach, your diaphragm, and finally your lungs. Hold this breath for five seconds ... 1-2-3-4-5 ... and exhale, allowing the breath to exit your lungs first, then your diaphragm, and finally your stomach. Take one more deep breath, and as you breathe in, feel the healing warmth of the sun around you, supporting your fingers, your toes, your legs, and your shoulders, even the top of your head. Hold the breath for seven seconds ... 1-2-3-4-5-6-7. As you exhale, feel all tension leave your fingers, your toes, your legs, and your shoulders, even the top of your head. Continue breathing deeply, in through your nose and out through your mouth. Feel the sun's light heating the top of your head. Allow the light and warmth to travel down your body, melting any excess stress. Feel your anxieties rolling off your body as your muscles release any tension, loosening and unwinding. (pause) You have never felt so relaxed, so secure, so calm.

You are walking in a rich forest dense with vegetation. Green, leafy trees tower above you on all sides as tiny herbal and flower shoots sprout from the leaf-matted ground. Vines snake along the ground, buried in the thick undergrowth and curling around tree trunks. A rudimentary, broken-down stone wall forms a barrier next to you, funneling your unsure feet onto a rough, narrow dirt path. The path is riddled with stones and doesn't appear to have been used for many years. Brown leaves, brittle and delicate, form a gentle carpet on the path; the spidery veins connect their broken tissues in an intricate web of frailty and mortality.

You pause, glancing up at the topmost branches of the trees and the splintering sky beyond. The sky is hidden by the heavy cover of leaves above you. You cannot tell if the sun shines brightly or if rain falls. Under the forest's canopy, all is gray and hidden and mysterious. Soft shadows creep from behind tree trunks and large boulders. Secrets hide in dark crevices and under mossy rocks. You are sure you hear something behind you, but when you turn to investigate, nothing is there. The wind sighs through the tree leaves as a bluebird softly calls to its mate. You shrug, turn back, and are greeted with a startling vision.

A large glowing ball floats before you. Golden, shining, and luminescent, it floats a few inches off the ground, neither moving forward nor back. It hovers, waiting for your response. You watch it warily, breathing calmly and deeply. Suddenly, the light expands outward in a powerful burst of energy. You cover your face and eyes until the light dims. When the spots finally stop dancing behind your eyelids, you look up and are astonished by what you see. In the midst of the glowing ball of light stands a small woman. Completely enveloped by the golden light, she is golden yellow with only a slight darkening of color under her eyes and in the shadows of her curving body. Her hair is slightly lighter and waves around her pixie face and delicate shoulders. Her eyes carry many lifetimes of wisdom, but that does not diminish their bright curiosity and love of life. You fall on your knees amid the forest deadfall and bow your head. The woman laughs, a light, tinkling sound that holds a hint of smoky warmth.

"Please, get up," the woman says, and when you stand, you see her smile is open and welcoming. "I am Sunna," she says, "Norse goddess of the sun, sister of Mani, daughter of Mundilfaeri, wife of Glen. Who are you?" You tell Sunna your name and a bit of your family lineage. (pause) Sunna nods and looks about her. "You are in the depths of the forest, my child," she says. "You are lost and need to see from greater heights." She points upward with her index finger while holding out a hand to you. You look around at the burgeoning vegetation and the decaying forest floor and decide to view this forest, the world, and your life from the perspective of Sunna. Grasping Sunna's hand, you decide to follow the path of the sun.

Sunna's hand is warm, but it does not burn. Indeed, when you step inside the golden ball of light, it is like stepping into a soft flannel blanket or a warm sauna or a fire-warmed room. The air feels close and comforting, warm and welcoming. The energy of the ball thrums around you in wavering lines of heat and light. (pause) The ball is in constant motion but is contained and confined. And its power is unbelievable. As Sunna starts to ascend to the sky, your head already feels a bit dizzy from the energy swirling around you. Your eyesight blurs around the edges, and your mind takes longer to understand words, pictures, and phrases. You feel like you are moving underwater, intoxicated and ecstatic.

Before long, you are in the sky, high above the clouds and the tallest mountain peaks. The ball of light has grown in size, and you and Sunna float effortlessly inside. The world stretches out before you, gloriously green and blue, brown, and yellow. The earth is a wonder, an object of art, a masterpiece of ingenuity and engineering. It is beautiful and terrifying, a tiny speck in the vast cosmic scope of life. (pause) You see the stars high above the atmosphere in the infinity of dark space. (pause) You shudder and Sunna rests a comforting arm across your shoulders. Your stomach feels slightly queasy as you look down on the rotating earth and look up at the star-strewn sky.

"We will not go into the sun," says Sunna, although you are sure you did not see her lips move. Her face slides quickly to the left and then corrects itself. You close your eyes and feel the energy of the ball thrumming through you. "The sun is too strong for your human body," the voice of Sunna continues through the darkness of your closed eyelids. "But we will ride the circuit of the day so you can taste the essence of my life and regain the power of your own." Suddenly, the glowing ball jerks forward, quick and steady. You open your eyes and see that you are no longer floating effortlessly in a circle of golden light. Instead, the ball has morphed into a brilliant chariot. (pause) Sunna stands next to you, grasping a set of reins and valiantly fighting to control two large, powerful horses. They are orange in color with flaming manes and tails, and hooves that spark fire with every step. Sunna looks very small next to them. You look even smaller as you sit on the seat next to Sunna.

"Heilsa Allsvinn ('Very Fast') and Arvak ('Early Rising')," calls Sunna, slapping the backs of the horses with the reins. "Faster boys, faster," she yells. The horses snort and whip their heads around as if in panic. Your stomach flips over as you see the earth spinning underneath you and you catch the scent of fear on the sweat of the horses. You lean over toward Sunna and yell in her ear, "What's going on?" The wind whips the words out of your mouth and you don't think that Sunna can hear you, but she smiles grimly and nods in comprehension. You lean into her shoulder and hear her say, "It's the wolf, Skoll." She motions with her head to the back of the chariot, and you look behind you at the fearsome giant wolf. (pause) Skoll's teeth gnash at the railings of the chariot, splintering wood and leaving slashes of his blood. His iron-sharp teeth reach for the chariot, tearing, gnawing, gashing through the soft wood. Sunna whips the horses into a faster pace, but Skoll is not so easily deterred. He lopes ever closer, his dark eyes mere slits in his angry face, his teeth and lips smeared with blood. He is a fearsome sight, an enemy that never gives up. He will not accept defeat.

You rip your eyes from the mesmerizing sight of Skoll and ask Sunna, "What does he want?" She smiles, tight-lipped, and answers, "Our deaths." You shudder as she pushes the horses faster, but then Skoll lunges and, clamping his teeth on the back of the chariot, catapults himself onto the seat with you. His throat emits snarling, growling sounds. He towers above you, all ravaging sinew and muscle and bone. (pause) You can smell the iron-rich scent of his spilled blood and feel his hunger and thirst for more. He pounces at you, but you scramble away to crouch behind Sunna.

"You must face him," calls Sunna over the roaring wind, over the howling wolf, over the snorting horses. "Only by facing the darkness can your light shine." You look at her like she's completely crazy, but Sunna has no more time to counsel you. The scent of the wolf has caused the skittish horses to shy and buck within their harnesses. She must focus all of her energy on controlling their frantic movements. You are left to your own skills, and the wolf knows it. He grins and relaxes slightly in anticipation of an easy kill. You take some deep breaths and peer intently at the wolf. Trying to understand the depths of his personality, his strengths and weaknesses, you gaze into his eyes. (pause) And there, in the very back, hidden behind the snarls and growls, is the part of your life that Skoll represents: the incident, the experience, the harsh words and criticism that give you pause and make you doubt, forcing your light to grow dim and small. (pause) Now that you have located the root of Skoll's power, you know the way to defeat him. (pause) Gather your energy, your knowledge, and your strength, and face down your fears. Find the weapon that will harm him, and hurtle him from the chariot. (long pause)

The wolf flies through the air and lands far away from the chariot. He is a dark speck on the light horizon, separated from you by fluffy clouds and thunderstorms and rainbows of color. He licks his paws and limps away to try his luck at swallowing the sun another day. Sunna grins at you and guides the suddenly calm horses toward the earth. Closer and closer they gallop as the choppy waves of the ocean and the soft mists of the rainforests envelop you. The world is clear and in sharp focus for you. The brilliant energy of the glowing ball no longer overwhelms your senses. You are one with the light, with the chariot, with Allsvinn and Arvak, and with the goddess Sunna. The energy of your body has connected with the energy of the sun. You are bright and glowing. You are powerful and fully alive.

The chariot touches down in the fruitful forest where you started your journey. You step out and look up at the brilliantly beautiful goddess Sunna. "You are sunlight, my darling," says Sunna, smiling down fondly at you. "No one can ever take that away. Shine. Shine so the whole world knows your wisdom! Shine and realize the wonder of yourself!" With those last words, Sunna flicks the reins, and Allsvinn and Arvak lift the chariot off the ground. In an instant, they are gone, a bright orb in the sky, racing from the clutches of the wolf Skoll, racing toward the future. You turn and follow the path out of the forest, back to your comfortable home.

Now, take a deep breath, in through your nose and out through your mouth. Take another deep breath, filling your stomach, your diaphragm, and finally your lungs. Hold this breath for five seconds … 1-2-3-4-5 … and exhale, allowing the breath to exit your lungs first, then your diaphragm, and finally your stomach. Breathe deeply once more, and as you breathe in, feel the energy and the wonder of the world around you in your fingers, your toes, your legs, and your shoulders, even the top of your head. As you exhale, wiggle your fingers and toes. Shake your legs and move your shoulders up and down. Take another deep breath and, as you exhale, move your head from side to side. Feel the ground under your body touching every nerve ending and muscle. Hear the rustlings of the people around you. Notice the movements outside. Continue breathing. Stretch your arms out above your head. You are returning to the present, to the here and now. Continue stretching. Continue breathing. When you are ready, open your eyes, blink and focus, and sit up.

INVOCATION TO SUNNA

Sunna,
Sun goddess of the Northern lands,
Your presence sustains me,
Warms me,
And nurtures me.
Without you,
My world is dark,
My psyche shadowed.

Ripped from your father's arms,
You shower love on us all.
Chased by the he-wolf Skoll,
You turn our year-wheel.
Destroyed at Ragnarok,

You birth hope and joy.

Without you, oh Sunna,
We are alone
In our darkest hour.
In death, in drudgery, in pain,
You appear,
Day-star,
Fair-wheel,
Light-bringer,
To lift us out of the gloom
So we may shine again.

In your radiance and beauty,
I honor you,
Sunna,
Shining-Bride of the North.

MAGICAL ACTIVITIES

Candle Magic: Opening to the Sun

Items needed: Twelve yellow votive candles (one for each month of the year), a wagon wheel, a lighter or book of matches, amber incense, a bottle of mead, a towel or blanket (optional), and your daily planner (optional)
Moon Phase: Waxing
Seasonal Cycle: Summer

Unless you live on a farm or have an antiques collector in your family, it might be difficult and expensive to locate a wagon wheel for this spell. Don't be afraid to ask around at local farms or farm stands to see if you can put down a refundable deposit on a wheel and then borrow it for the day. This way, the farm is covered in case you fall in love with your wheel and don't wish to return it, and you are removed from having to spend fifty to a hundred dollars on a wagon wheel that will molder in your basement. If you simply cannot find a real, authentic wagon wheel, just draw one on paper or use a tire.

Whatever you choose, remember that the wheel symbolizes movement, specifically the turning of the year.

Gather all of your items together on a bright, sunny Sunday in the summer. Go to a sacred spot that is in direct sunlight and lay out your wagon wheel in front of your towel or blanket in a fairly comfortable sitting space. (Take care to look for beehives and anthills. There's nothing worse than having your spellwork interrupted with a bite from some of nature's creatures.) Place all of your candles at regular intervals around the wheel. It is best if they can balance on the wheel itself; however, you can place them around the circumference of the wheel as well.

Return to your sitting space, light the incense, and meditate in the warm sun. (If you are fair of skin, don't forget the sunblock.) Allow the sun's rays to melt away any tension and anxiety. Feel yourself relax. Ground and center as you normally do, and then walk to the candle in the north direction. This candle represents the month of January. Think back on your most recent experiences in January. What feelings and activities do you recall? Do you have any extremely positive or negative memories? Did you go on vacation? Have a fun time after midnight on New Year's? If you have your daily planner, look through it to jog your memory. Consider everything that you can remember about January, and then make a decision to bring the sun into your life the following January. Envision the sun's bright rays and her healing warmth pervading your January events and emotions, bringing a lightness of being and a burst of renewed energy. When you feel ready, light the January candle, tip your face up to the sun, and say, "Hail Sunna, shining bride of heaven!" Then move to the next candle and the next month in the year (February) and perform the same recollection exercise. Do this for each of the candles, ending at December.

When all of the candles on your wheel are ablaze, return to your towel. Form the Sowilo rune with your body, using runic yoga. Feel the might and main of the sun enter your body, coursing through your bones and blood. Allow her free access to your emotional center, brightening and lightening your outlook on life. When you feel altered, unwind from your runic position, sit down, and offer your mead to the goddess Sunna with these words:

Mead from the honey bees
Your companions in sweet harvest.
Goddess Sunna,

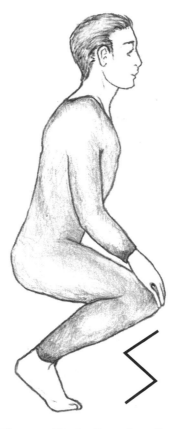

Figure 13: The Sowilo runic stadha.
(Source: http://www.sunnyway.com/runes/stadha.html.
The stadhas can also be found in Edred Thorsson's *Futhark: A Handbook of Runic Magic*
[York Beach, ME: Weiser Books, 1984], page 52.)

I honor you
And thank you
For your transforming warmth
For your dazzling light.
Hail Sunna!

Pour a good amount of mead near the wagon wheel and then take a sip yourself. Allow the candles to burn out naturally if possible. If not, snuff them reverently with a candle snuffer and gather them up to use throughout the year as reminders of your opening to the sun.

Crystal Magic: As the Hvel Turns

Items Needed: A gold rutilated quartz crystal, a sunstone, a citrine crystal, purified
    water, a glass container, and vodka
Moon Phase: Full
Seasonal Cycle: Spring or summer

For this spell, you will be creating a gem elixir: magical water that will help you to manifest your goals and dreams. In this case, the elixir is designed to utilize the power and energy of the sun to balance your energy centers. The sun will burn away any negativity, removing any blockages while bringing creativity, warmth, love, and light into your body. If you do not wish to include the vodka in your elixir, simply leave that ingredient out of the recipe and replace it with water. Many crystal workers believe that the vodka helps to draw out the essence of the crystal to a higher degree than water. However, if you do not drink alcohol, don't feel obligated to add the vodka; the water will draw out the crystal's energy as you need it. Don't change your ideals and morals for one spell.

Once you have gathered all of your items together, go to a warm, sunny place in your house or apartment. Pour some purified water in your glass container, leaving approximately a quarter of the space for your vodka. Add your vodka to the water, allowing it to mix. (You will have one part vodka to three parts water in your concoction.) Take your sunstone in your hands and activate it using your energy, requesting that it help you in reaching the sun's energy in order to clear and activate your Norse energy centers, known as hvels (Old Norse for "wheel"). (The hvels are similar to the more well-known chakras of the Indian Hindu religion and are a modern concept. To my knowledge, there is no mention of a "hvel energetic system" in the Eddas or Sagas.) Hold your sunstone so that the light of the sun surrounds it, and say, "Return me to the source, oh sunstone. Remove unnecessary ties to my hvel system. Build me up and make me strong." Drop the sunstone in the glass container of water and vodka.

Hold the citrine in your hands and ask for the power of the sun to radiate through this crystal, energizing your entire hvel system. Hold the citrine up to the sun and say, "Sustain and balance me, oh citrine. Remove any negative energy housed in my hvels and transmute it into shining sunlight. Keep me upbeat and sustain my confidence." Drop the citrine in the glass container of water and vodka.

Hold the rutilated quartz in your hands and ask the sunlight to illuminate your hvel system, removing barriers to spiritual growth. Hold the golden rutilated quartz up to the sun and say, "Cleanse and energize me, oh golden rutilated quartz. Enlighten my soul with knowledge from afar, linking me to the wisdom of the goddess Sunna. Open my hvels and protect their energy." Drop the golden rutilated quartz in the container of water and vodka.

Cover the container and shake it while you chant Sunna's name nine times. Keep the elixir in the sunlight for the space of a month, shaking it and chanting every day. At the end of a month, remove the rocks from the elixir and pour the elixir into various spray bottles and drinking containers. You can use this gem elixir as a liquid supplement to your daily diet, as a cleansing tool for ritual items, or as a clearing agent to remove unwanted energy in a room.

Written Magic: Heal Thyself

> Items Needed: A piece of parchment paper; a red pen; a copy of the runic alphabet; a copy of the second Merseburg charm; a flat rock; red ochre paint; a paintbrush; four small bowls; honey; appropriate offerings to Sunna, such as mead, flowers, and food; wet cloth (optional); a thesaurus (optional); and a spoon (optional)
>
> Moon Phase: Any, but especially the new moon
>
> Seasonal Cycle: Any, but especially around the summer and winter solstices

On a bright, sunny day, gather all of your spell materials and sit in the sun. Place your four small bowls at each of the cardinal points in your sacred space: east, south, west, and north. Return to the center of your space and, in a cross-legged position, meditate on an aspect of yourself that you feel needs to be healed. This can be a physical infirmity in your body or an emotional scar on your psyche. Take as much time as you need to locate and name this part of yourself. You may wish to focus on some of your shadow aspects or on incidents that left a lasting negative impression on your soul. Consider the possibility that your physical ailments are actually indicators of the need for deep, emotional cleansing work.

Once you have decided on an aspect of yourself that you would like to heal, hold that idea in your mind, pick up the honey, and walk to the bowl in the east. Pour some honey in the bowl, being sure to taste a small drop with your index finger. Hold the bowl up to the sun and say:

This honey, sweet on my tongue, resonates with the innocence of youth and the promise of dawn. I honor you, Spirits of the East, and ask for you to witness and aid my rite.

Place the bowl back on the ground and walk to the south. Pour some honey in the bowl, once again tasting a small amount. When you are ready, hold the bowl up to the sun and say:

This honey, sweet on my tongue, pulses with the passion of motherhood (fatherhood) and the power of noontime. I honor you, Spirits of the South, and ask for you to witness and aid my rite.

Return the bowl to its place and walk to the west. Pour and partake of some honey in the west, and then hold the bowl up to catch the light of the sun, saying:

This honey, sweet on my tongue, reverberates with the knowledge of queens (kings) and the decline of twilight. I honor you, Spirits of the West, and ask for you to witness and aid my rite.

Put the bowl back on the ground and walk to the north. Pour the honey into the northern bowl, being sure to taste one precious drop. Hold the bowl up to the sun and say:

This honey, sweet on my tongue, pulses with the wisdom of the crone (sage) and the mystery of midnight. I honor you, Spirits of the North, and ask for you to witness and aid my rite.

Return to the center of your sacred space and sit down in a comfortable position. (If your hands are sticky, use the wet cloth to clean them.) Read your copy of the second Merseburg charm. Consider ways to substitute your healing wish with that expressed by the poem. The second Merseburg charm is a spell designed to heal a physical wound, such as a cut or gash. Therefore, the words used reflect a bringing together or weaving, knitting, or binding spell. Your healing may take the form of a removal or digging out or an acceptance of some kind. Find words that reflect your own individual healing needs. Using these new words, write out the second Merseburg charm, with your healing in mind. First write it in English (or your native tongue) and then translate it into runes, using your runic alphabet. When you are done, hold your charm up to the sun and request the bright rays of Sunna to see and grant your healing wish.

Take your written charm, your flat rock, and your red paint and paintbrush to a sunny location that will not be disturbed for a week. This location should be easily accessible for you, so it is best if it is in your house, apartment, or yard. Ideally, the charm and the rock would be kept outside, but any location that receives the sun's rays will work. Put your charm at your location, word side up, toward the sun, and then cover it with your flat rock. Draw a Sowilo rune on top of your rock with your red paint and paintbrush. When you are done, say, "By the light of Sunna, I see my success before me." Then leave a physical offering to the goddess beside your charm and rock. For the next seven sunny days (cloudy days do not count), you must leave an offering by your charm and rock. (Be sure to clear away the old offerings the day after you've given them to Sunna. So if you leave flowers on a sunny Monday, you should clear them away on Tuesday, even if it is cloudy and rainy.) Every time you leave an offering, say the phrase: "By the light of Sunna, I see my success before me."

After you have placed your charm and rock and given your first offering, return to your sacred space and walk to the north. Pick up the bowl of honey and pour it onto the ground, saying:

By the wisdom of the crone (sage) and the mystery of midnight, I return this sweetness to the earth in praise and thanks to the Spirits of the North.

Figure 14: Sowilo

Make sure all of the honey is out of the bowl before moving to the west. (You may want to use a spoon to scoop the honey out of the bowl.) Pour out the honey in the western bowl and say:

By the knowledge of the queen (king) and the decline of twilight, I return this sweetness to the earth in praise and thanks to the Spirits of the West.

Once all of the honey has been removed from the bowl, walk to the south. Pour the honey in the south onto the ground while saying:

By the passion of motherhood (fatherhood) and the power of noontime, I return this sweetness to the earth in praise and thanks to the Spirits of the South.

Continue to scoop out all of the honey until the bowl is empty. Then, walk to the east and begin to pour out the honey, saying:

By the innocence of youth and the promise of dawn, I return this sweetness to the earth in praise and thanks to the Spirits of the East.

Finish pouring out the honey and then return to the center of your sacred space. Raise your arms up to the sky in honor of the goddess Sunna and say:

Hail Sunna, Sun Goddess of the North!

Your spellwork is complete. Remember to gift Sunna with offerings for the next seven sunny days. On the eighth sunny day, take your charm and burn it outside in a sacred manner. (Be aware of the plants and weather conditions around you. If it is very dry or windy, burn the charm inside. You don't want to inadvertently start a fire.) Take the painted rock and add it to your altar or to a rock wall outside. This rock will always be infused with the power of the Sowilo rune and can be utilized in other spells and magic.

BIBLIOGRAPHY

Ariannon. "Arianrhod." *Facets of the Goddess.* http://www.geocities.com/ariannon/index .html (accessed January 2008).

Aswynn, Freya. *Northern Mysteries and Magick: Runes and Feminine Powers.* St. Paul, MN: Llewellyn Publications, 1998.

Bellows, Henry Adams. *The Poetic Edda.* Princeton, NJ: Princeton University Press, 1936. Available online at http://www.sacred-texts.com/neu/poe (accessed January 2008).

Best, R. I., Osborn Bergin, M.A. O'Brien, eds. "Lebor Gabala Erenn." *Irish Texts Archive.* http://www.ancienttexts.org/library/celtic/irish/lebor.html (accessed January 2008).

Bianca. "Arianrhod: Goddess of the Milky Way." *Order of the White Moon.* http://www .orderwhitemoon.org/goddess/Arianrhod.html (accessed January 2008).

Biti-Anat, Lilinah. "The Major Dieties in the Myths of Ugarit." *Qadash Kinahnu: A Canaanite-Phoenician Temple.* http://www.geocities.com/SoHo/Lofts/2938/majdei .html (accessed January 2008).

Bray, Dan, trans. "The Old Norwegian Rune Poem." *Northvegr Foundation*. http://www.northvegr.org/lore/runes/003.php (accessed January 2008).

Bromwich, Rachel, ed. and trans. *The Welsh Triads*. As quoted in *Mythic Crossroads*. http://www.mythiccrossroads.com/triads.htm (accessed January 2008).

Bullfinch, Thomas. *The Age of Fable*. Ridgewood, NJ: BookRags, 2004. http://www.bookrags.com/ebooks/4928/419.html (accessed January 2008).

Byock, Jesse L., trans. *The Saga of the Volsungs*. As quoted in *Germanic Goddesses*. http://www.wyrdwords.vispa.com/goddesses/frigg/volsung.html (accessed January 2008).

Carr-Gomm, Philip and Stephanie. *The Druid Animal Oracle*. New York: Fireside, 1994.

Church of Y Tylwyth Teg. "Water and the Sacred Well" and "The Celts and Sacred Wells." *The Sacred Well Resource Page*. http://www.tylwythteg.com/Entrance/sacred-well-1.html (accessed January 2008).

Collins, Morris. "The Arthurian Court List in Culhwch and Olwen." *The Camelot Project at the University of Rochester*. http://www.lib.rochester.edu/camelot/CULlist.htm (accessed January 2008).

Cross, Tom P., and Clark Harris Slover, eds. and trans. *Ancient Irish Tales*. New York: Henry Holt and Company, 1936. Available online at http://www.ancienttexts.org/library/celtic/ctexts/lebor5.html (accessed January 2008).

Cunningham, Scott. *Cunningham's Encyclopedia of Magical Herbs*. St. Paul, MN: Llewellyn Publications, 1985.

Davis, Karen. "Arianrhod." *Encyclopedia Mythica*. http://www.pantheon.org/articles/a/arianrhod.html (accessed January 2008).

Deacon Paul of Warnfriet. *The History of the Langobard Folk*. As quoted in *Germanic Goddesses*. http://www.wyrdwords.vispa.com/goddesses/frigg/deaconpaul.html (accessed January 2008).

Dillon, Myles, ed. and trans. *The Cycle of the Kings*. Oxford: Oxford University Press, 1946. Available online at http://www.ancienttexts.org/library/celtic/ctexts/phantom.html (accessed January 2008).

Enright, Michael J. *Lady with a Mead Cup*. Portland, OR: Four Courts Press, 1996.

Epstein, Angelique Gulermovich. *The Morrígan and Her Germano-Celtic Counterparts*. Los Angeles: University of California Press, 1998.

Evans, Dyfed Lloyd. "Gwyn fab Nudd." *Nemeton: The Sacred Grove; Home of the Celtic Gods*. http://www.celtnet.org.uk/gods_g/gwyn.html (accessed January 2008).

———. "Nudd/Lludd/Nodons." *Nemeton: The Sacred Grove; Home of the Celtic Gods*. http://www.celtnet.org.uk/gods_n/nudd.html (accessed January 2008).

Ford, Patrick K. *The Mabinogi and Other Medieval Welsh Tales*. Los Angeles: University of California Press, 1977.

Gifford, Jane. *The Wisdom of Trees*. New York: Sterling Publishing, 2000.

Graves, Robert. *The White Goddess*. New York: Farrar, Straus and Giroux, 1975.

Gray, Elizabeth A., trans. "The Second Battle of Mag Tuired." *Internet Sacred Text Archive*. http://www.sacred-texts.com/neu/cmt/cmteng.htm (accessed January 2008).

Green, Miranda. *Celtic Goddesses: Warriors, Virgins, and Mothers*. New York: George Braziller, 1996.

Gundarsson, Kveldúlf Hagan, ed. *Our Troth*. North Charleston, SC: BookSurge, 2006.

Higley, Sarah, trans. "Preiddeu Annwn: The Spoils of Annwn." *The Camelot Project at the University of Rochester*. http://www.lib.rochester.edu/camelot/annwn.htm (accessed January 2008).

Jones, Gwyn, and Thomas Jones, trans. *The Mabinogion*. London: Everyman's Library, 1996.

Jordan, Michael. *Encyclopedia of Gods: Over 2,500 Deities of the World*. New York: Facts on File, 1993.

Kaldera, Raven. "Northern-Tradition Shamanism Herbal." *Cauldron Farm*. http://cauldron.jovi.net/herbal/herbal.html#frigga (accessed January 2008).

Keating, Geoffrey. *The History of Ireland (Book I and II)*. Cork, Ireland: CELT (Corpus of Electronic Texts), 2002. http://www.ucc.ie/celt/published/T100054.html (accessed January 2008).

Kinsella, Thomas. *The Tain*. Oxford: Oxford University Press, 2002.

Larrington, Carolyne, trans. *The Poetic Edda*. New York: Oxford University Press, 1996.

Macalister, R. A. S. *Lebor Gabala Erenn*. Dublin: Irish Texts Society, 1956.

Matthews, John. *The Elements of the Grail Tradition*. Dorset, UK: Element Books, 1990.

Meyer, Kuno. *The Wooing of Emer.* Cork, Ireland: CELT (Corpus of Electronic Texts), 2004. http://www.ucc.ie/celt/published/T301021/text031.html (accessed January 2008).

Monaghan, Patricia. *The New Book of Goddesses & Heroines.* St. Paul, MN: Llewellyn Publications, 2002.

Mountfort, Paul Rhys. *Ogham: The Celtic Oracle of Trees.* Rochester, VT: Destiny Books, 2002.

Order of Bards, Ovates, and Druids. "Ivy: Hedera Helix & Friends." *Order of Bards, Ovates, and Druids.* http://www.druidry.org/obod/trees/ivy.html (accessed January 2008).

Paxson, Diana L. "Beloved." *Hrafnar.* http://www.hrafnar.org/goddesses/frigga.html (accessed January 2008).

———. "Sif: From Loss to Joy." *SageWoman,* Winter 2005.

Schmitt, Dirk. "Sunna and Mani: An Investigation into the Sun and Moon in the Germanic Folkway." *Assembly of the Elder Troth.* http://www.aetaustralia.org/articles/ardssunnamani.htm (accessed January 2008).

Skye, Michelle. *Goddess Alive!* St. Paul, MN: Llewellyn Publications, 2007.

Storms, Godfrid, ed. and trans. *Anglo-Saxon Magic.* Folcroft, PA: Folcroft Library Editions, 1975.

Sturluson, Snorri. *Edda.* Rutland, VT: Charles E. Tuttle, 2002.

———. *Heimskringla.* Translated by Lee M. Hollander. As quoted in *Germanic Goddesses.* http://www.wyrdwords.vispa.com/goddesses/skadhi/yngling.html (accessed January 2008).

Thorn, Thorskegga. "How Sif Got Her Golden Hair." *Thorshof.* http://www.thorshof.org/howsif.htm (accessed January 2008).

Thorpe, Benjamin, trans. *The Edda of Sæmund the Learned.* Lapeer, MI: Northvegr Foundation, 2002. http://www.northvegr.org/lore/pdf/poetic_thorpe.pdf (accessed January 2008).

Thorsson, Edred. *Futhark: A Handbook of Rune Magic.* Maine: Samuel Weiser, Inc., 1984.

University Corporation for Atmospheric Research. "About the Sun." http://www.hao.ucar.edu/Public/education/basic.html (accessed January 2008).

Ward, Christie. "Courtship, Love and Marriage in Viking Scandinavia." *The Viking Answer Lady*. http://www.vikinganswerlady.com/wedding.shtml (accessed January 2008).

Welch, Lynda C. *Goddess of the North*. York Beach, ME: Weiser Books, 2001.

INDEX